AF262930

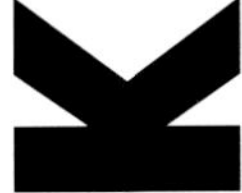

First published in Great Britain in 2026 by Laurence King,
an imprint of The Orion Publishing Group Ltd, Carmelite House,
50 Victoria Embankment, London EC4Y 0DZ

An Hachette UK Company

The authorised representative in the EEA is Hachette
Ireland, 8 Castlecourt Centre, Dublin 15, D15 XTP3, Ireland
(email: info@hbgi.ie)

10 9 8 7 6 5 4 3 2 1

Text © 2026 Amy Dempsey
Foreword © 2026 Hettie Judah

The moral right of Amy Dempsey to be identified as the author of this
work has been asserted in accordance with the Copyright, Designs and
Patents Act of 1988.

All rights reserved. No part of this publication may be reproduced,
stored in a retrieval system, or transmitted in any form or by any means,
electronic, mechanical, photocopying, recording, or otherwise, without
the prior permission of both the copyright owner and the above
publisher of this book.

A CIP catalogue record for this book is available from the
British Library.

ISBN (Hardback) 978 1 39962 673 6
ISBN (eBook) 978 1 39963 472 4

Commissioning Editor: Laura Paton
Art Director: Liam Relph
Design: Dan Jackson & Liam Relph
Picture Researcher: Emily Taylor
Senior Production Controller: Sarah Cook

Origination by F1 Colour
Printed in China by C&C Offset Printing Co. Limited

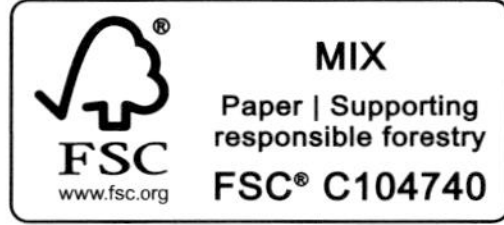

www.laurenceking.com
www.orionbooks.co.uk

THE FEMALE BODY IN ART

AMY DEMPSEY

Laurence King

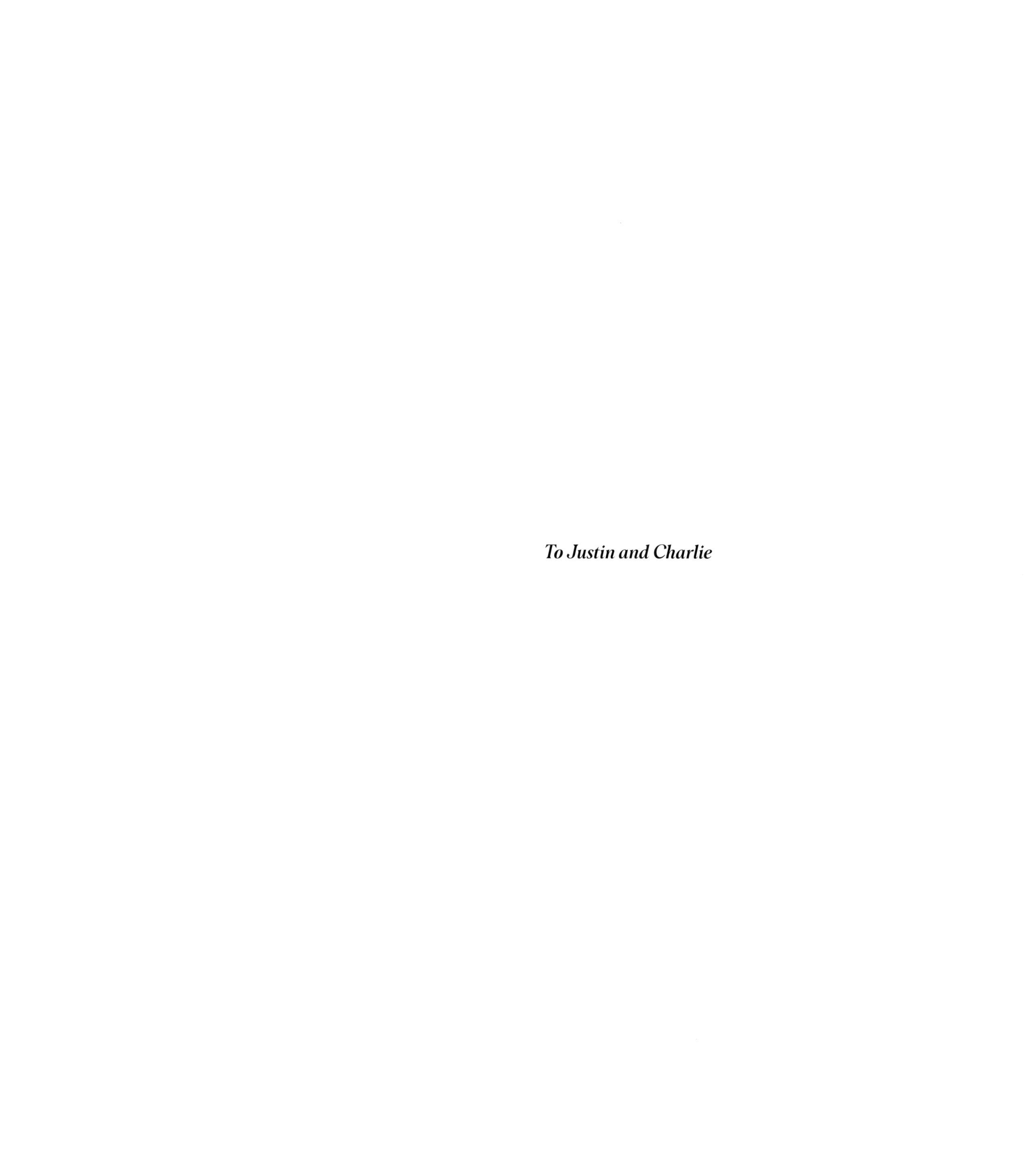

To Justin and Charlie

CONTENTS

IV. 1960 to 1999

V. 2000 onwards

FOREWORD

"Do women have to be naked to get into the Met Museum?" the feminist collective Guerrilla Girls asked in 1989. Their famous poster carrying that slogan appears towards the end of Amy Dempsey's book. By the time you reach it, you will recognize the painting it is based on.

In Jean-Auguste-Dominique Ingres's *La Grande Odalisque* (pp. 66–69), a creamy skinned white woman is seen from behind, naked but for a jewelled turban and a few strings of beads. Her nipples, pubic hair and the cleft between her buttocks are artfully concealed, but we can see the side of her breast and a tantalising portion of her flawless bottom. We appear to have wandered into a fantastical Turkish boudoir, but the naked woman doesn't seem to mind. Dempsey notes the 'knowing look' she casts over her shoulder, and the licence that gives for us 'to gaze back' in return.

The exotic setting and complicit gaze are among the many techniques artists have deployed to give viewers the permission to gaze at naked women. Almost all of the nudes in Dempsey's book (and there are many) are painted as anonymous archetypes – they are not intended as representations of identifiable women. For most of the period covered by *The Female Body in Art*, it was not considered respectable for a woman to display her exposed body outside of the wedding chamber (and perhaps not even there). That prohibition is removed from the painted nude because she represents Venus, the goddess of love, or a culture that abides by different social codes, or an enslaved woman evoking our sympathy. As Dempsey explains, these constructions 'allowed polite society to gawp at nakedness in a safe manner.'

Ingres's La Grande Odalisque has been idealized to anatomically improbable proportions. Dempsey compares the painter's pictorial tricks to a photographer's use of Photoshop. Just as fashion photos and celebrity portraits in our own time have been smoothed, slimmed, elongated and manipulated to otherworldly perfection, so painters since the 15th century have presented unattainable ideals of feminine beauty – smooth, hairless, shapely, eternally young.

La Grande Odalisque is but one imaginary body within a long history of women painted as impossible objects of desire, whether in the guise of mythic characters such as Venus or women of fashion such as Georgiana, Duchess of Devonshire (p. 56) and Virginie Gautreau (better known as John Singer Sargent's notorious *Madame X* (p. 88). Among other things, *The Female Body in Art* charts ideals imposed on the female body across 500 years.

We might well ask the Guerilla Girls in return: Do naked women have to be young and beautiful to get into the Met Museum? Well, not always, as Dempsey reminds us, but when older women are pictured, they are seldom treated kindly. In Hans Baldung's engraving *The Witches* (p. 20), an 'old shrieking hag … serves as a reminder' of what the young witches will soon become. Another engraving, based on a painting by Bernado Strozzi, shows an old woman extravagantly dressed and accessorised, gazing in the mirror (p. 44). It is not a sympathetic portrayal. The message of the picture seems to be that if you are no longer young, you might as well give up on beauty or fashion.

Dempsey also finds artists who cast older women in sympathetic light. The three sisters painted playing chess by Sofonisba Anguissola (pp. 28–31) are watched over by their grey-haired governess, who 'has not been made into an evil hag because of her age but appears to be a well-loved member of the household.'

In his eighties, the Dutch artist Franz Hals painted a group of elderly women who ran an almshouse for old men (p. 46). Hals portrays them as knowing and powerful: 'real people, with unique features – including wrinkles and age spots.' Not all women were allowed to age with grace, as Dempsey observes. Queen Elizabeth I, who appears here in a portrait by Nicholas Hilliard (p. 32), issued a proclamation to control her image as she aged. So long as she retained a 'mask of youth' in official portraits, she hoped to banish unsettling thoughts of death and succession among her subjects. The ageing female body remains taboo, and it is significant that the final work in this book is a sculptural self-portrait by Julie Rrap (p. 220). Made when she was in her early seventies, it shows her naked body not once, but twice.

There are magnificent women artists here, among them Artemisia Gentileschi (p. 36) and Élisabeth Vigée Le Brun (p. 58). Nevertheless, for many centuries almost all female bodies in art have been produced by men, who have painted and sculpted them according to their fantasies and desires, and those of their assumed male audience.

For feminist artists of the 20th and 21st centuries, taking back control of the depiction of the female body became an important project. In the scandalous performance work *Meat Joy* (p. 156), Carolee Schneemann suggests that a naked woman could be an artist as well as an art object. Paula Rego's *Abortion Series Triptych* (pp. 190–193) is a campaigning work opposing the control of women's bodies under the law. In three monumental pastel paintings, women of different ages and social classes are shown in a backstreet abortion clinic. Rego's works proved persuasive in the 2007 referendum to legalize abortion in Portugal. Feminist artists argue for the importance of art that shows real female bodies, derived from real women's experiences.

Why look back, then, to the female body in art history? This book opens with Sandro Botticelli's *The Birth of Venus*, c. 1486 (pp. 14–17), a painting that Dempsey notes was inspired by the idealized bodies of Greek and Roman statuary. Botticelli's Venus is thus connected to a long history of nudes that preceded it, but it also influenced how the female body was shown in art in the centuries that followed. Like many of the works in these pages, it remains an important cultural reference, influencing artists, photographers, fashion designers and even celebrities on the red carpet. Art may have moved on, but Venus continues to be reborn, again and again.

Hettie Judah

INTRODUCTION

The Female Body in Art explores how women have been portrayed in art from the Renaissance to the 21st century – as the 'good, the bad and the ugly' – and how these archetypes and stereotypes, both idealized and misogynistic, have developed and manifested themselves in artworks. It also examines how, over time, these representations have been questioned, dismantled and replaced or supplemented with new, different images.

The story is told through artworks by 80 artists from a range of cultures and traditions to show the different ways the female form has been portrayed, from Sandro Botticelli's *The Birth of Venus*, c. 1486 (pp. 14–17), which ushered in an ideal of feminine beauty that is still with us today, to Julie Rrap's *SOMOS (Standing On My Own Shoulders)* of 2024 (p. 220), which asserts that the ageing female body should also be represented in visual culture.

In her pioneering book *Woman in Art: From Type to Personality* (1944), art historian Dr Helen Rosenau (1900-1984) explored how representations of women progressed from 'Type' (goddess, lover, warrior, mother, mistress) to 'Personality' (individualized people and characters). In *The Female Body in Art*, too, we will see the evolution of women from being seen as types or objects to being represented as complex individuals with their own personalities, traits and stories. We will also see the invisible made visible, the under-represented represented and social mores and taboos being questioned, changed or overturned.

Art can make you think about the world or yourself in a different way or see things in a new light. It can also provide a way into another time, place or culture. What do these depictions of women tell us about the times in which they were made? About the worlds we inhabit now? The work is presented chronologically so that we can see how major world events – political upheaval, the abolition of slavery, the industrial revolution, women's suffrage – are reflected in art, as well as allow us to see dialogues between artists and artworks as they emerge over time.

Key themes and catalysts include:

The purpose of the art:
Who was it for? Who would see it? Where would it be seen? In our modern, image-rich lives, it is hard to imagine a time when artworks were only seen by a few people in a few locations – churches or palaces – and were signs and tools of power, control, education and prestige. This began to change with the rise of the middle classes and new patrons wanting art that reflected their lives and concerns. Art also became more accessible with the establishment of art schools, museums, galleries and public exhibitions. As art became part of everyday life for more and more people, so it began to reflect and represent us all – including images of female bodies of all shapes and sizes, beyond the heteronormative tradition.

The impact of new technologies and inventions:
The impact of the invention of the printing press in the 15th century cannot be overstated. It facilitated the spread of ideas and images like never before, much like the internet and social media have done for us today. Images of the 'ideal' female body could be shared far and wide, while the invention of the flat, full-length mirror allowed women to compare themselves to it and printed beauty manuals told them how to achieve it. Photography also transformed

the way the world was seen and influenced how art was made, while expanded modes of reproduction allowed posters, prints and books to reach an ever-wider audience.

Impact of travel:
The excitement about new discoveries, the fusion of traditions and artistic practices, and the exchange of materials, ideas and imagery through travel and immigration have all informed artmaking and contributed to the various depictions of the female form in art.

Changing fashions:
The notion of the 'ideal' body has changed dramatically over the years, and these trends have directly influenced the portrayal of women in art. Changing fashions in the art world also affect what subjects and themes are deemed suitable for portrayal in art.

Sadly, there is plenty of sexism, ageism, misogyny, racism and discrimination on show in art through the ages, as artists and their work reflect and contribute to the socio-political cultural environments of which they are a part. There is also plenty of art that reveals and comments upon man's inhumanity to man, and man's inhumanity to women. Although my selection acknowledges this (I think it is important to see how these ideas arise and are spread), it leans towards art and artists that I find more intriguing, inspiring and pivotal, countering some of the nastiness with more positive, inclusive images.

I have tried to give a voice and presence to a wide range of participants, but no selection can be entirely exhaustive. If certain cultures, artists, periods and traditions may seem to be missing, this is not a deliberate exclusion; it may be that their content and practice was not concerned with the female form and falls outside the remit of this book. Inevitably, the selection is personal, but it is not arbitrary. There will be some familiar names and artworks, and hopefully some that are new to you. In either case, there is plenty to think about – to argue about – and to inspire, encourage, consider and enjoy.

Dr Amy Dempsey

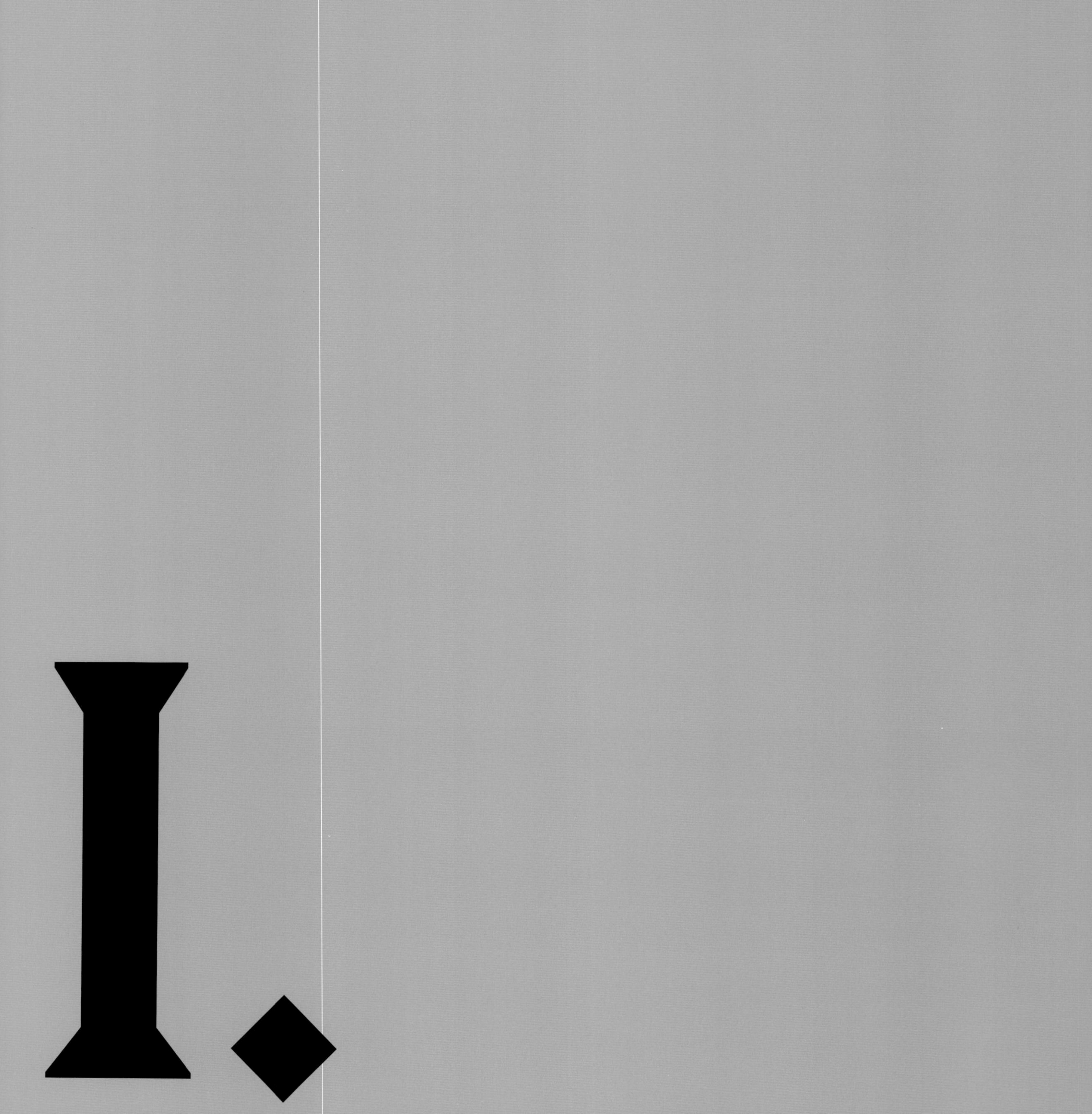

RENAISSANCE to 1799

THE BIRTH OF VENUS _c. 1486_

Sandro Botticelli's *The Birth of Venus* is one of the most beloved paintings in the world. It was groundbreaking on many levels, from its subject matter – a life-sized standing female nude in a pagan setting – to its patronage and audience. It was not commissioned by the Church as a religious devotional image, but most likely by a member of the wealthy Florentine Medici family as a source of pleasure and decoration for one of their homes.

Venus, the Roman goddess of love and beauty, was conceived when seawater was fertilized by semen from her father, Uranus, the god of heaven (whose son castrated him and threw his genitalia into the sea). Botticelli depicts this celestial Venus – the offspring of the union of the sacred and the profane – as she is blown to shore on a shell to bring love and beauty to the earth. This secular mythological scene and figure set forth an image of 'ideal womanhood', both human and divine, that was inspired by admiration for the art and philosophy of ancient Greece and Rome, as well as the Renaissance drive to imagine how this beacon of beauty and virtue would manifest itself in physical human form.

'The embodiment of the ideal female is a young woman with pale, delicate skin, a sensuous hourglass figure and flowing golden hair. The archetypal goddess of beauty had arrived'

To arrive at his concept of female beauty and virtue, Botticelli turned to both the classic 'Venus Pudica' (Venus of Modesty) pose, in which the figure attempts to cover her nakedness with her hands, and to descriptions of natural beauties in ancient texts. The resulting embodiment of the ideal female – beautiful and virtuous, who inspires love and goodness – is a young woman with pale, delicate skin, a sensuous hourglass figure and flowing golden/ strawberry blonde hair. Botticelli applied gold highlights to her hair and alabaster powder on her skin to heighten these effects and give her a shimmering, ethereal presence. The archetypal goddess of beauty, which has endured for centuries, had arrived.

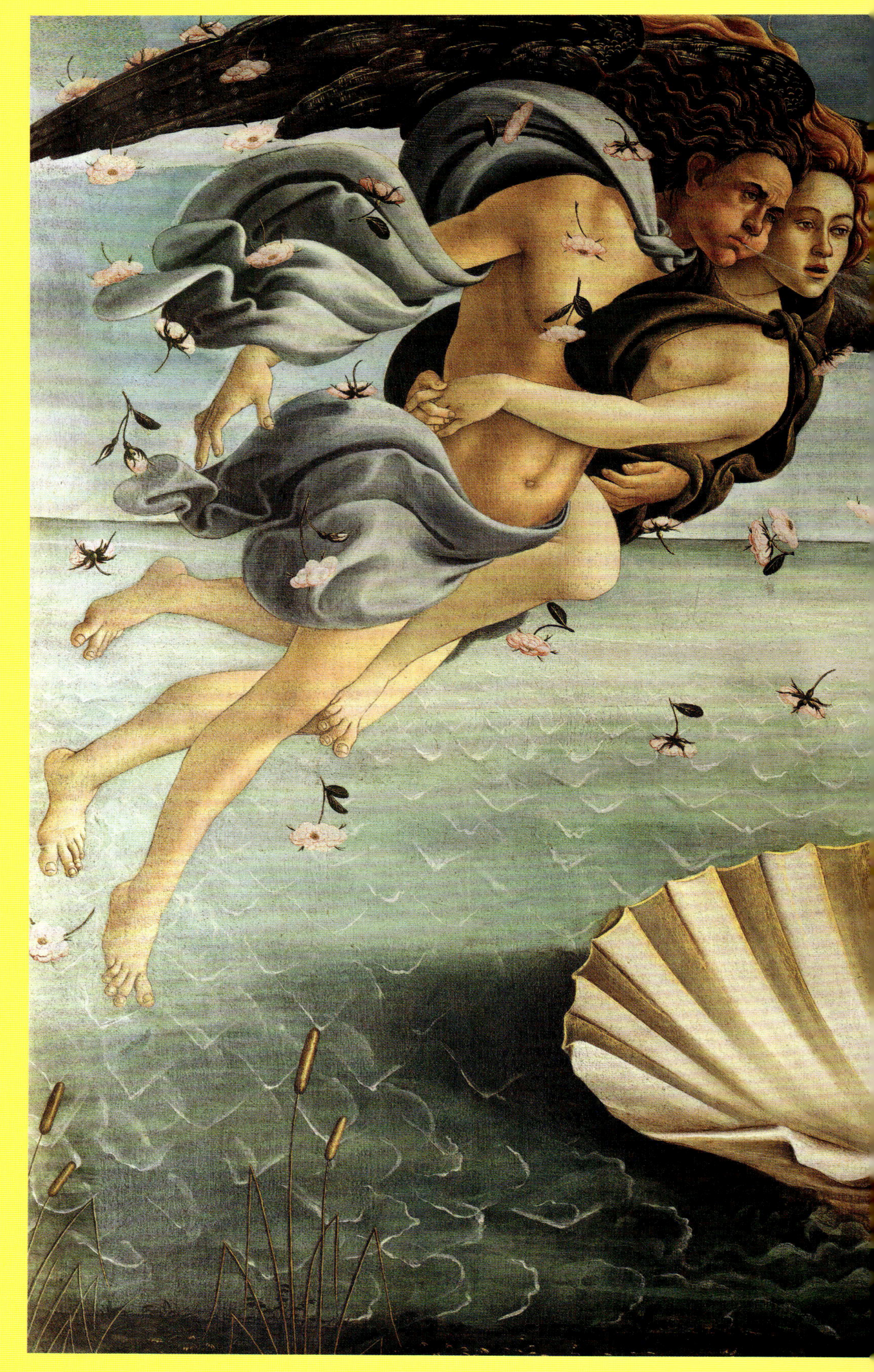

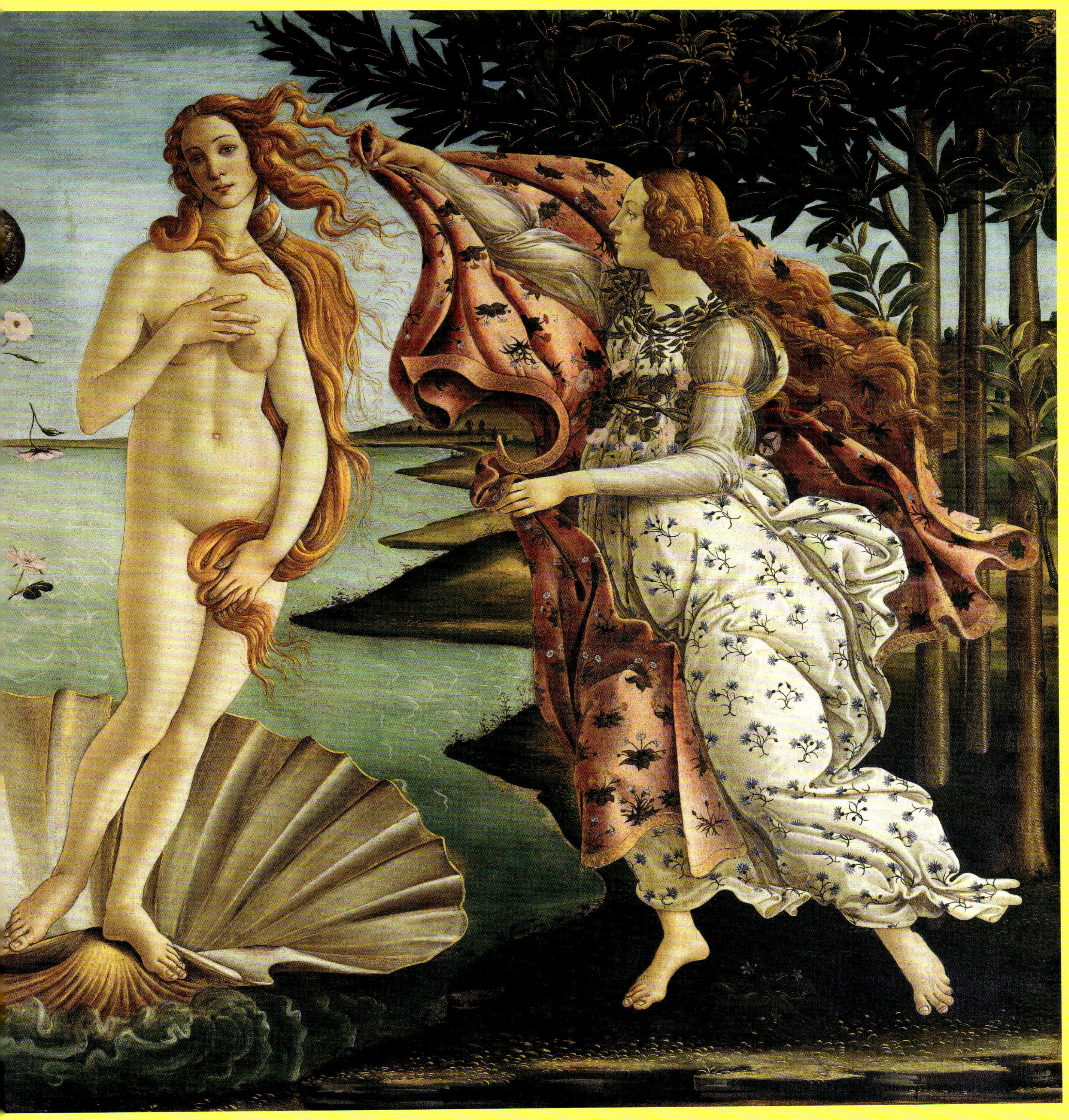

MONA LISA *1503–1519*

Mona Lisa, by the artist, scientist and thinker, Leonardo da Vinci, must be the most famous portrait in the world. Certainly, it is the most referenced, copied and parodied work of art in history – you can even pick up a copy for yourself at the furniture giant, IKEA. The sitter is generally believed to have been Lisa Gherardini, wife of the Florentine merchant Francesco del Giocondo. Leonardo worked on the portrait with her for three years, but continued to tinker with the painting until his death in 1519.

With this portrait, Leonardo introduced a number of influential innovations. Instead of just a bust, his composition extends below the waist to include her arms and hands, giving her a much more commanding presence. She is also sitting in front of a landscape, instead of in her home, as was more customary for portraits of women at the time. While most earlier portraits were in profile, Leonardo offers a three-quarter view, so his sitter is looking out at the viewer, taking them on with her enigmatic expression and gaze. She appears self-possessed, slightly bemused and with a hint of a smile.

That smile amazed Leonardo's contemporaries and has continued to intrigue for 500 years since. Giorgio Vasari, an artist and author of *The Lives of the Most Excellent Painters, Sculptors, and Architects* (1550), wrote at the time that 'the mouth, joined to the flesh-tints of the face by the red of the lips, appeared to be living flesh rather than paint ... [and] ... there was a smile so pleasing that it seemed divine rather than human; and those who saw it were amazed to find that it was as alive as the original.'[1]

Leonardo left us with a portrait of a real woman with individual features facing the viewer with an expression that continues to intrigue and captivate. Enter the archetypal beautiful woman of mystery.

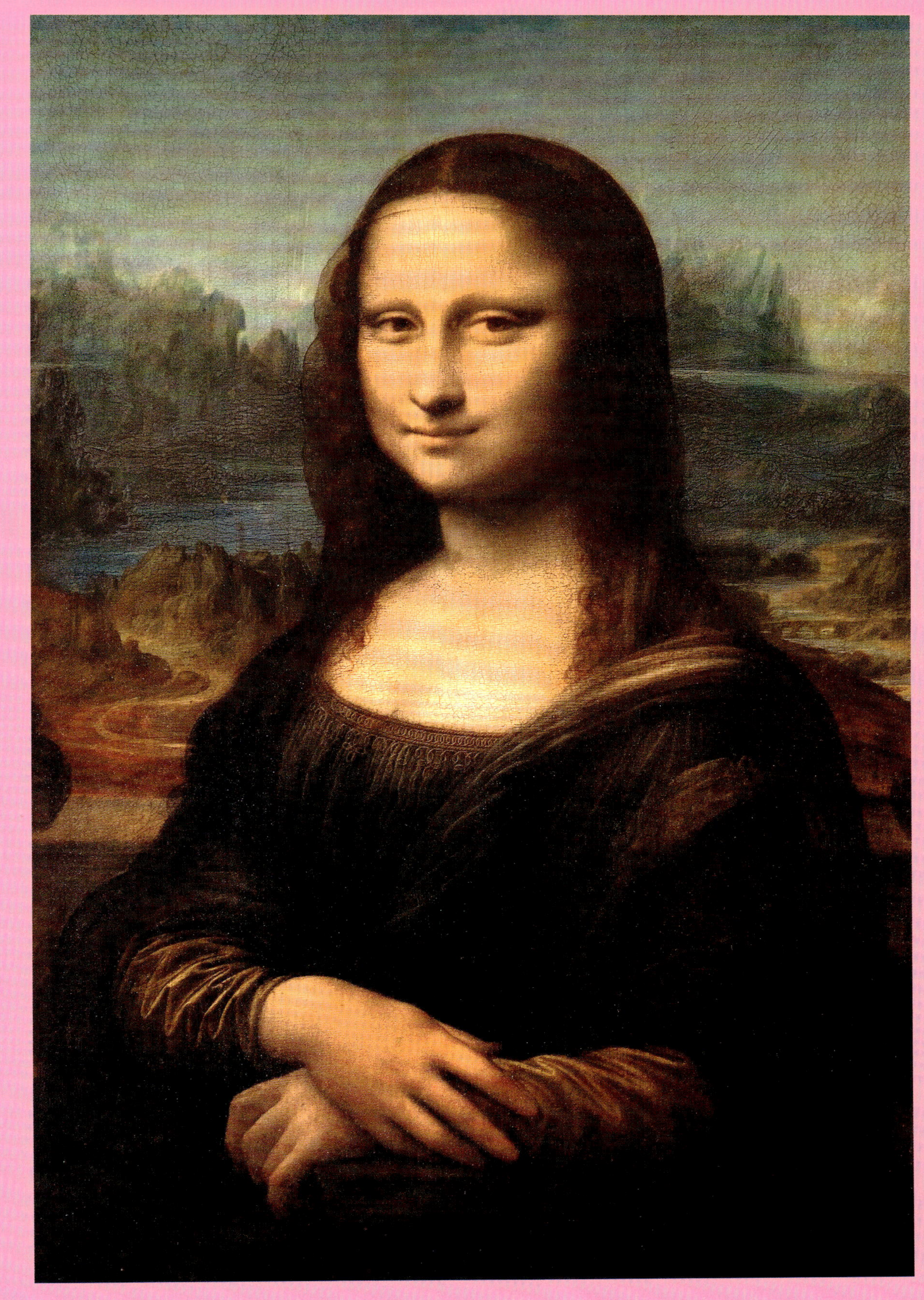

Hans Baldung
(German, 1484–1545)

THE WITCHES *1510*

At the same time as Botticelli was conceptualizing his image of ideal femininity (pp. 14–15), a pair of Dominican friars – Heinrich Kramer and Jacob Sprenger – were writing their vicious witch-hunters' guide, *Malleus Maleficarum (The Hammer of Witches)* (1486). This hateful book 'proved' in no uncertain terms that witchcraft existed and warned of witches' powers and activities, such as cavorting with demons and kidnapping and eating babies.

The book contained instructions on how to identify and convict witches in order to eliminate them, and revealed how 'all witchcraft comes from carnal lust, which is in women insatiable', and that love magic is 'the best known and most common form of witchcraft'.[2] While men could be witches, more often than not they were victims of the sorcery of women doing Satan's work. Those singled out for vitriol were old women, midwives, nuns, healers and women who made potions and cosmetics – especially love potions and charms. Artists such as Hans Baldung provided visuals for these personifications of evil, so that everyone could identify the witches in their midst.

In *The Witches*, a group of nude witches prepare for a mass gathering – a 'sabbath' – underlining the fear of gatherings of groups of women and the activities that are their exclusive domain. Two young, seated witches are shown with an old shrieking hag between them, who serves as a reminder of what they will become. The trio is seen making a magic potion. Its smoke rises to the flying temptress above, who rides backwards on a goat as she eyes the viewer seductively (riding backwards is a symbol of evil, while goats are associated with the devil and lust). With their loose, scraggly hair, Baldung's women are free and dangerous, as opposed to the refined, respectable women of the day who wore their hair pulled back and contained (see Anguissola, p. 28 and Carracci, p. 34).

The invention of the printing press in 1440 allowed the misogynistic fearmongering of *Malleus Maleficarum* to be spread far and wide. More than 30 editions were printed between 1486 and 1669 – the prime years of witch trials in Europe – while prints such as Baldung's helped cement the notion that female sexuality was evil and dangerous. They also showed what it looked like: the witch was either an old hag or a sexy femme fatale luring innocent men to an awful fate.

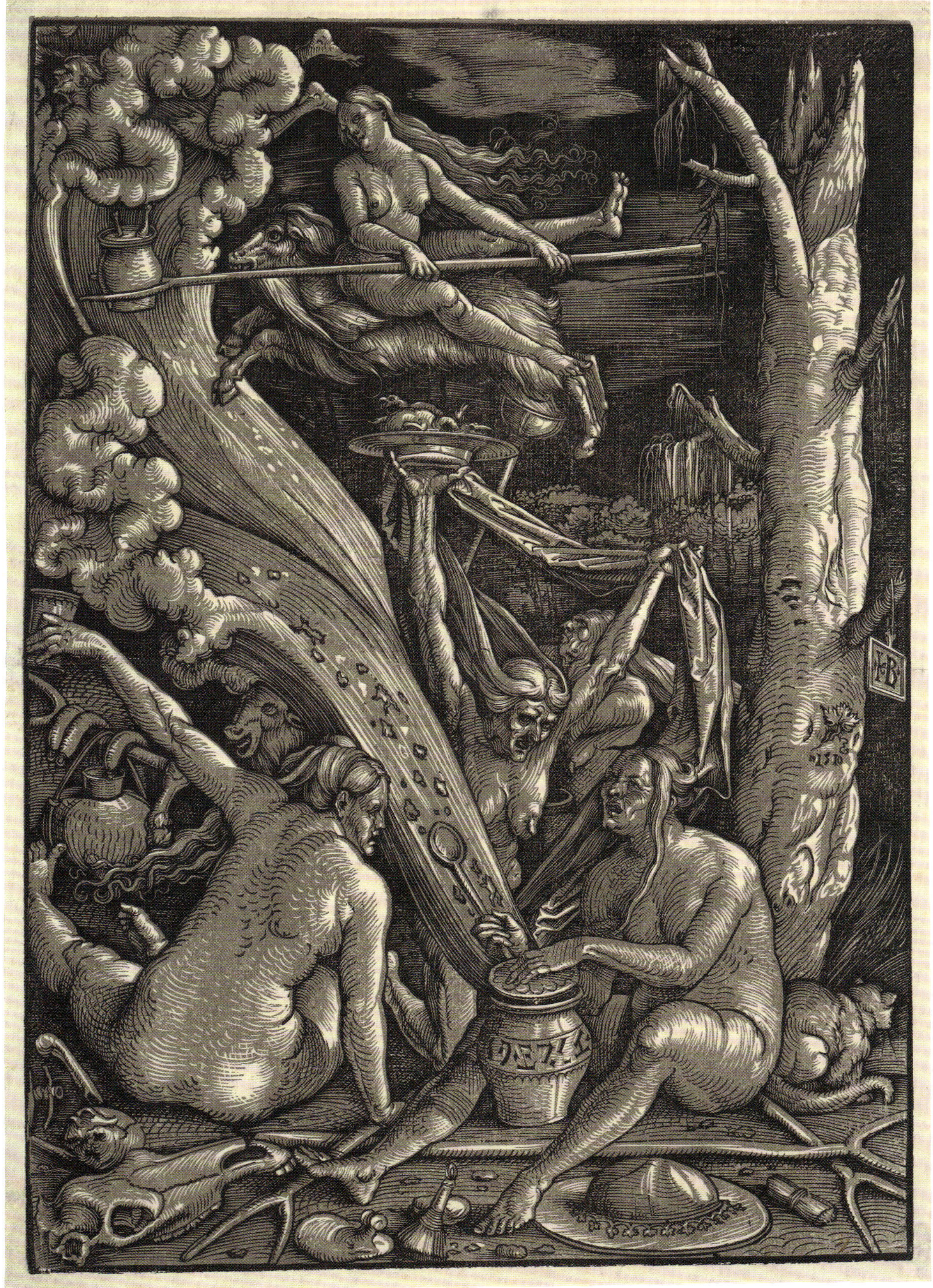

MADONNA DELLA SEDIA _1514_

Raphael is renowned for his exquisite Madonna paintings and idealized visions of beauty, especially female beauty. *Madonna della Sedia* (*Madonna of the Chair*, also known as *Madonna and Child with St John*) is by far his most humanist portrayal of the Virgin Mary. While the clues are there that this is a Madonna painting – Mary is wearing her signature blue dress and there are faint halos behind her and the toddler (St John) who is praying and holding a tiny cross – Mary definitely reads as a realistic human mother with her children. This certainly allows for greater identification with the viewer than many other religious paintings of the time.

In most of Raphael's Madonna paintings, Mary is portrayed looking at the Christ Child, but here she is looking out at the viewer, holding her child in a tender, protective embrace – trying to protect him from his fate, perhaps? In this image, we see Mary more as the mother of baby Jesus, rather than Mary, the Mother of the Church. Even if the viewer knows that this is a painting of the Madonna and Child with St John the Baptist, it is not the Virgin Mary as Saint, but Mary as more of an 'everywoman' or 'everymother' that comes across. She is further humanized by the contemporary fashionable headscarf and shawl that she is wearing.

Raphael's characters are physically beautiful and definitely human (they were based on studies of live models instead of classical statues) and are imbued with a divine serenity. Here, Renaissance Humanism and Christian beliefs conflate in the motherly love of the Virgin Mary (who is both divine and human) for her child Jesus. It is an image of ideal motherhood, of exalted maternal love; loving and protecting, sacred and natural.

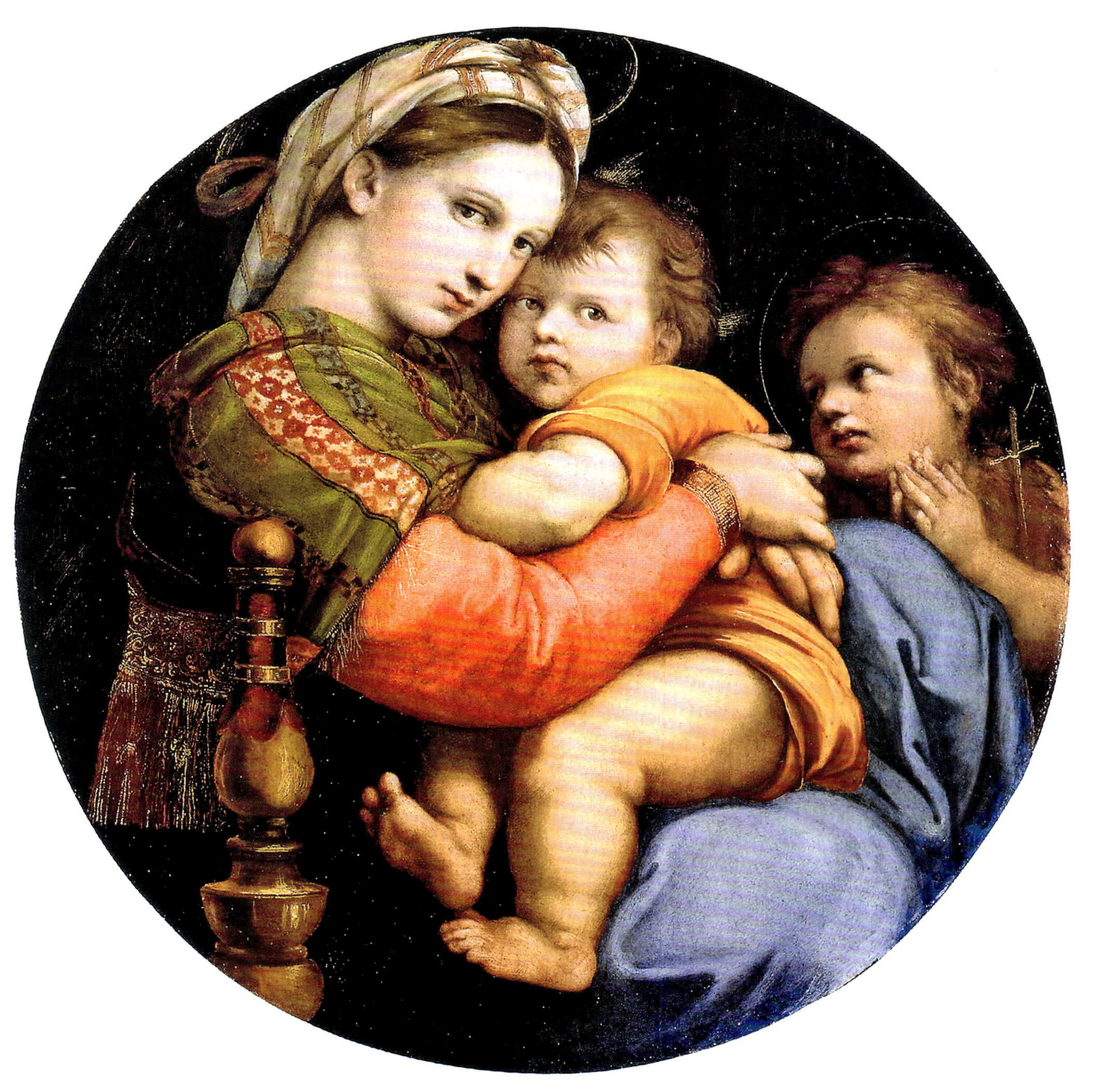

VENUS OF URBINO *1538*

If we take Botticelli's Venus (p. 14) as occupying a liminal space between goddess and human being, as transitioning between marble statue and human flesh, then Titian's Venus is most definitely of this world. She is an earthly, human woman; erotic, titillating, gazing at the viewer with a 'come hither' expression. This recumbent Venus was painted for the Duke of Urbino's private chambers and shows the goddess of love lying on rumpled sheets. One hand casually covers her genitals while the other holds a posy of red roses (one of the emblems of Venus); a dog sleeps at her feet (a symbol of faithfulness in marriage).

Images of real – albeit idealized – versions of the female body, such as this, began to appear across Italy in the 16th century, in art, in print and in (and on) public buildings and public spaces, along with the classical statues that inspired them. Pygmalion-like, artists such as Titian brought the classical stone statues to life, turning them into seductive flesh.

The result was the fashion for the ideal physical female nude to be hourglass-shaped with small, pert breasts and no body hair (those ancient statues do not have body hair). In his book, *The Ornaments of Ladies* (1562), Giovanni Marinello wrote that 'when hair is superfluous over the entire body, as with many ladies who become so hairy that they look like a wild beast, one has to remove it, which one can do excellently in the bath.' He also explained that 'both the ancient and the modern poets and painters want the hair belonging to a beautiful woman to be long, soft, thick, curled and of a blond colour like gold.'[3]

'Images of real – albeit idealized – versions of the female body began to appear across Italy in the 16th century, in art, in print and in public buildings and public spaces, along with the classical statues that inspired them'

Calling her Venus – the mythological goddess of love – allowed polite society to gawp at her nakedness in a safe manner, with the mythical assignment preserving everyone's propriety. There she is in all her glory, laid out for men and women to admire and desire, for women to compare themselves to and aspire to become. Marinello's book was just one of many books and pamphlets that were published with recipes for cosmetics, hair dyes and body hair removal, as well as diet tips to make sure that you weren't too fat or too thin. In short, to help women become more 'Venus-like'.[4]

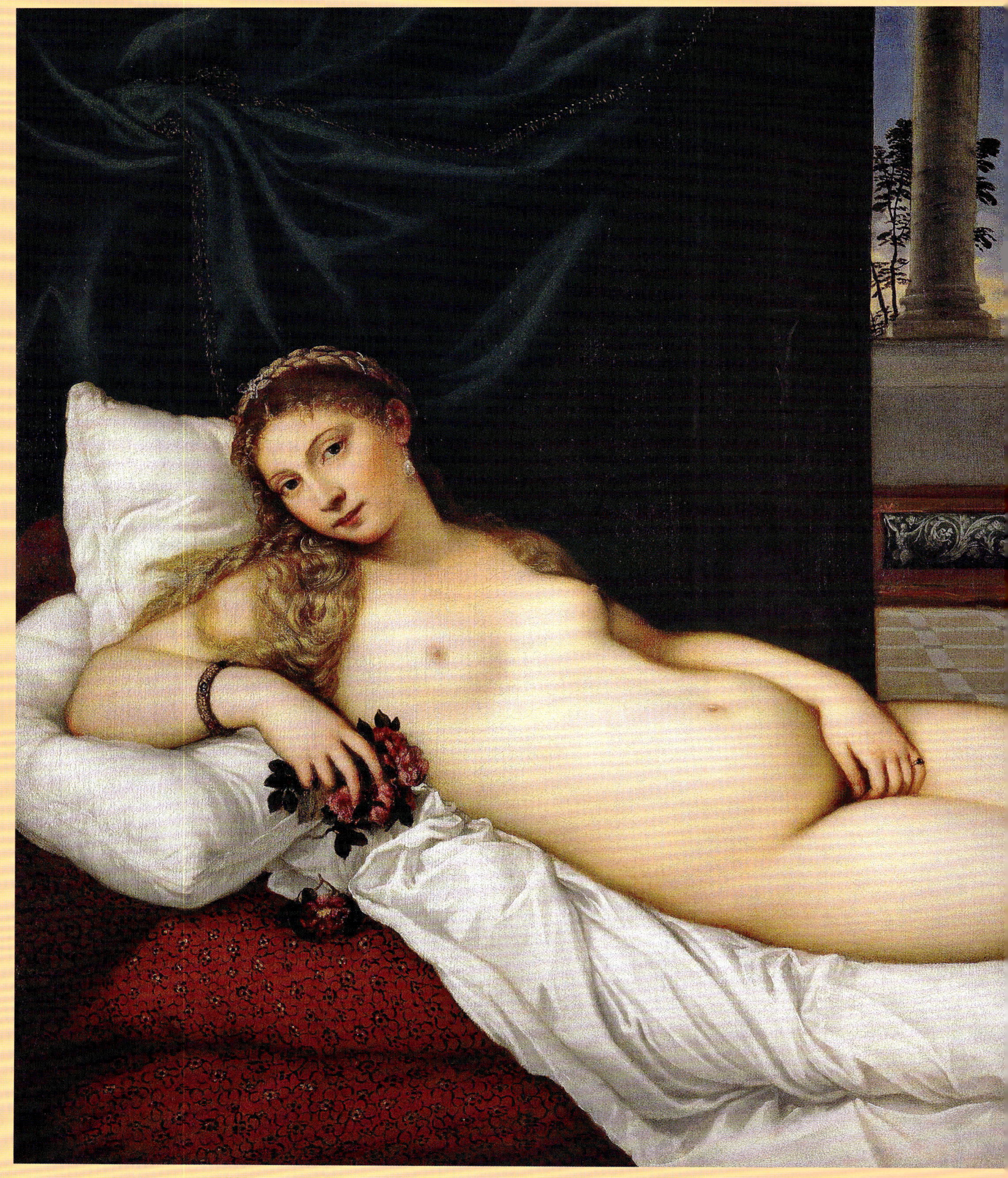

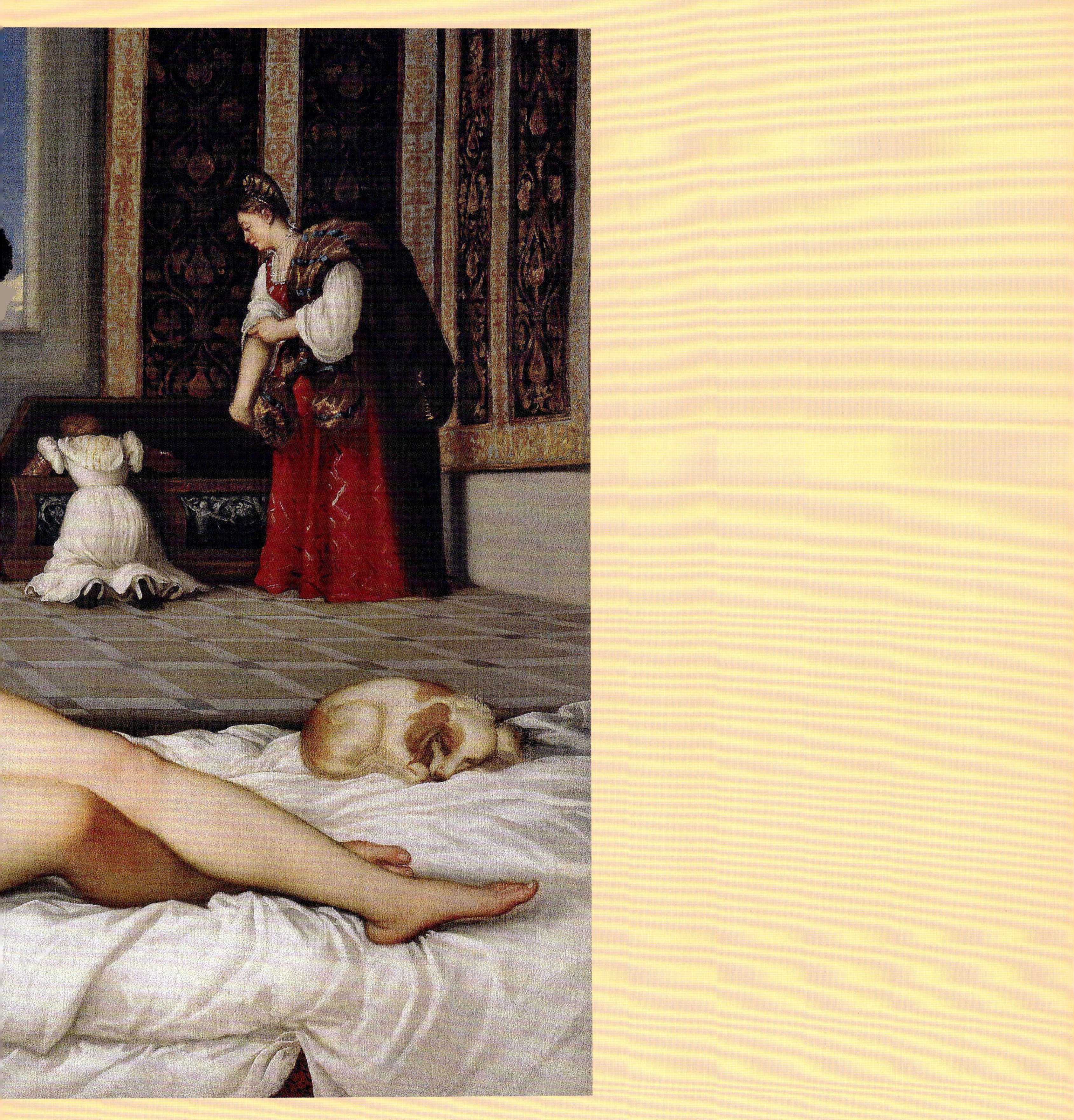

THE CHESS GAME

(Portrait of the Artist's Sisters Playing Chess) <u>1555</u>

Sofonisba Anguissola was a popular Renaissance portrait painter, known for her self-portraits and portraits of her family. She was given an extensive humanist education, as befitted members of minor Italian nobility and, unusually for a female, professional art training. She was enormously successful in her own lifetime and was invited to join the court of King Philip II of Spain, where she served as a painter and lady-in-waiting to his young queen, Elisabeth of Valois, from 1559 to 1573.

Anguissola made her name with intimate family scenes such as this, which depicts three of her sisters playing chess. The youngest sister in the middle, Europa, is watching and learning with an impish grin on her face as the middle sister to the right, Minerva, puts her hand up in defeat or protest – or perhaps to ask a question. Meanwhile, the oldest sister, Lucia, holds the queen in her hand and looks out at the viewer from the left of the painting. She has a slightly smug 'got her' look on her face, or perhaps it is a look to say that we might be young women, but we are educated and intelligent and can play chess too – it is not just the preserve of men. Anguissola includes herself in the picture by signing the chess board with her name, the title and date in Latin.

The sisters in this painting are chaperoned by their governess, an old woman protecting their virtue, or maybe even helping with the game. In contrast to Baldung's print of a group of young women accompanied by an old woman (p. 20), here the older maid looking on is rendered in a caring, tender fashion. She has not been made into an evil hag because of her age but appears to be a well-loved member of the household. The same governess also appears in one of Anguissola's later self-portraits.

'The oldest sister, Lucia, holds the queen in her hand and looks out at the viewer – perhaps to say that we might be young women, but we can play chess too'

Giorgio Vasari wrote about the painting in the second edition of his famous book, *The Lives of the Most Excellent Painters, Sculptors, and Architects* (1568): 'Speaking, then, of Signora Sofonisba [...] I must relate that I saw this year in the house of her father at Cremona, in a picture executed with great diligence by her hand, portraits of her three sisters in the act of playing chess, and with them an old woman of the household, all done with such care and such spirit, that they have all the appearance of life, and are wanting in nothing save speech.'[5]

These fresh-faced girls are a picture of Renaissance beauty ideals, with their peachy complexions, clear broad foreheads, bright dark eyes, thin eyebrows and rosy lips. Their long, dark, golden hair is worn with centre partings, curled in front and pulled back with braids wrapped around their heads, and adorned with lavishly jewelled headbands.[6] They are not threatening, but attractive, healthy and intelligent young noblewomen who would make good catches for worthy suitors.

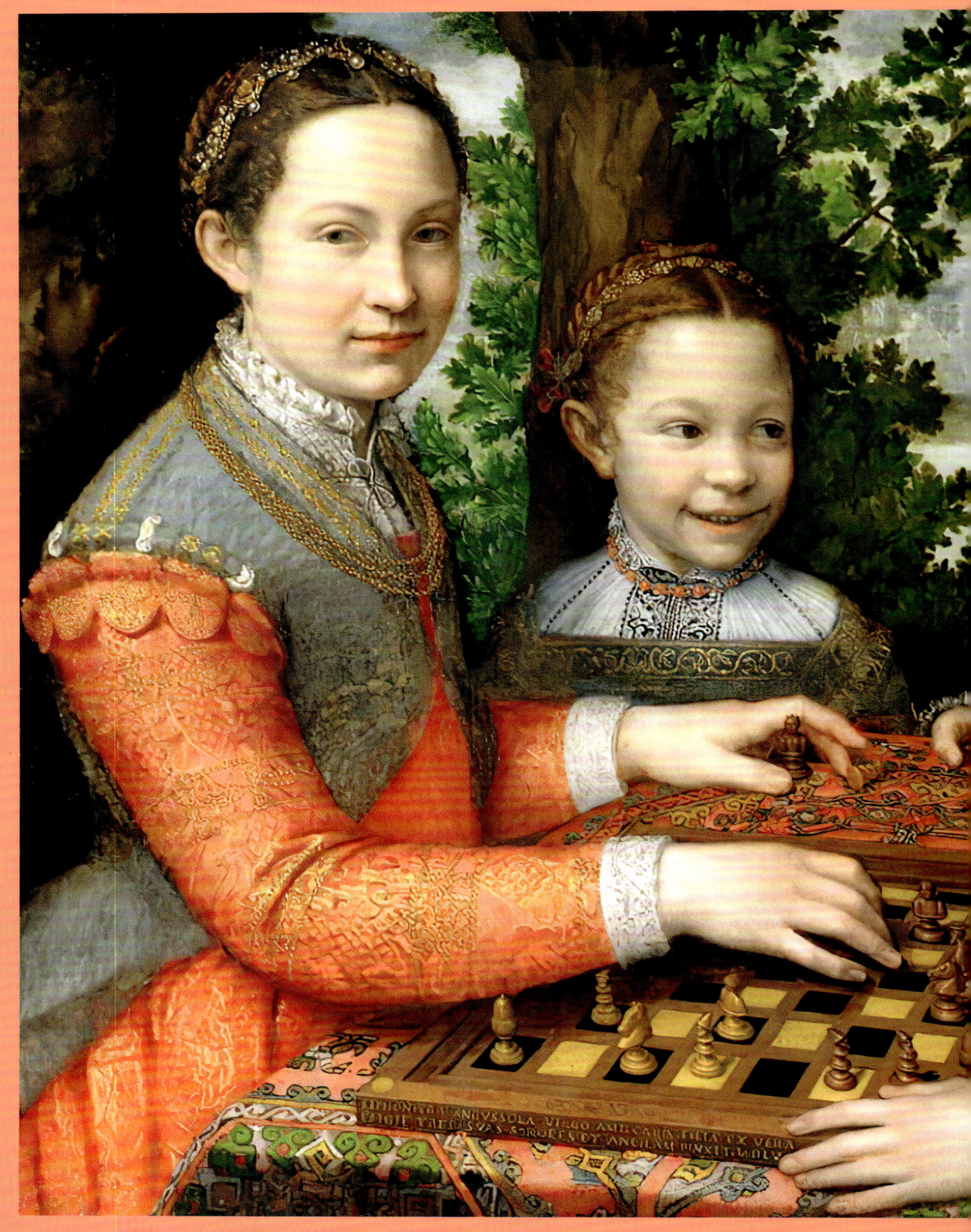

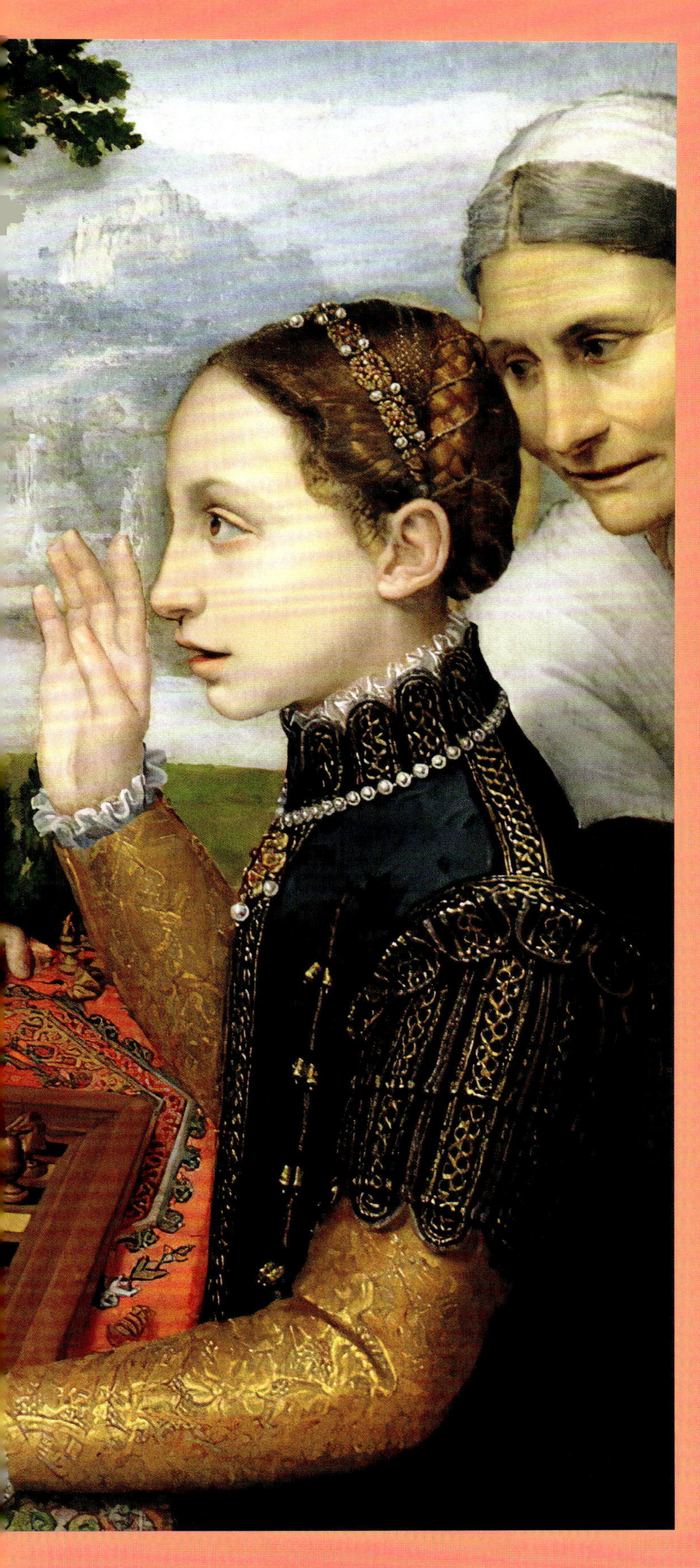

ELIZABETH I WITH A PELICAN EMBLEM *c. 1574*

In the male-dominated 16th century, Elizabeth I (1533–1603), Queen of England and Ireland, had to command the respect and loyalty of her all-male government. Far from being hindered by her gender and unmarried state, Elizabeth used these circumstances to suit her own purposes. Her decision not to marry was portrayed as an act of self-sacrifice, and her virginity came to stand for national independence: Elizabeth was not an old maid, but the Virgin Queen.

Nicholas Hilliard was the most important English artist working in Elizabethan London, and one of the very few who had the opportunity to paint the monarch from life – most artists had to work from approved 'face patterns' derived from official portraits. In *Elizabeth I with a Pelican Emblem*, several devices are used to communicate messages about Elizabeth, including pearls (purity), the Tudor rose (unity) and the pelican pendant pinned on her chest (love). Mother pelicans were believed to pluck their own breasts to feed their starving young, dying in the process. Elizabeth used this symbol of self-sacrifice and motherly love to represent her as the 'mother' of her nation and to show her commitment to her subjects.

In later portraits, Hilliard continued to portray the Queen as an idealized young woman, and it is worth recalling that the function of royal portraits was to serve as an emblem of monarchy. The aim was not to portray a real woman in her fifties or sixties, but to glorify Elizabeth as an object of beauty and virtue. As Elizabeth aged, her image was more tightly controlled, with an official proclamation in 1596 ordering any 'unseemly' portraits to be destroyed. While the so-called 'mask of youth' was flattering to Elizabeth, it also served a broader purpose: by this time, she had become an icon of stability and national independence, and it was far better that she remained forever young than raise questions about what might follow her death.

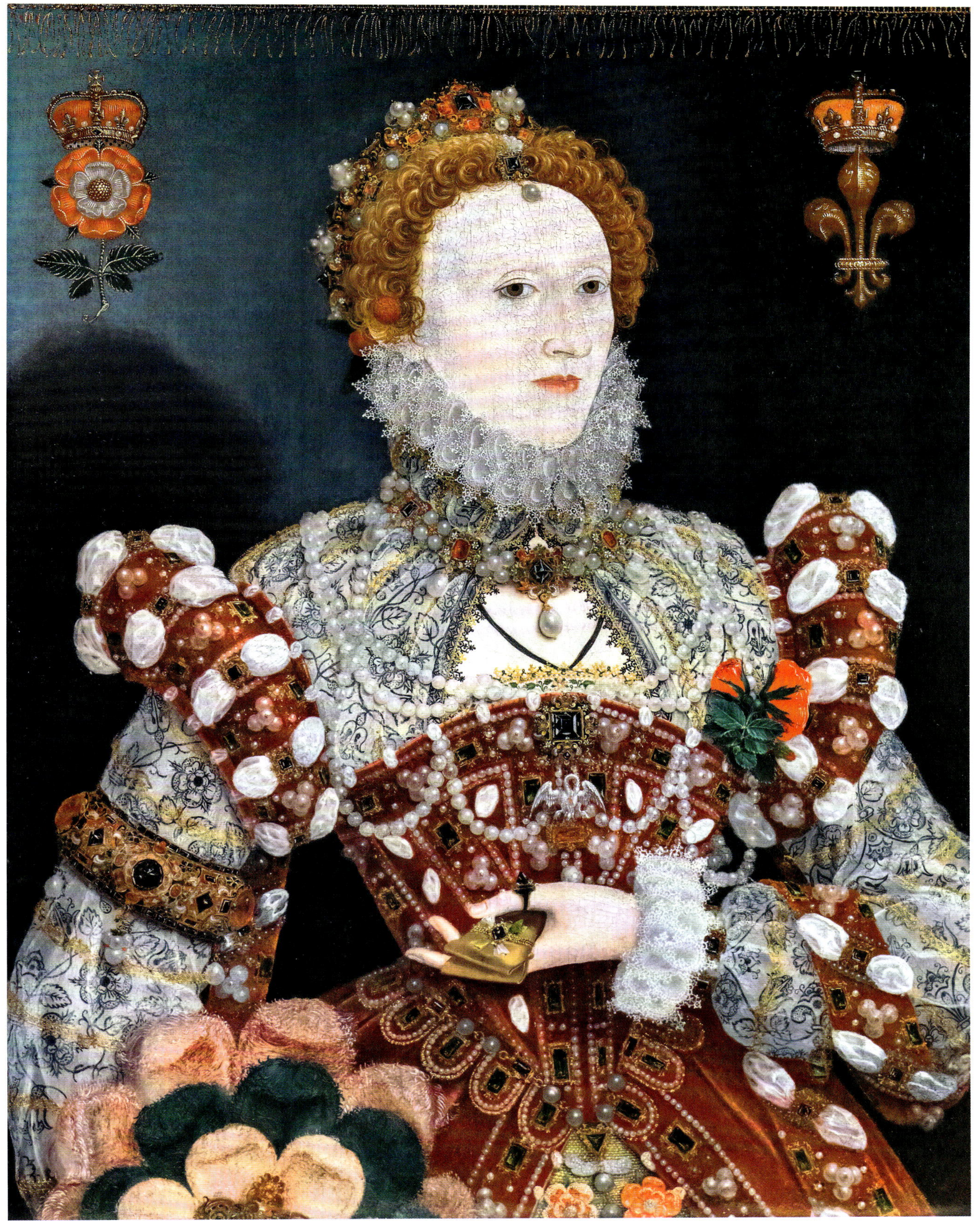

PORTRAIT OF AN AFRICAN WOMAN HOLDING A CLOCK

c. 1583–1585

This portrait of an unidentified Black woman is a fragment rescued from a larger, damaged painting attributed to Annibale Carracci. A finely dressed woman wearing an elegant day dress, an expensive coral necklace and gold and pearl earrings looks us right in the eye while presenting an ornate gilt bronze table clock. Her high, broad, unblemished forehead, rosy lips and cheeks, and hairstyle all conform to Renaissance beauty standards. The elaborate clock is definitely a status symbol, whether hers or the person cut out of the picture, as it was a sign of luxury and also the latest advanced technology.

The mystery of who the sitter was continues to intrigue. She does not appear to be enslaved or used as a 'prop', and fashion historians interpret her attire as that of a middle- or merchant-class woman, as her dress is of expensively dyed black fabric, but does not have an elaborate, ornate collar or ruff, such as the one that is just visible in what remains of another sitter. The pins and needle in her bodice have led to speculation that she was a seamstress or housemaid, while the prominence of the clock has caused others to wonder if she was part of a larger group portrait of clockmakers or goldsmiths.[7]

Most portraits of the time were of the very wealthy or aristocracy, but this appears to be a rare example of a more 'normal' person of average means and circumstances. Although the rest of the painting has been lost, this portrait was saved and has been cherished for more than 450 years by owners that have included King Philip V of Spain and Arthur Wellesley, 1st Duke of Wellington, among others. Exactly who this woman was – and what kind of life she led – remains to be discovered, but despite the mystery surrounding her identity it is obvious that she is a distinct individual, rather than a generic 'type'.

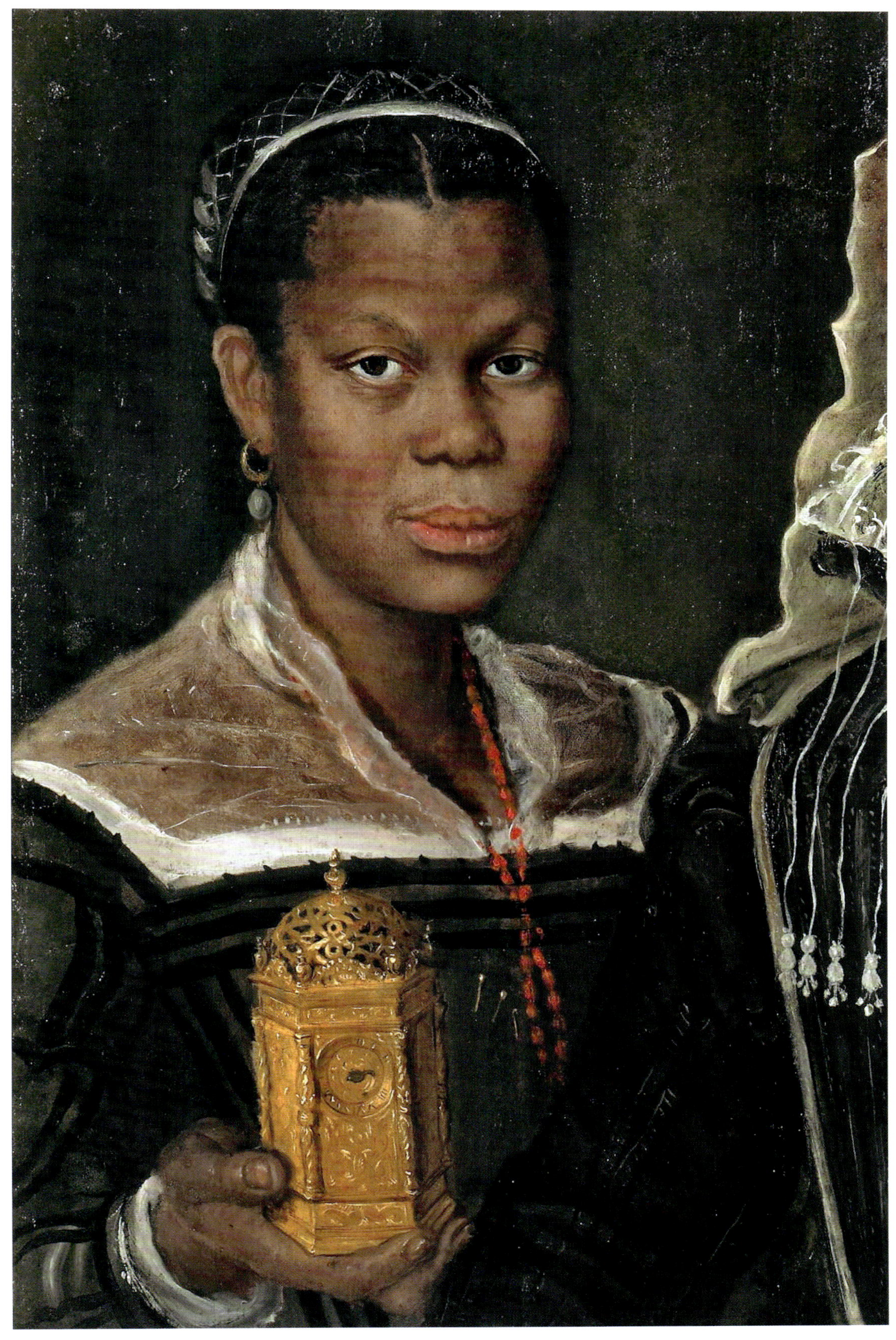

JUDITH BEHEADING HOLOFERNES *c. 1620*

Artemisia Gentileschi was the leading Italian female artist of the Baroque period and through her strength of character, formidable talent and choice of subject matter, the 'strong independent woman' enters our pantheon of types. Gentileschi's powerful female leads are out for revenge or to save the day, and one of her favourite characters was the Old Testament heroine, Judith, who – through a mix of beauty, brains and strength – saved herself and her people from subjugation.

According to the story, Judith used her feminine wiles to get herself invited to dine with the enemy general, Holofernes. Holofernes is so enchanted with her that he drinks too much and passes out. Judith seizes the moment and, with the help of her maidservant, Abra, uses his sword to decapitate him. The theatrical lighting, blood spurting on the women's arms and breasts, and sense of the sheer force needed to hold Holofernes down and drive the sword through his neck – and the fact that he has woken during the attack and is trying to fight the women off – all lend Gentileschi's painting the feel of a gruesome horror film.

Even if you don't know the story, you can still read the scene of two determined young women taking control. This biblical story has not only come to stand for female rage and empowerment in general, but also for the artist's own backstory, which saw her survive the trauma of being violently raped by her art teacher when she was a teenager and the subsequent public trial (during which she was subjected to thumbscrews to prove that she was telling the truth). Gentileschi would go on to become very successful in Rome, Florence, Venice, Naples and England; the support and admiration of her colleagues and patrons was made clear in 1616 when she became the first woman to be admitted to Florence's Accademia delle Arti del Disegno (Academy of the Arts of Drawing).

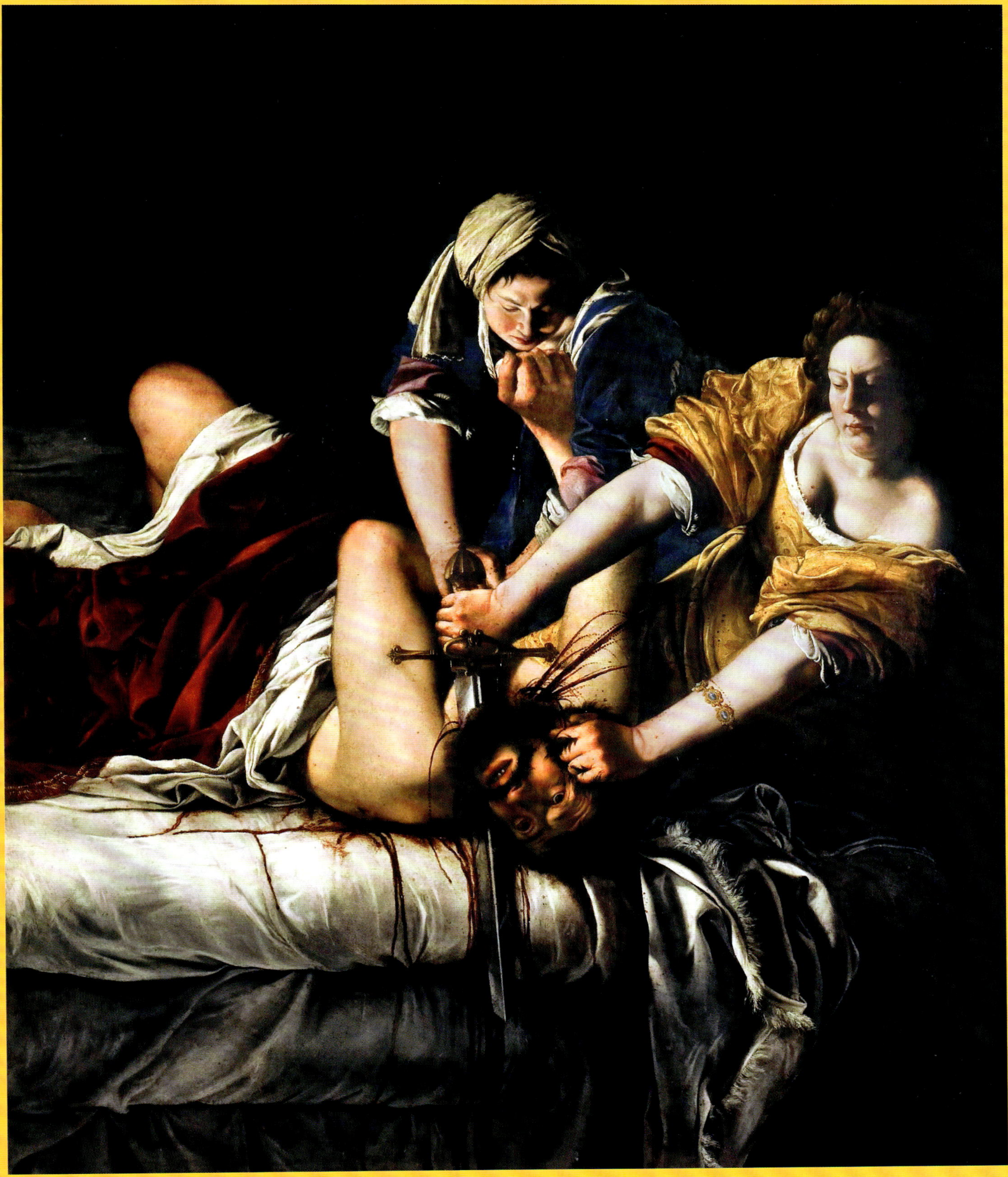

Peter Paul Rubens
(Flemish, 1577–1640)

THE THREE GRACES *1630–1635*

Peter Paul Rubens was the most influential Baroque painter in northern Europe, with an international career and commissions from royal courts in Italy, Spain, England and France. In general, the Flemish painter was less concerned with capturing everyday life than some of his contemporaries (such as Frans Hals, p. 46), instead preferring a rapturous exploration of the human body in sumptuous, theatrical allegorical scenes.

In Greek mythology, the Graces are three minor deities who often accompany and assist Venus, adding desirable feminine traits to the mix of beauty, love and virtue that she represents, such as charm, pleasure, friendship and gratitude. For Rubens, they provided an opportunity to paint three female nudes and the circular composition allowed him to depict – and us to see – the female body in different positions, front and back. And what bodies they are! Luscious bodies in a luscious background, swaying gently or dancing in a circle, framed by a tree draped with clothes and a fountain, both of which echo the shapes of their curvaceous forms.

For Rubens, the ideal female body was fuller-figured and fleshier than those of Botticelli (p. 14) and Titian (p. 24). Indeed, so closely entwined are the artist and this particular representation that 'Rubenesque' has entered our vocabulary to describe the voluptuous female physique that he preferred.

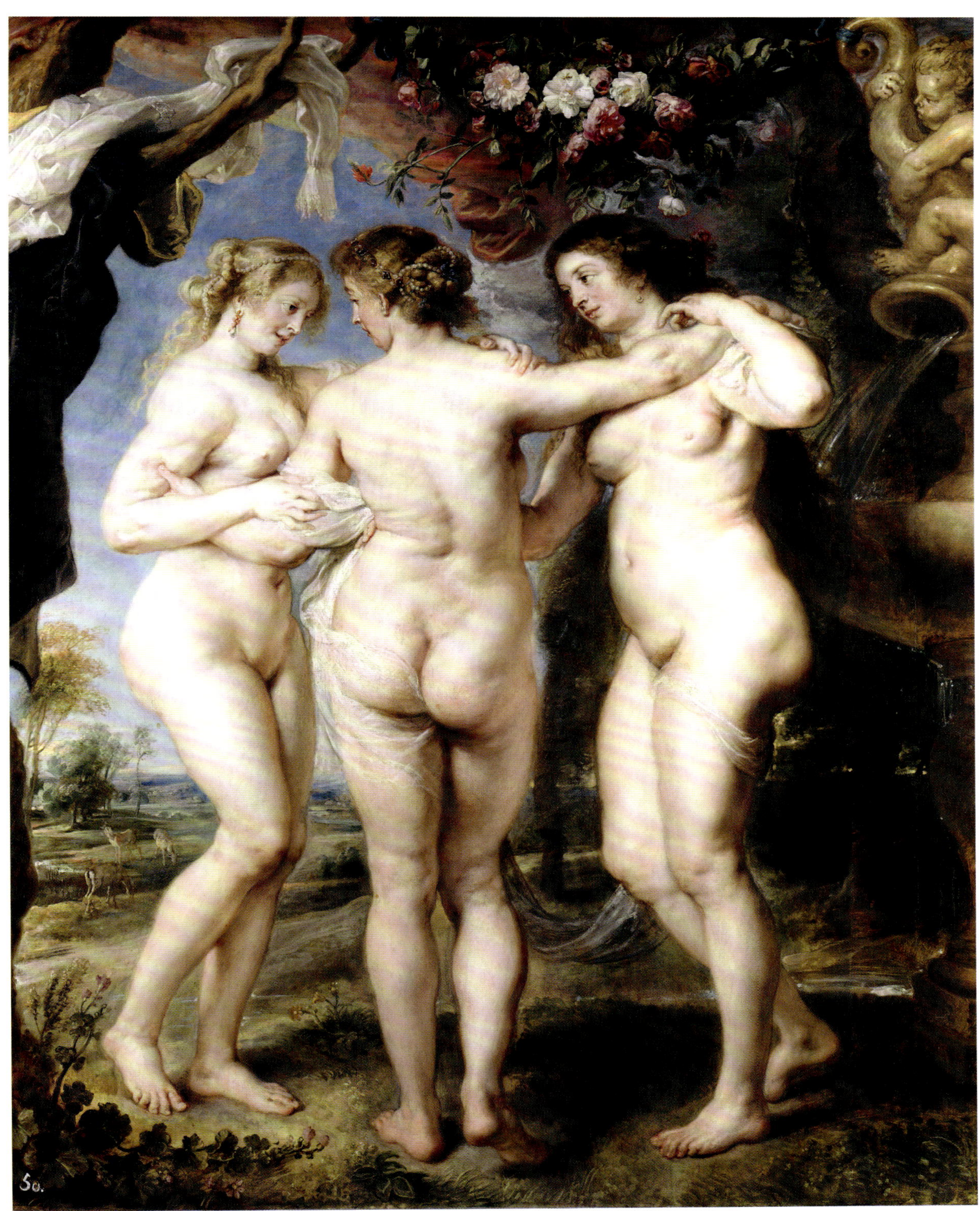
5o.

THE TOILET OF VENUS

('The Rokeby Venus') c. 1647–1651

The Rokeby Venus, by the Spanish artist Diego Velázquez, is at once intensely naturalistic and idealized – and unusual. Most reclining Venus paintings show the goddess facing the viewer, as in Titian's painting (p. 24) or, if Venus is looking in a mirror, she is in a sumptuous setting and adorned with finery, as is the case with the old woman in Falck's print (p. 44). However, Velázquez confounds expectations on both fronts.

First, his nude is seen from the back and is much less explicit than other full-frontal Venuses. Second, there aren't any jewels or accessories to tell us more about her; the only thing that assigns the figure to the realm of myth is Cupid in the corner, holding up the mirror. She is not in a particularly luxurious setting, either. It definitely looks like she is on a set in an artist's studio, which turns the nude into an actual woman whose identity is being protected by her blurred-out face.

This is Velázquez's only surviving female nude, which adds a frisson of danger to the story. Painting the female nude was forbidden in Spain at the time, as was owning a painting of a female nude (even though the King had one of the finest collections of female nudes). Although Velázquez was the King's first painter, this painting was not in the royal inventory.

Inspiration for the pose of Velázquez's lithe, sinuous nude came from the Borghese Hermaphrodite, an ancient sculpture of a sleeping figure that looks like a woman from the back, but from the front is revealed to be intersex.[8] When Velázquez saw this sculpture in Rome, he ordered a bronze copy for his main patron, King Philip IV of Spain. As Caroline Vout explained: 'Everything about [the sculpture] was originally designed for the "big reveal", when what the viewer thought was an off-duty sex goddess, or a vulnerable maiden is realized as Hermaphroditus. Already in the 17th and 18th centuries, the sculpture was thought beautiful, but its beauty can be a source of fear as well as pleasure.'[9]

Does the knowledge of Velázquez's inspiration for the pose suggest another reading for the work? Look again at the subject's out-of-focus face in the mirror and the look she is giving us. Is it provocative? Smirking? Getting ready for a 'big reveal'?

Velázquez's painting certainly conceals more than it reveals. You cannot walk around and find out what this Venus looks like from the front any more than you can bring her face into sharp focus, so she remains an enigma. Perhaps it is because the painting hints at much, but reveals little, that it continues to intrigue and remain relevant to new audiences.

Velázquez was known for his intense visual realism, use of mirrors and creating scenes within scenes, such that things are not always what they seem at first. So it seems to me quite possible that the artist meant to confound the viewer on many levels. Perhaps he is cautioning us to be wary of illusion – of the illusion of beauty, our assumptions and certainties about people and beauty? Velázquez's nude certainly allows the audience to take part in finishing the picture and its story; to imagine their own version of the goddess of love.

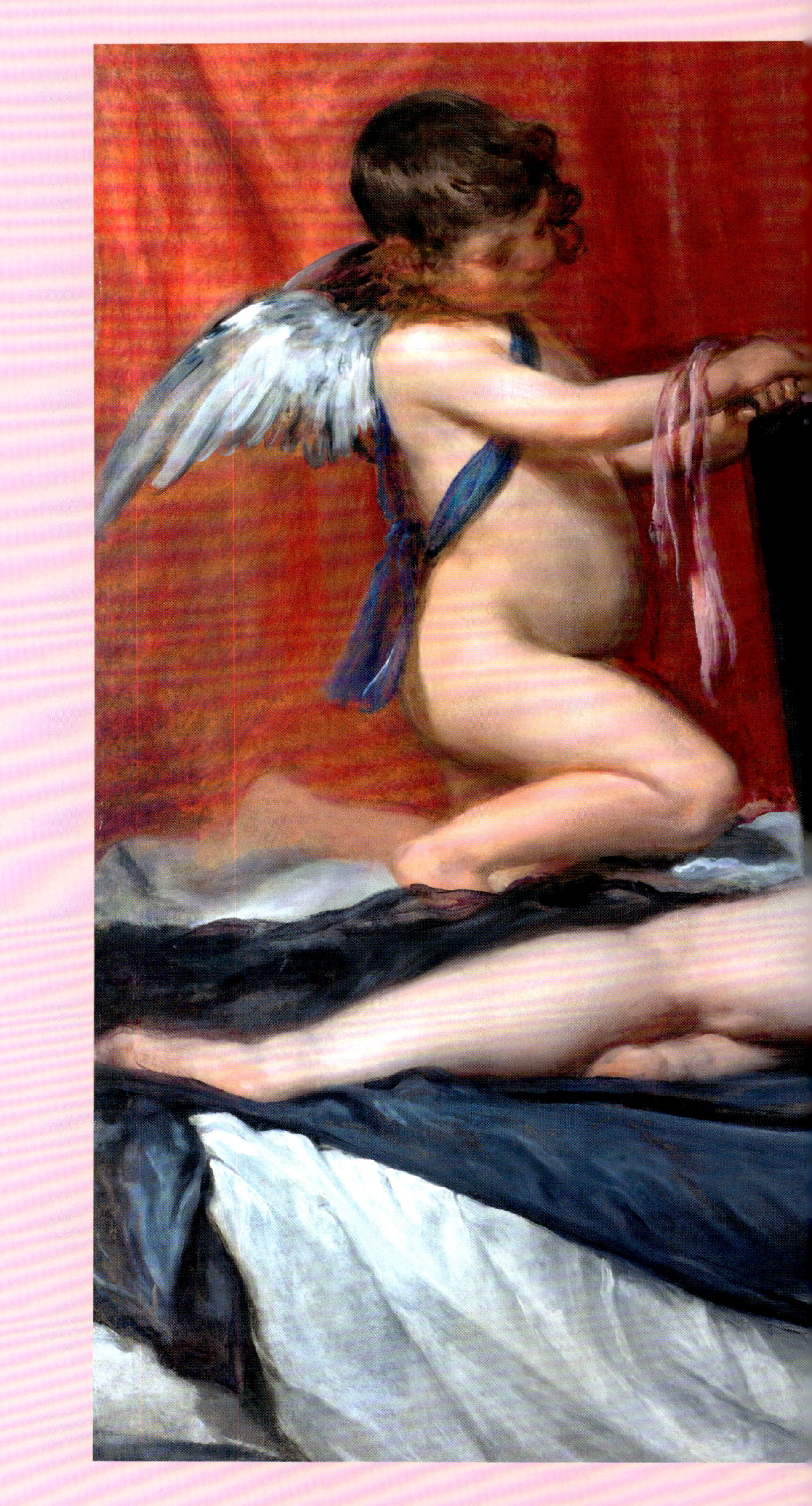

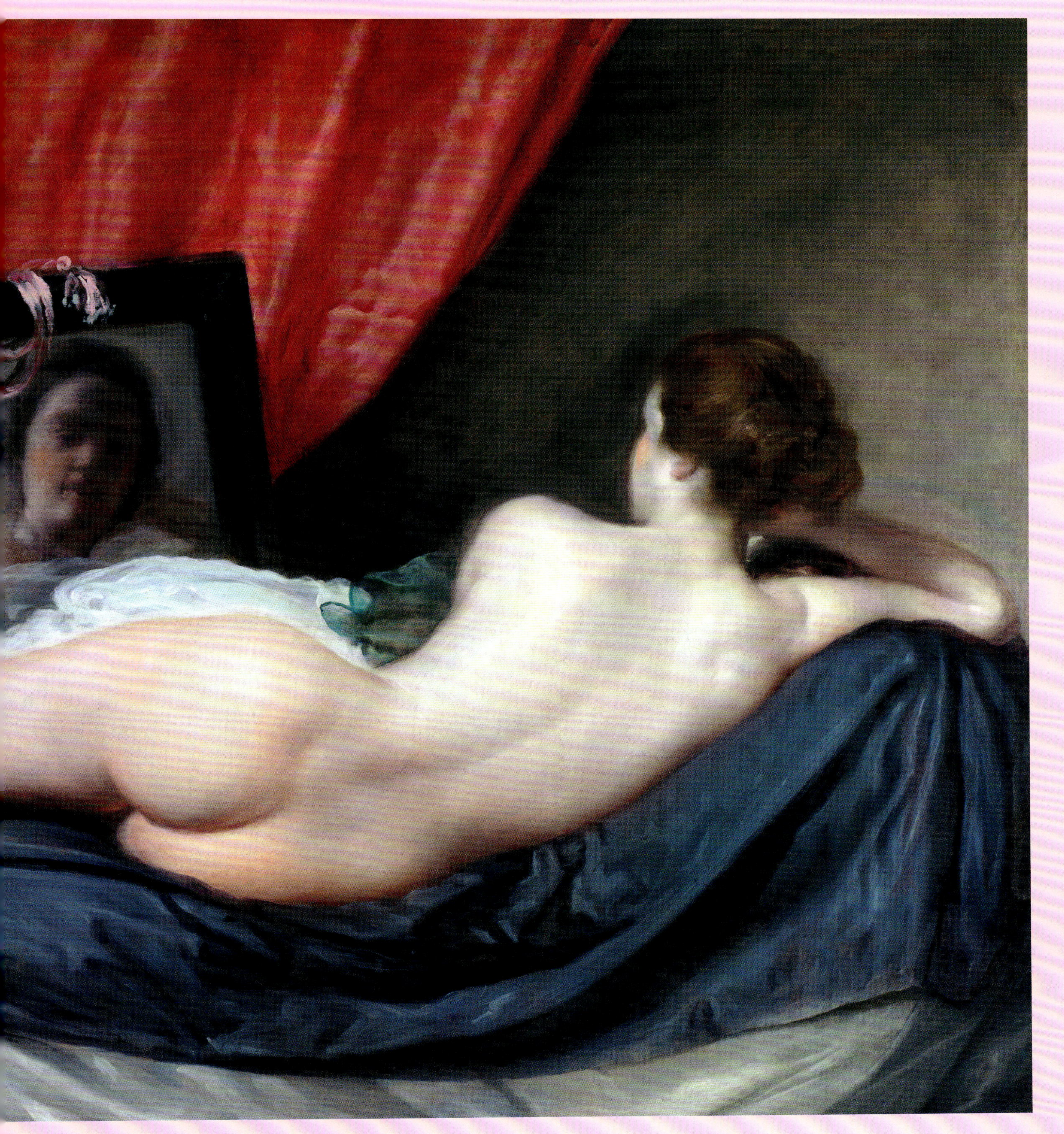

Jeremiasz Falck
(Polish, *c.* 1610–1677), after painting by
Bernardo Strozzi (Italian, 1581–1644)

THE OLD WOMAN AT THE MIRROR *1655–1657*

'Vanitas' paintings were popular in the 17th century, especially in northern Europe. They served as reminders of the transience of life, the fleeting nature of earthly pleasures and the certainty of death. Bernardo Strozzi's painting of 1615 of an old woman sitting at her dressing table, surrounded by signs of wealth and beautification (perfume, pearls, jewels) speaks to this theme. It also warns of the dangers of a Narcissus-like yearning for youth and beauty. Signs of impermanence include the choice of flowers (representing love, beauty, matrimony and death) and the fact that they grow, bloom, wither and die. The old woman, whose shrivelled bare breast is slipping out of her opulent, low-cut dress, is brought face to face with the fact that time has taken its toll by one of the younger women in attendance, who holds up a mirror for her to see herself as others see her.

Are the three women having fun together? Or are the younger women mocking the old woman? Are they seeing what is in store for them? Considering the various titles for the image – *The Ageing Wanton, The Old Coquette, Vanitas* – one can't help but read the image as a moralizing judgement about the vanity of women, especially old women trying to look beautiful or seductive, rather than a scene of celebration of female old age or camaraderie between women.

While not portrayed quite as cruelly as the 'witch-hag' of Baldung (p. 20), the old woman certainly seems to be a figure of fun, someone to be scorned or pitied rather than cherished. This scene also calls to mind the evil stepmother and stepsisters from *Cinderella*, preparing to head off to the prince's ball. This brings another trope to the table – that of the evil, jealous stepmother – as well as derogatory descriptions of older women being 'mutton dressed as lamb'.

Strozzi's popular painting was made into an engraving by Jeremiasz Falck for an album of prints of the collection of the Reynst brothers, Gerard and Jan.[10] This allowed the image and the messages it conveyed to spread far and wide.

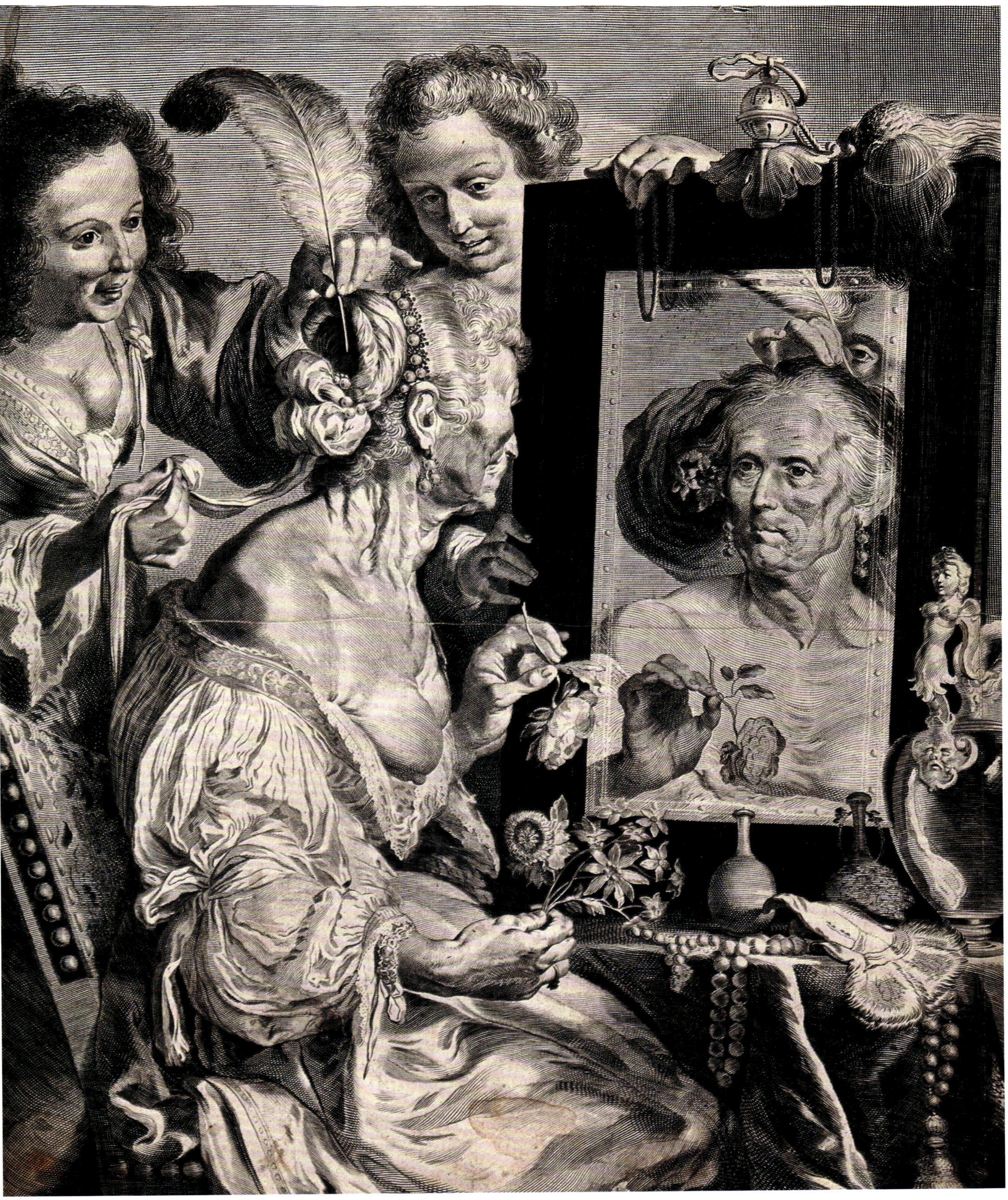

REGENTESSES OF THE OLD MEN'S ALMSHOUSE *1664*

The Dutch Republic (now the Netherlands) flourished after it gained independence from Spain in 1648, following 80 years of war. In doing so, it became a major centre for the arts, whose main patrons were from the newly prosperous middle class, rather than the Church or the aristocracy. Consequently, religious imagery started to be replaced by scenes that celebrated the accomplishments of individuals and organizations of the new republic, and group portraits that expressed national or civic pride were prized commissions.

The most celebrated portrait artist of the Dutch Golden Age was Frans Hals. He is particularly known for his large group portraits, which include *Regentesses of the Old Men's Almshouse*. The elderly women in the picture are the directors of a care home for poor old men. They are not mocked or belittled in their old age, as in the Falck print on p. 44, nor are they portrayed as generic 'types'. They read as real people, with unique features – including wrinkles and age spots.

> *'The elderly women in the picture are not mocked or belittled in their old age, nor are they portrayed as generic "types". They read as real people, with unique features – including wrinkles and age spots'*

As the art historian Helen Rosenau wrote in 1944: 'Here the women are seen highly differentiated and individualized ... The spirituality of faces and hands is emphasized, and the dignity of old age coupled with distinction of personality.'[11] At the time that he painted this portrait, Hals was himself in his eighties and this perhaps added to his desire to create a thoughtfully considered image of the wisdom and frailty that can accompany old age.

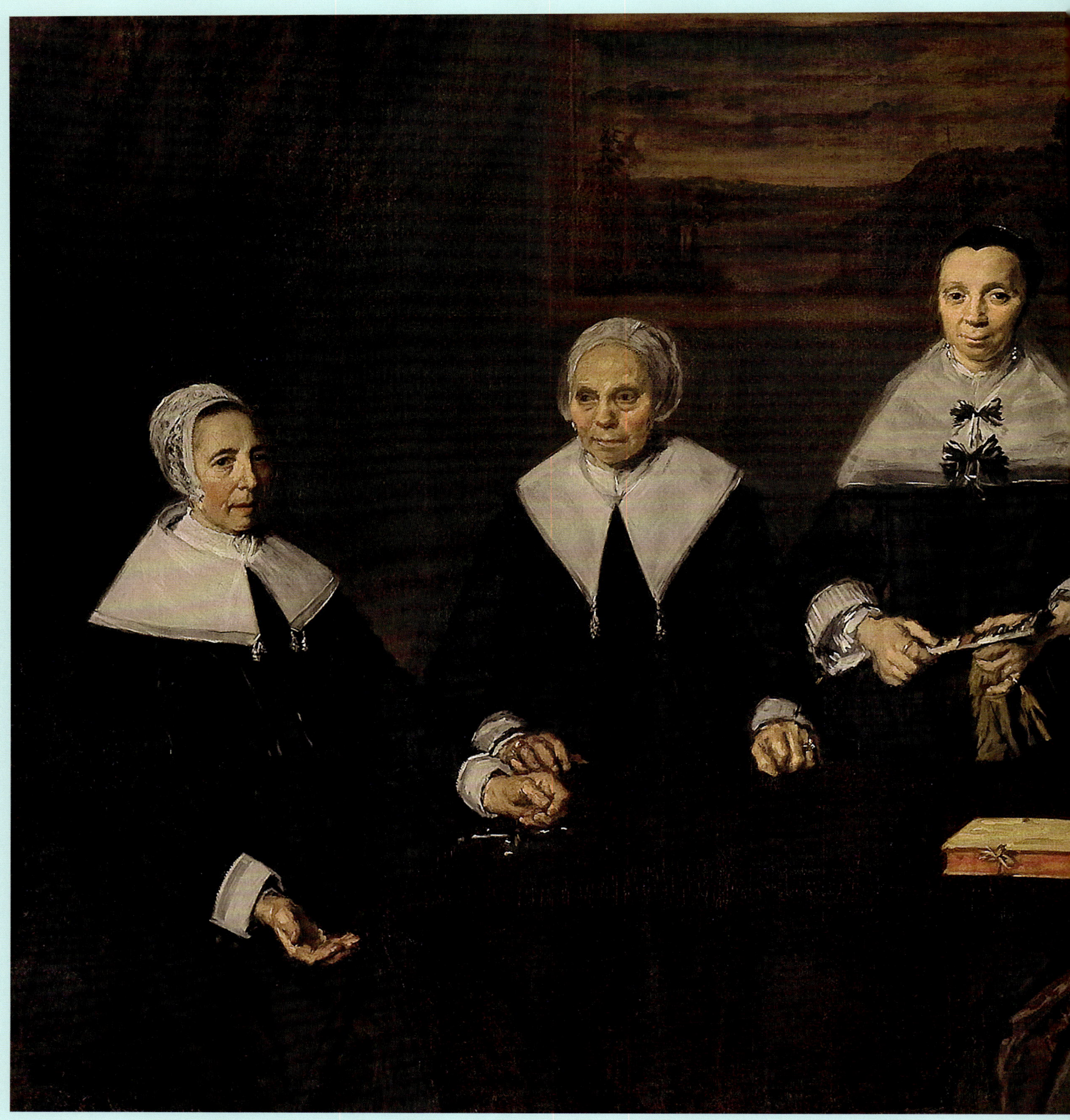

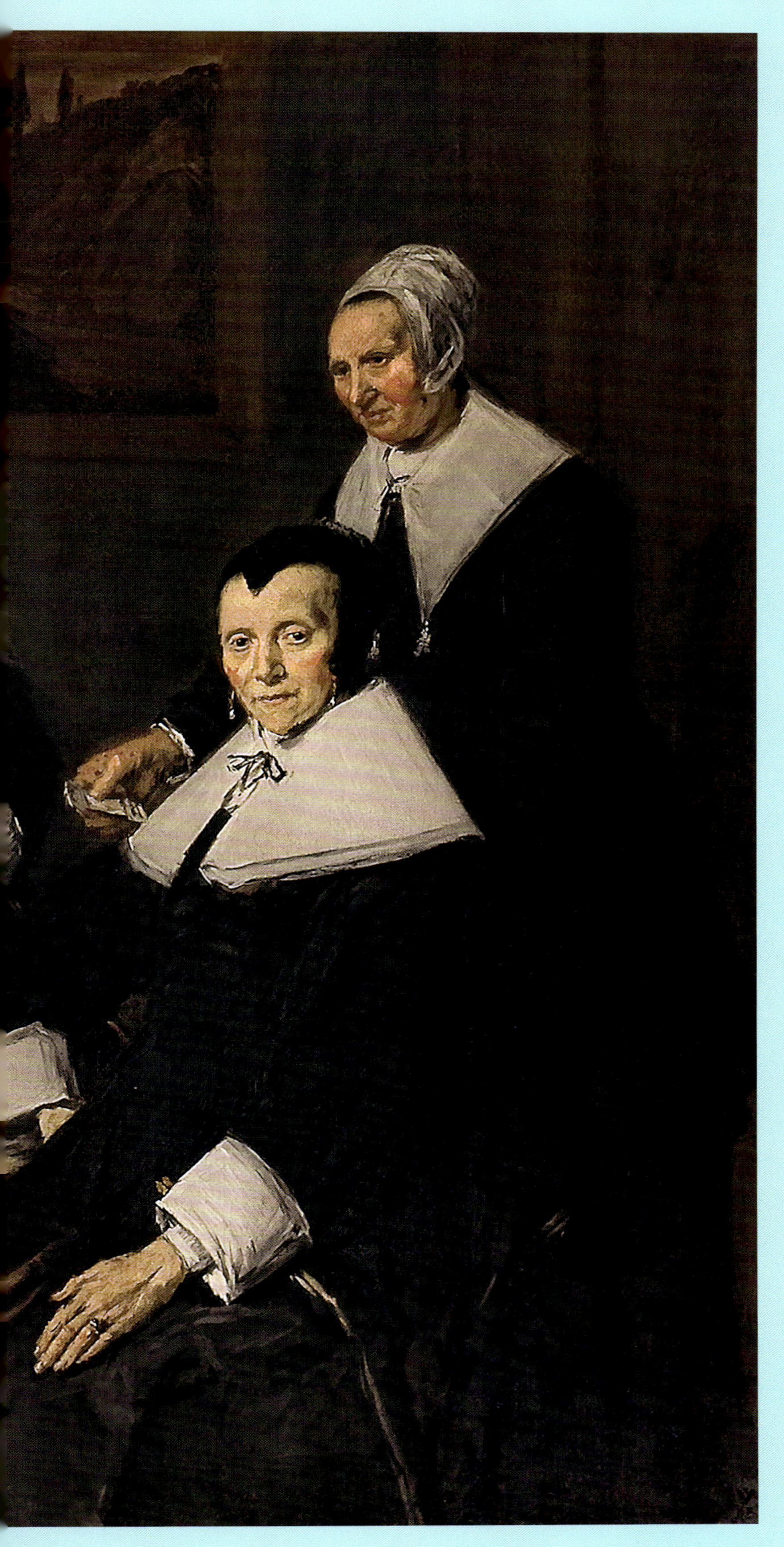

GIRL WITH A PEARL EARRING *1665*

Nicknamed 'Mona Lisa of the North', Johannes Vermeer's *Girl with a Pearl Earring* pictures a beautiful mysterious woman of the Dutch Golden Age. Like Leonardo's *Mona Lisa* (p. 18), it is left to the viewer to determine what the girl is thinking as she looks out, lips parted as if about to say something.

There has been much speculation about the identity of the girl, but unlike the Mona Lisa, Vermeer's painting is not a portrait of a specific person. It is what the Dutch call a *tronie* – a study of facial expression and costume, to make an imaginary character or ideal 'type'. Vermeer's girl is wearing a jacket that was fashionable dress of the day, but her headdress of blue and yellow scarves was not worn by Dutch women of the time, making her an idealized 'young woman in exotic dress'.

In most of Vermeer's other paintings of women, the subject is often alone, performing mundane activities in domestic interiors – the women are not looking out and connecting with the viewer as this one does. There is something about this girl's 'strike a pose' stance, looking over her shoulder with sparkling eyes and moist lips, combined with being dressed-up in a costume, that makes her seem familiar and contemporary, like a fashion model on a catwalk or photoshoot.

The painting only became known to the public when it was sold at auction in 1881 in The Hague, Netherlands, but has since become one of the world's most recognizable paintings. It has provided inspiration for numerous books, plays, films and other artworks imagining the life of the girl, as well as that of the artist, whose own life remains almost as mysterious as the subject of his painting.

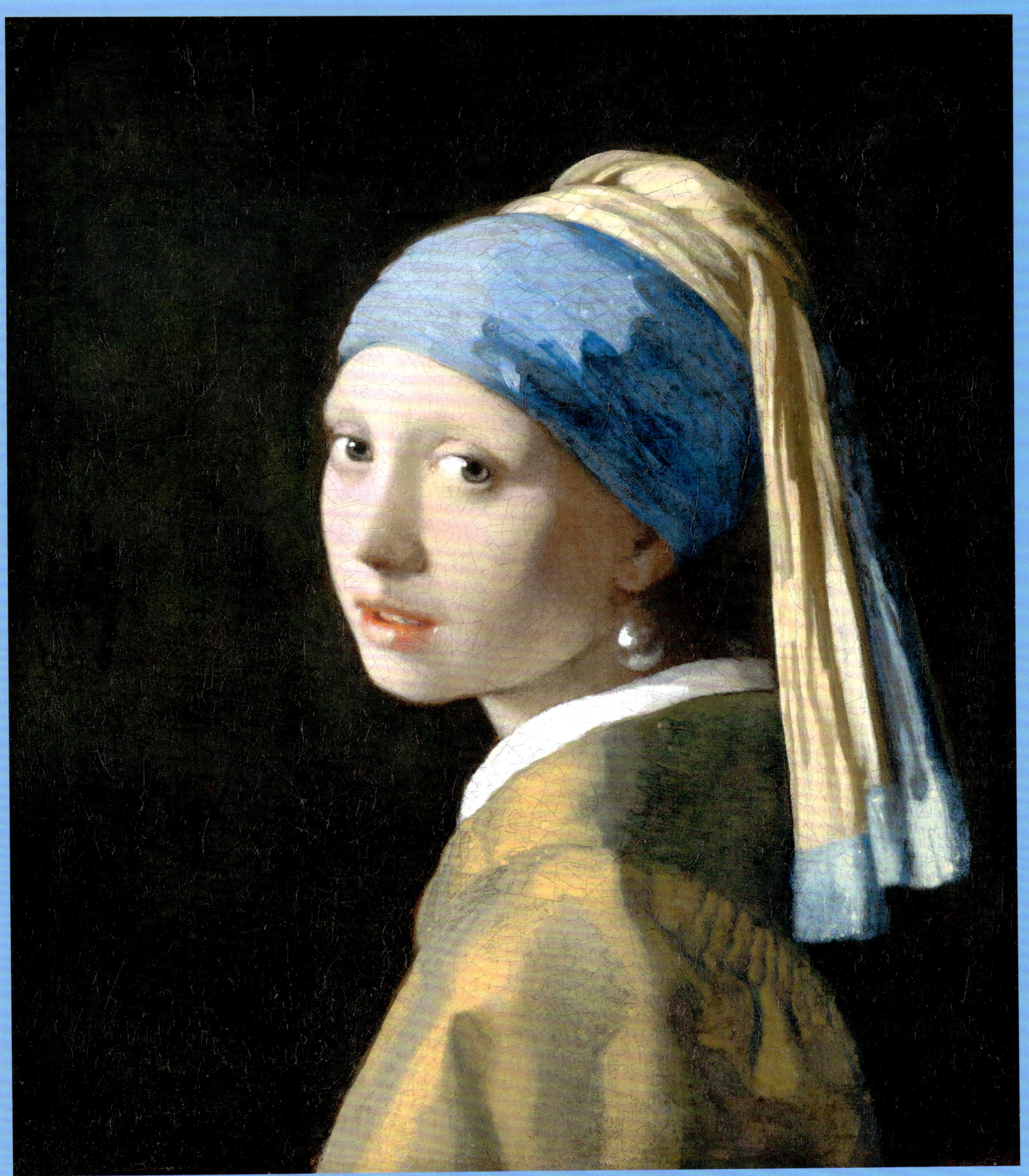

MISS VAN ALEN *c. 1735*

Religious painting was not permitted in early Puritan America, as it would be presumptuous to paint what one cannot see (such as angels) and idolatrous to paint God. As genre painting, landscape and still life were considered frivolous, this really only left portraiture.

Early New England portraits served two functions: to create a record of the sitter and as a status symbol. They were painted by limners (meaning 'to illuminate'), who were untrained artisans that were anonymous in both identity and technique. Their portraits were naïve, strongly patterned, flat and linear. The Gansevoort Limner is so-called because of the number of portraits he or she painted of the Gansevoort family, a prominent Dutch-American family in the Hudson River valley area of New York.

Miss Van Alen is a popular example of early American Colonial portraiture. The subject is portrayed in fashionable dress and jewellery, suggesting a certain wealth and status. She is depicted in a realistic manner, painted from life but without much mastery of physiognomy. There is a sense of it being a particular person, as opposed to a generalized, idealized portrait of a young woman, despite the fact that the same pose and composition were used in a number of portraits of young women, presumably by the same artist.

The painting was exhibited widely during the 1930s, appearing in exhibitions of early American painting and folk art throughout the United States and in Paris, France. It was admired for its simplicity, directness and functional nature by those looking for American sources in their quest to develop a distinctly modern American art. This included the American Precisionist, Charles Sheeler (1883–1965), who had a reproduction of this painting hanging in his home.

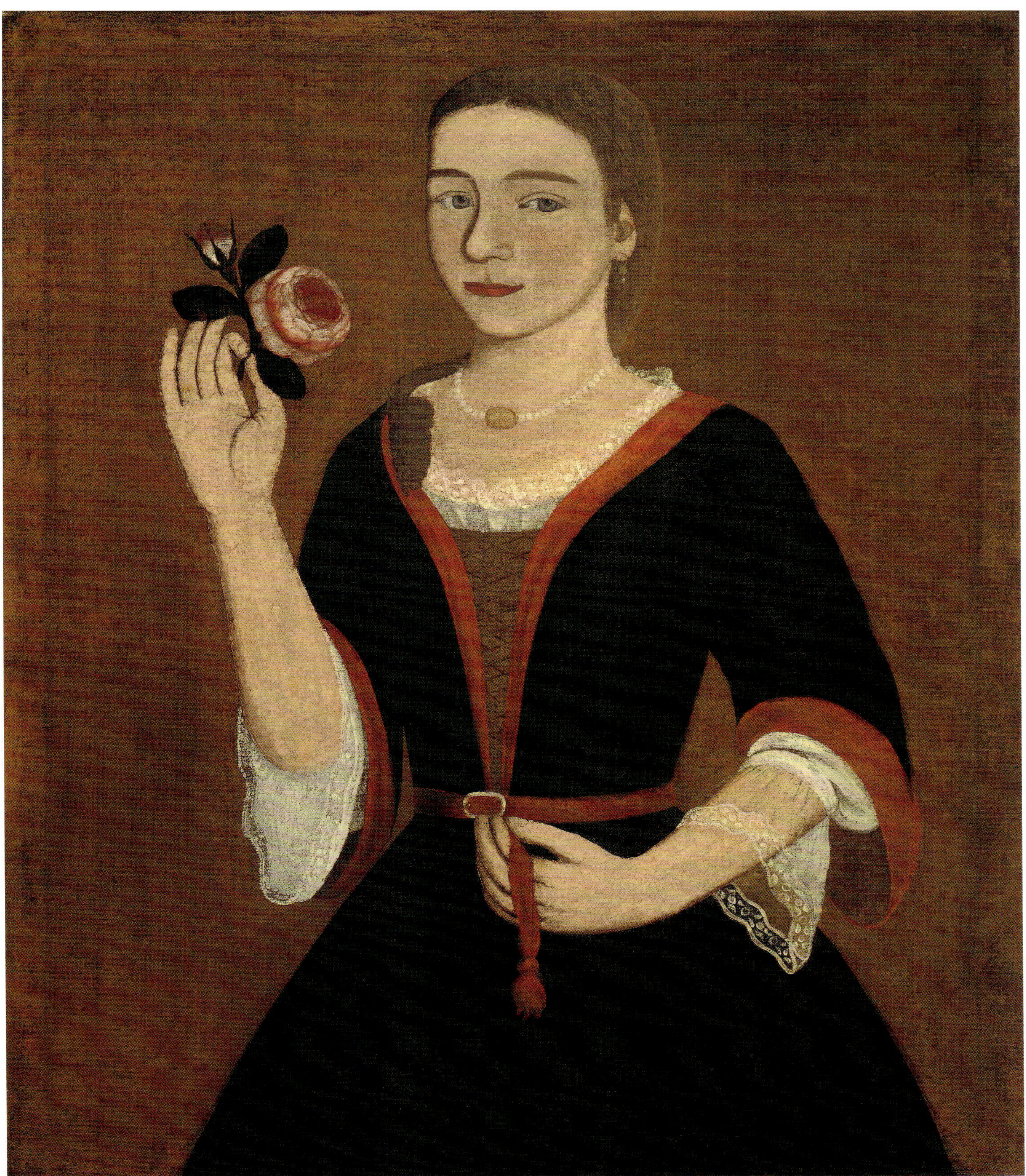

THE NIGHTMARE *1781*

The late 18th century witnessed both the American War of Independence and the Industrial Revolution in Great Britain. Gothic horror stories provided escape from the traumas of these major societal upheavals, while paintings with strange and fantastic images drawn from the imagination – rather than history or the Bible – shocked and titillated in equal measure.

One such painting was *The Nightmare* by Swiss artist Henry Fuseli, which has been variously interpreted as a sleeping woman in the midst of a nightmare; a woman overcome by her erotic dream or fantasy; a scene inspired by a dream of Fuseli's about an unrequited love; or the evil 'other' capturing a beautiful woman.[12] When it was put on display at the Royal Academy in London in 1782, his dramatic, theatrical painting of a damsel in distress frightened visitors and quickly gained notoriety. A print soon followed, popularizing the image and enabling it to reach a wider audience.

Fuseli's helpless woman is but one of a cast of overwrought, swooning, sleeping or unconscious women who appear in various guises throughout art history. Sex and fear, horror and fantasy, dreams and imagination, attraction and repulsion are all played out on the body of a defenceless woman. Fuseli's exploration of the dark side of the human subconscious made *The Nightmare* an inspiration for Gothic writers such as Mary Shelley and Edgar Allan Poe. His fascination with the supernatural and dreamworlds – and especially with disturbing sexual undertones – make him a precursor of Surrealism, with psychoanalyst Sigmund Freud supposedly among those who owned a print of the painting. However you read it, and wherever it takes you, the macabre image has had an enormous influence on art and popular culture since.

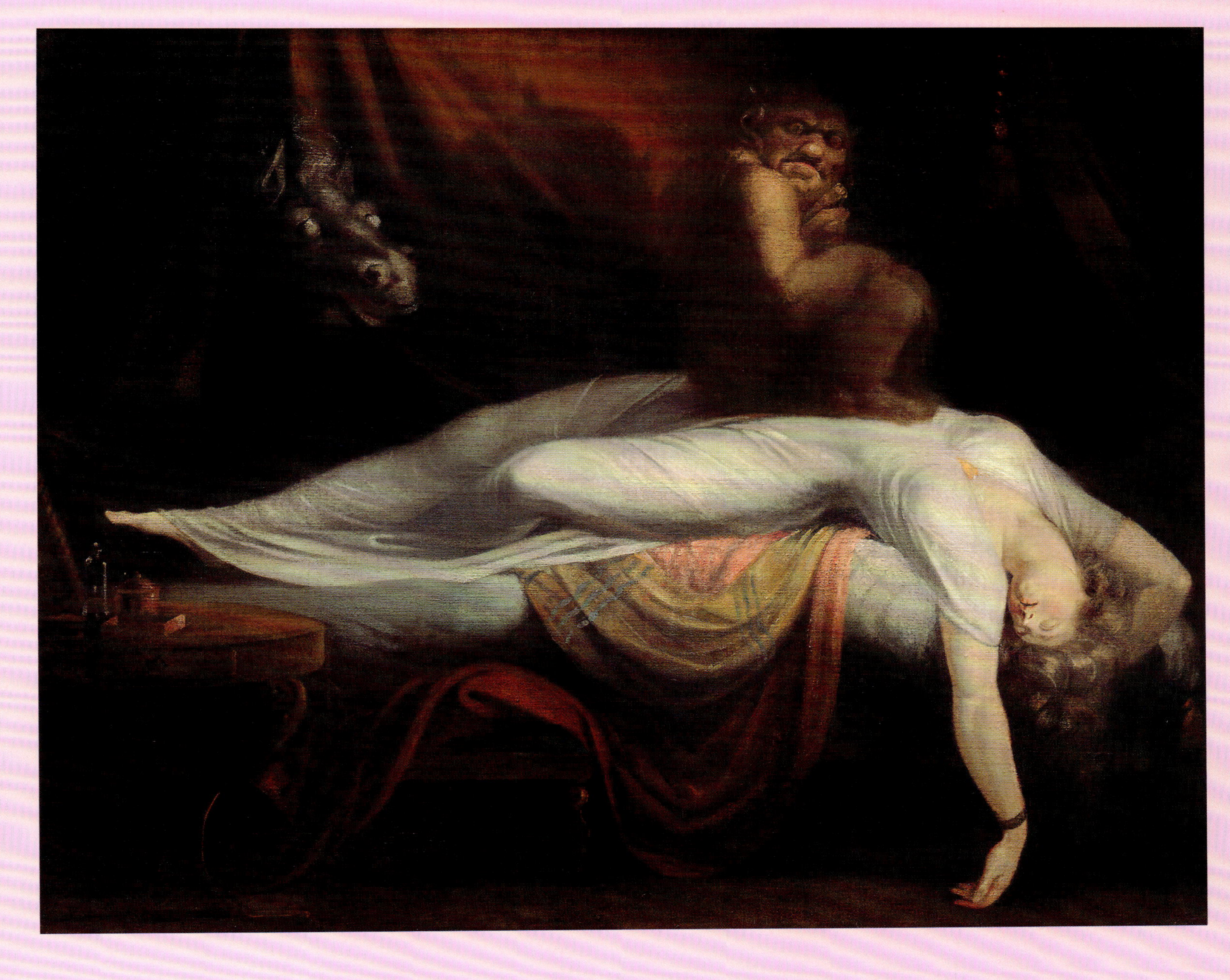

Thomas Gainsborough
(British, 1727–1788)

PORTRAIT OF GEORGIANA, DUCHESS OF DEVONSHIRE *1785–1787*

Thomas Gainsborough was one of the leading portrait artists of Georgian high society in England, while Georgiana Cavendish (1757–1806) was one of its most prominent and colourful characters. Georgiana was known for her charisma and kindness, lavish parties, affairs with men and 'romantic friendships' with women, political activism and a gambling addiction that left her in enormous debt. She was hugely popular, and the press and the public followed her every move, be it commenting on her political activities, dress sense or her gossip-worthy, unconventional love-triangle marriage to the Duke of Devonshire.[13]

A trend-setting celebrity of her day, Georgiana's outfits and hairstyles were immediately copied by all; she helped instigate the fashion for higher and higher hairstyles and ostrich-feather headdresses. In this portrait, Georgiana is wearing a fabulous hat that she designed with drooping black ostrich feathers, which sits perched atop her signature big hair. Once seen, milliners were beset with requests for 'the Duchess of Devonshire's picture hat'. Similar hats soon appeared in fashionable society and in other portraits, becoming known as the 'Gainsborough hat'.

The painting, like its sitter, went on to have its own famous history, having been lost and found, bought and stolen, and along the way getting cut down from a full-length Grand Manner portrait to its current size to fit over a fireplace. The painting now resides at the Devonshires' ancestral home, Chatsworth, in central England.

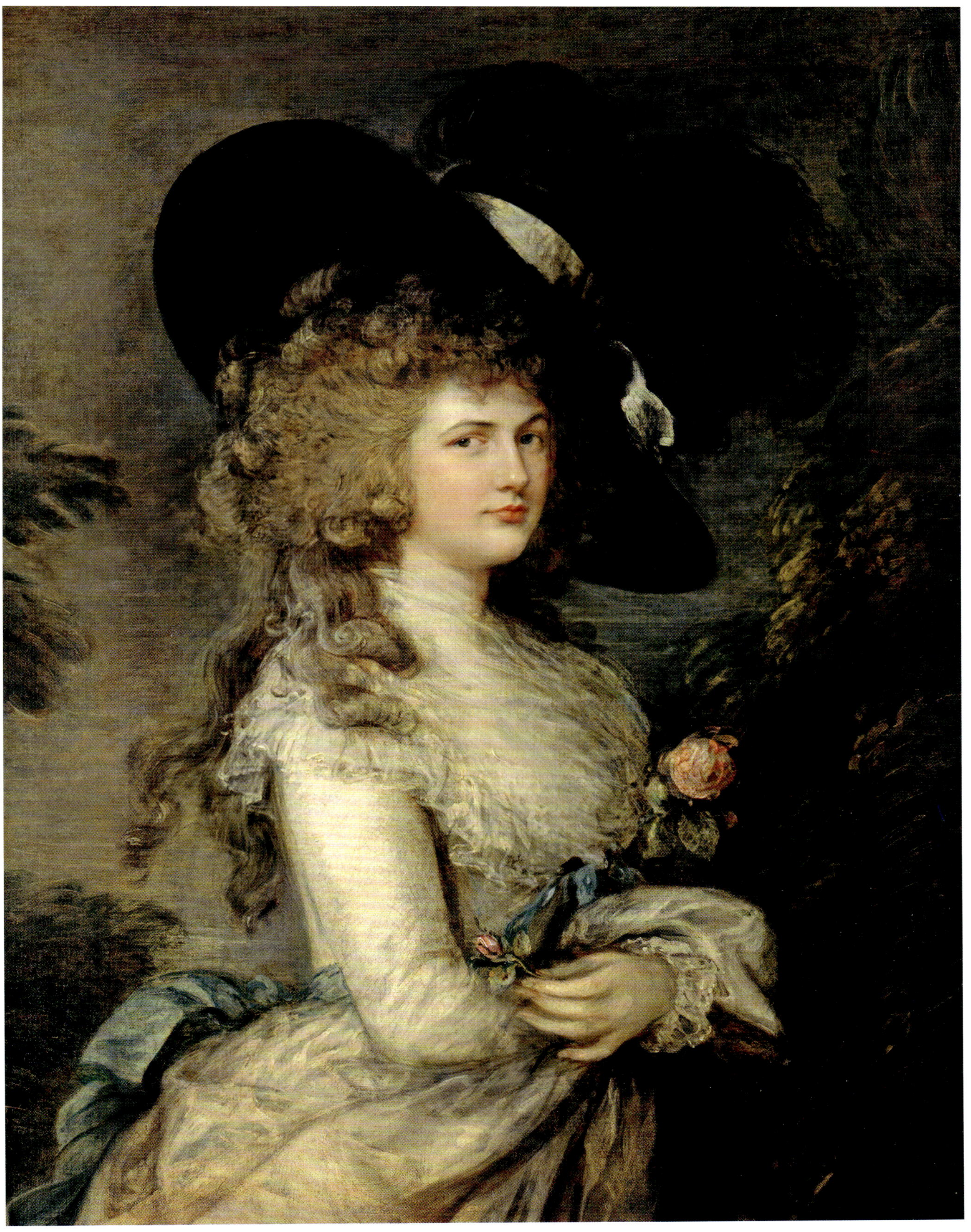

SELF-PORTRAIT *1790*

In 1778, when she was only in her twenties, Élisabeth Vigée Le Brun became the favourite painter of Marie Antoinette, Queen of France. While the patronage of the Queen brought Vigée Le Brun fame and fortune, this turned to danger with the onset of the French Revolution. Deemed an 'enemy of the people' by the revolutionaries, Vigée Le Brun left her husband and France in October 1789, fleeing to Italy.

Without the financial support and social standing that came with being a court painter, Vigée Le Brun had to reinvent herself in order to support herself and her young daughter. Known for her fashionable, often sensual portraits of French nobility in elaborate dress and lavish surroundings, Vigée Le Brun had to both refer to her reputation as a successful and admired royal portrait painter to attract new clientele, while simultaneously distancing herself from the French queen.

In her self-portraits of 1790 and 1791, we see Vigée Le Brun doing just that. She presents herself wearing a modest but fashionable outfit in an anonymous studio setting that underlines her serious profession as an artist. As a calling card to advertise herself, it is interesting to note that the first version of this self-portrait shows her in the act of drawing a portrait of Marie Antoinette, reminding the viewer of her royal patronage. However, in the copy that she made in 1791 she replaces the Queen's portrait with one of her daughter, now presenting herself as an artist and mother.

In both paintings, she appears younger than her actual age, demonstrating her ability to convey charm and beauty in a 'natural' wholesome fashion – desirable skills for flattering portraits of prospective clients. Vigée Le Brun had a successful second career abroad in Italy, Austria, Germany, Russia, Switzerland and England, before returning to France after 12 years in exile.

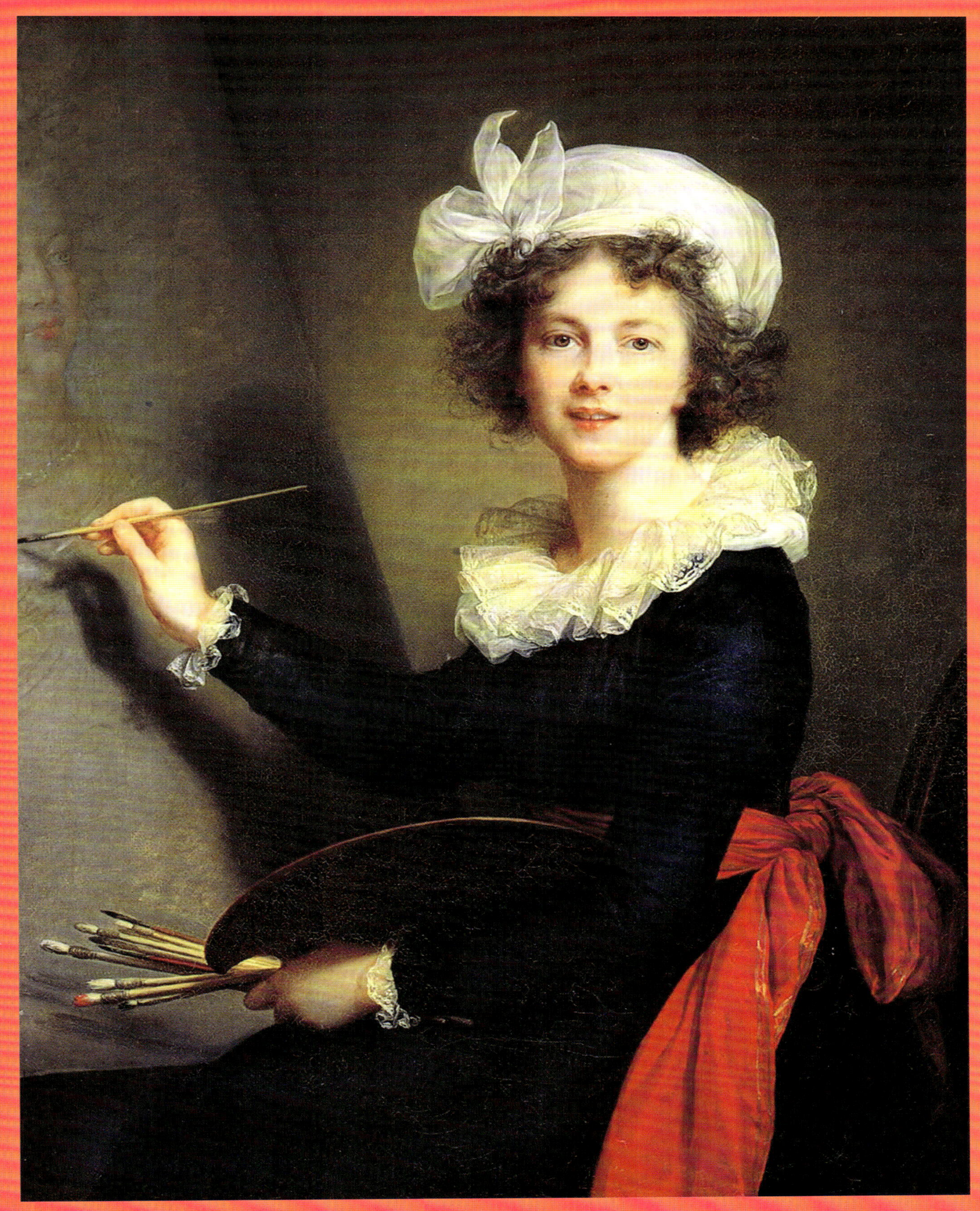

Kitagawa Utamaro
(Japanese, 1753–1806)

COQUETTISH TYPE *c. 1792–1793*

Kitagawa Utamaro rose to fame in Japan in the 1790s with his *ukiyo-e* ('pictures of the floating world') depictions of Japanese beauties with elegant, elongated features. He was known for his more realistic, individualized portrayals of women of different ages, social classes and backgrounds, often in intimate moments, such as this one, where the woman is emerging from a bath, her hair and gown in disarray. The evolution and development of woodblock printing allowed these images to be widely distributed, although only in Japan, as the country had closed its ports to almost all international trade in the 1640s.

When Japan ended its self-imposed seclusion in the mid-19th century, rapid Westernization followed, and the West became fascinated with all things Japanese. Japanese art and crafts were included in the enormously popular international expositions held in Europe and the United States, bringing the work of Utamaro and others to Western audiences. The Japanese-style of *ukiyo-e* woodblock prints with their flowing graphic lines, decorative surface patterns and large areas of flat colour were particularly inspirational for many Art Nouveau, Impressionist and Post-Impressionist artists that followed, such as Edgar Degas (p. 90) and Mary Cassatt (p. 92).

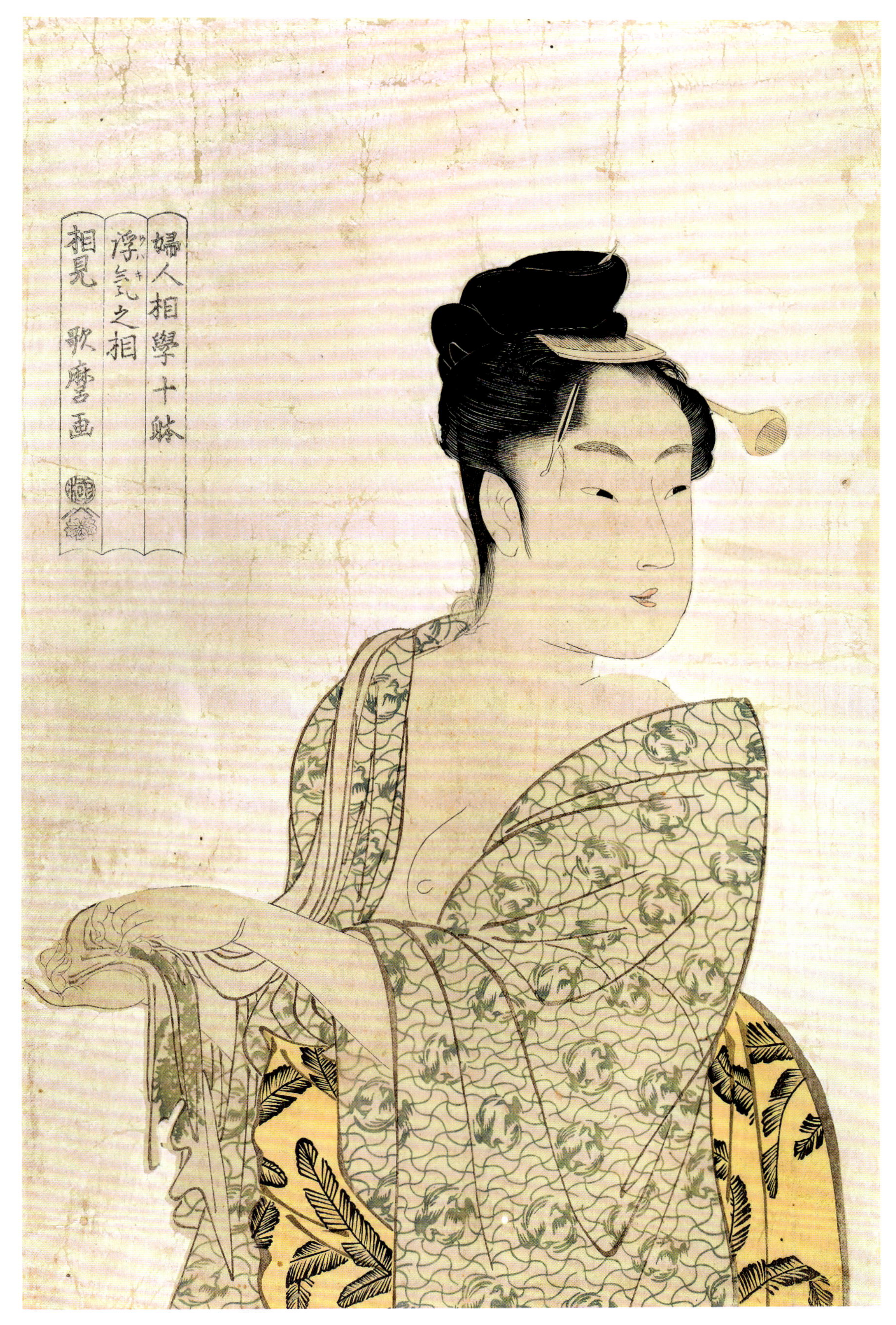

婦人相學十躰
浮気之相
相見　歌麿画

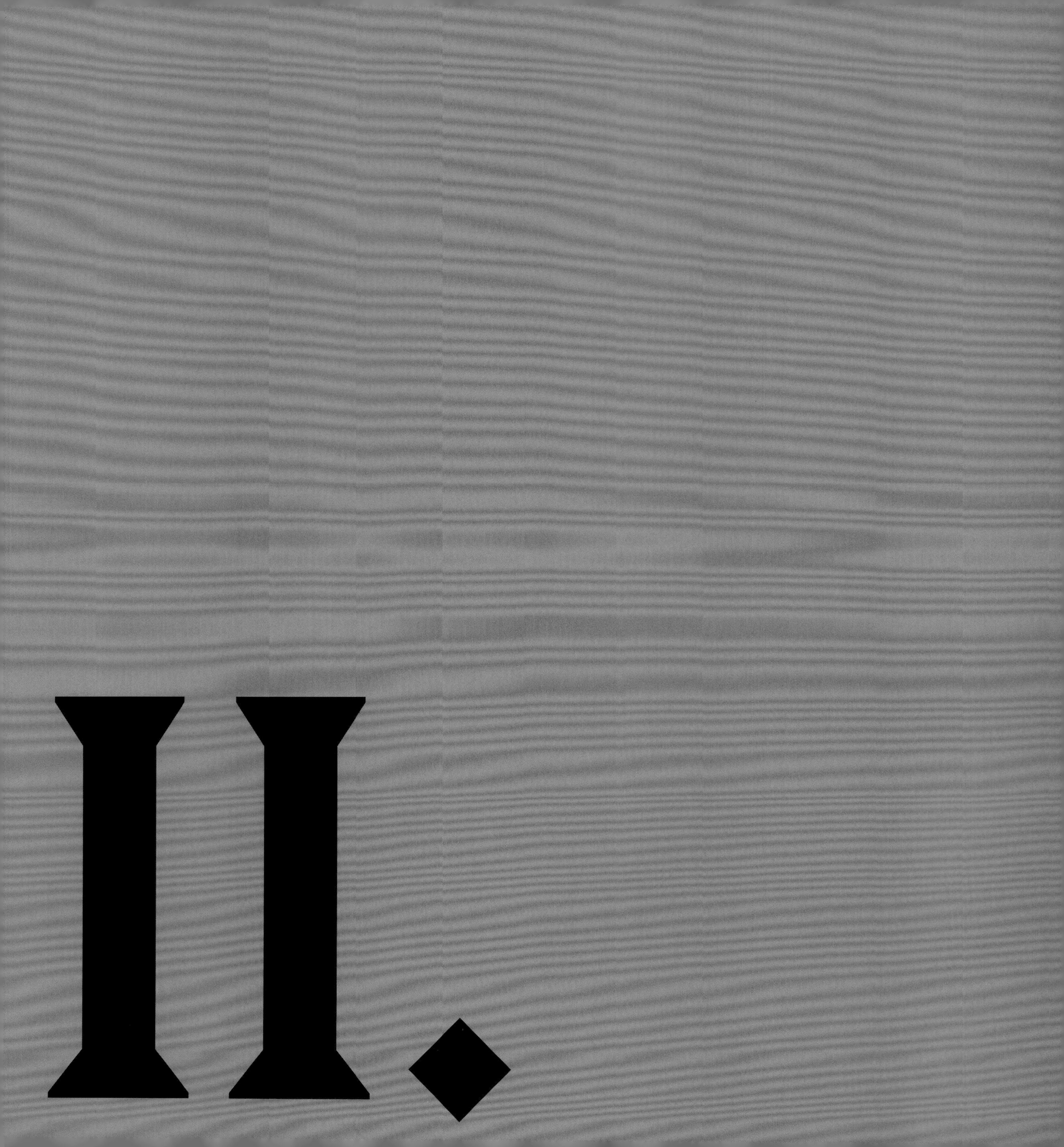

II.

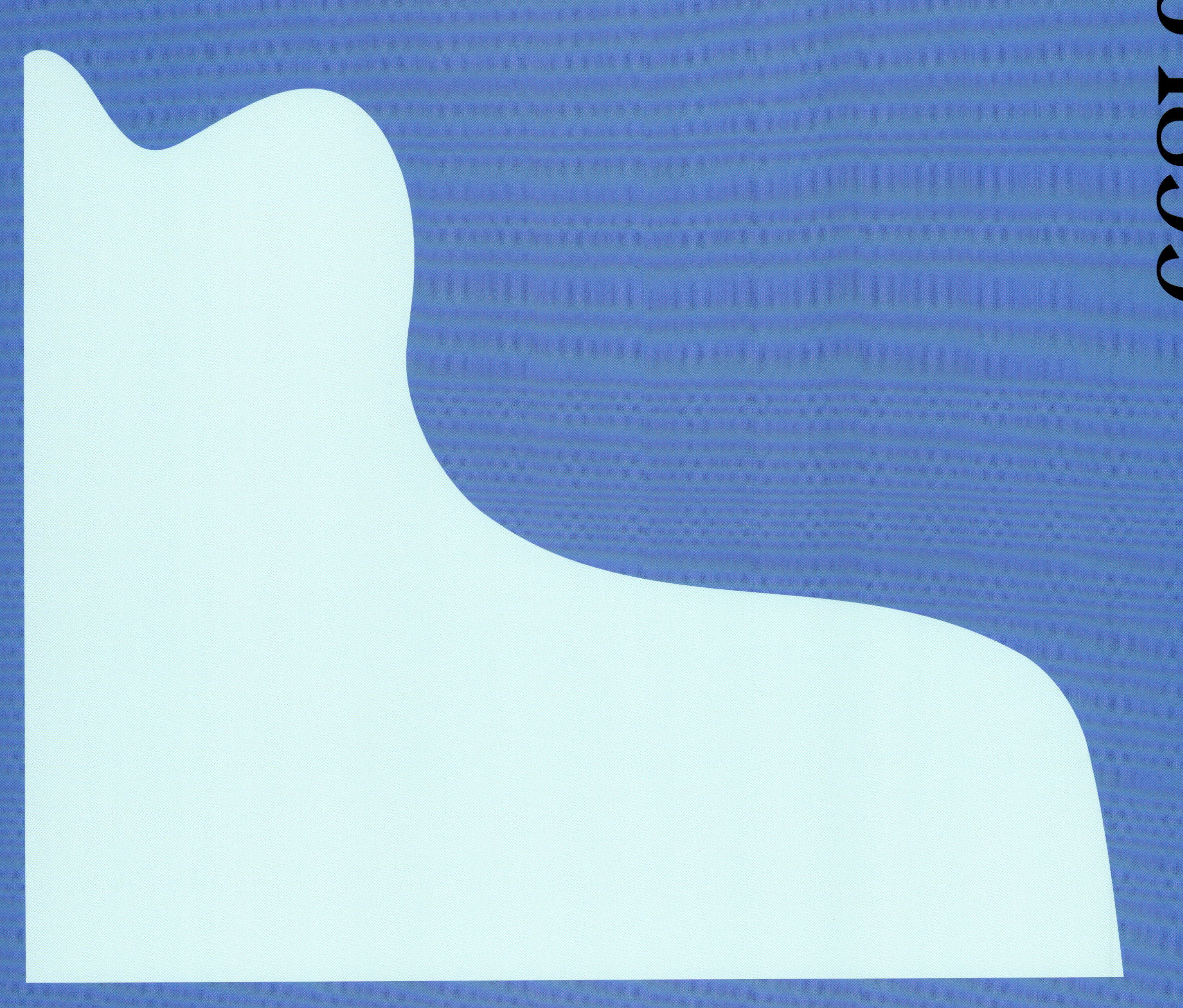

1800 to 1899

PORTRAIT OF MADELEINE *1800*

Portrait of a Black Woman (also known as *Portrait of Madeleine*) is an arresting image of a dignified young Black woman looking directly at the viewer. Unnamed at the time, the sitter is now believed to have been a former slave, named Madeleine, from Guadeloupe, who worked for the artist's in-laws. Significantly – and unusual for European art of the time – this Black woman is not portrayed as a servant or attendant, or a symbol to demonstrate a white master's wealth or status.

Instead, French artist Marie-Guillemine Benoist portrayed Madeleine in the fashionable attire and setting of conventional society portraiture. With its beautiful Black sitter wearing the blue, white and red colours of the *tricolore* flag adopted by the French Revolutionary government in 1790, the painting seems to function somewhere between an actual portrait and an allegory for post-revolutionary France. In 1791, the government opened France's official art exhibition – the influential Paris Salon – to all artists for the first time, regardless of gender or membership of the Royal Academy, while in 1794 it abolished slavery in all French territories. Benoist painted her portrait in the heroic neoclassical style favoured by those espousing the ideals of the new democratic nation, and it brought her fame when it was exhibited at the Paris Salon in 1800.

Whether it was intended as such, or not, *Portrait of a Black Woman* seems to put forth a face for the new republic and call for its motto of 'liberty, equality and fraternity' to apply to all, including women and people of colour. Poignantly, this striking image of a freed Black woman in the colours of the French Republic, painted by a female artist who herself was experiencing greater freedoms in her career of choice than before, projects the hopes and possibilities for Black and female emancipation from the gains made by the French Revolution. Yet at the same time, progress in both causes was eroding and would be dashed by Napoleon in the years that followed.[14]

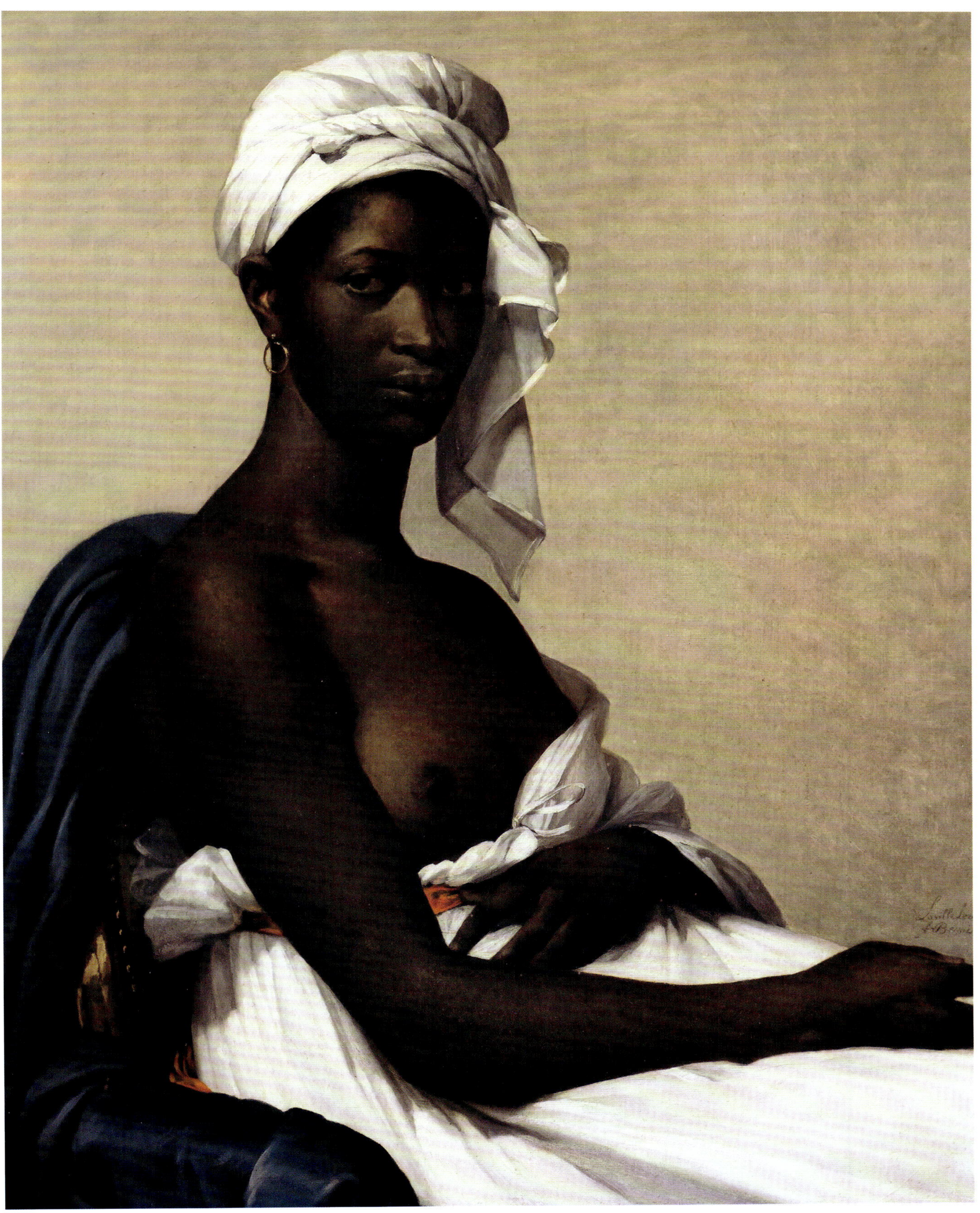

LA GRANDE ODALISQUE *1814*

When *La Grande Odalisque* was first exhibited in 1819, Jean-Auguste-Dominique Ingres was criticized for sacrificing anatomical correctness in his quest to convey a new feminine ideal. Although the French artist's painting is in the tradition of reclining female nudes, such as those by Titian (p. 24) and Velázquez (p. 40), Ingres has not cloaked his nude in classical mythology by calling her a Venus. Instead, he is vehemently declaring her to be a real (albeit imagined) person: a concubine in a Turkish harem.

Ingres never went to Turkey, but he imagined his beauty from travel writing and contemporary French notions of the exotic and erotic lives of those who lived in the Ottoman Empire. As such, his nude is an *idea* of feminine beauty. It is a fantasy, rather than a specific individual, and this sense is heightened by her stylized, elongated curved torso.

Ingres's sensual beauty has a knowing look as she gazes over her shoulder at the viewer, who is allowed in turn to gaze back upon her – after all, she is a fantastical exotic 'other', rather than a real (European) woman. Within his painting, Ingres references other artists' versions of feminine beauty, notably that of his hero, Raphael, with the woman's face and headdress drawn from (or a homage to) Raphael's *Madonna della Sedia* (p. 22). The serpentine line and smooth, marble-like skin of Ingres's nude set among the rich, detailed textiles and other exotic accessories, add to the slightly abstract feeling of the woman's physically impossible body.

'Ingres imagined his beauty from travel writing and contemporary French notions of the exotic and erotic lives of those who lived in the Ottoman Empire. As such, his nude is an idea of feminine beauty. It is a fantasy, rather than a specific individual'

Looking at the painting from a 21st-century perspective, brings to mind the contemporary practices of artists and editors who Photoshop and edit images, as well as the physical adjustments people make to their own bodies in pursuit of an idealized version of 'perfection'. Ingres made various versions of this odalisque during his life, as have other artists throughout history, such as the Guerrilla Girls (p. 180).

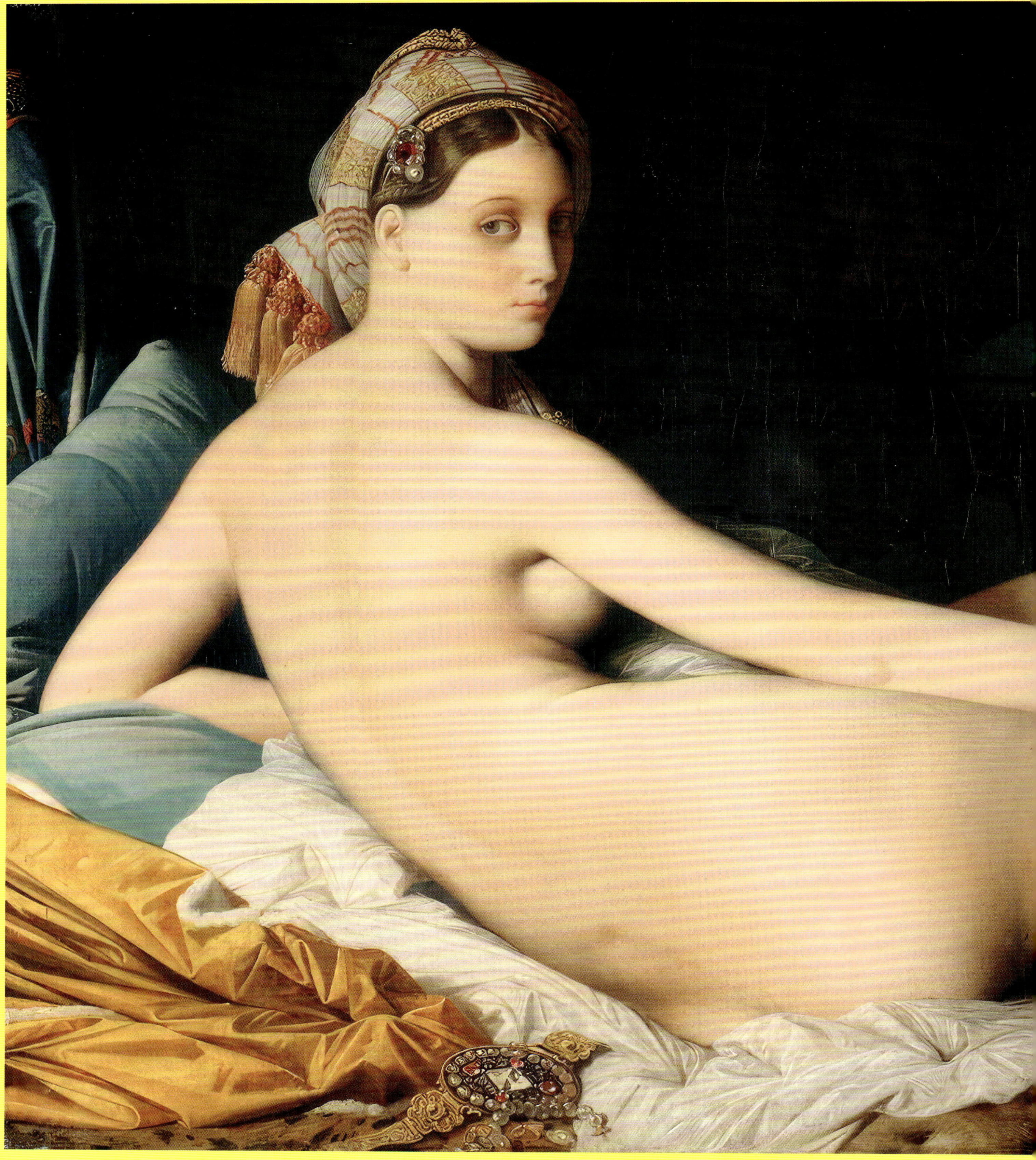

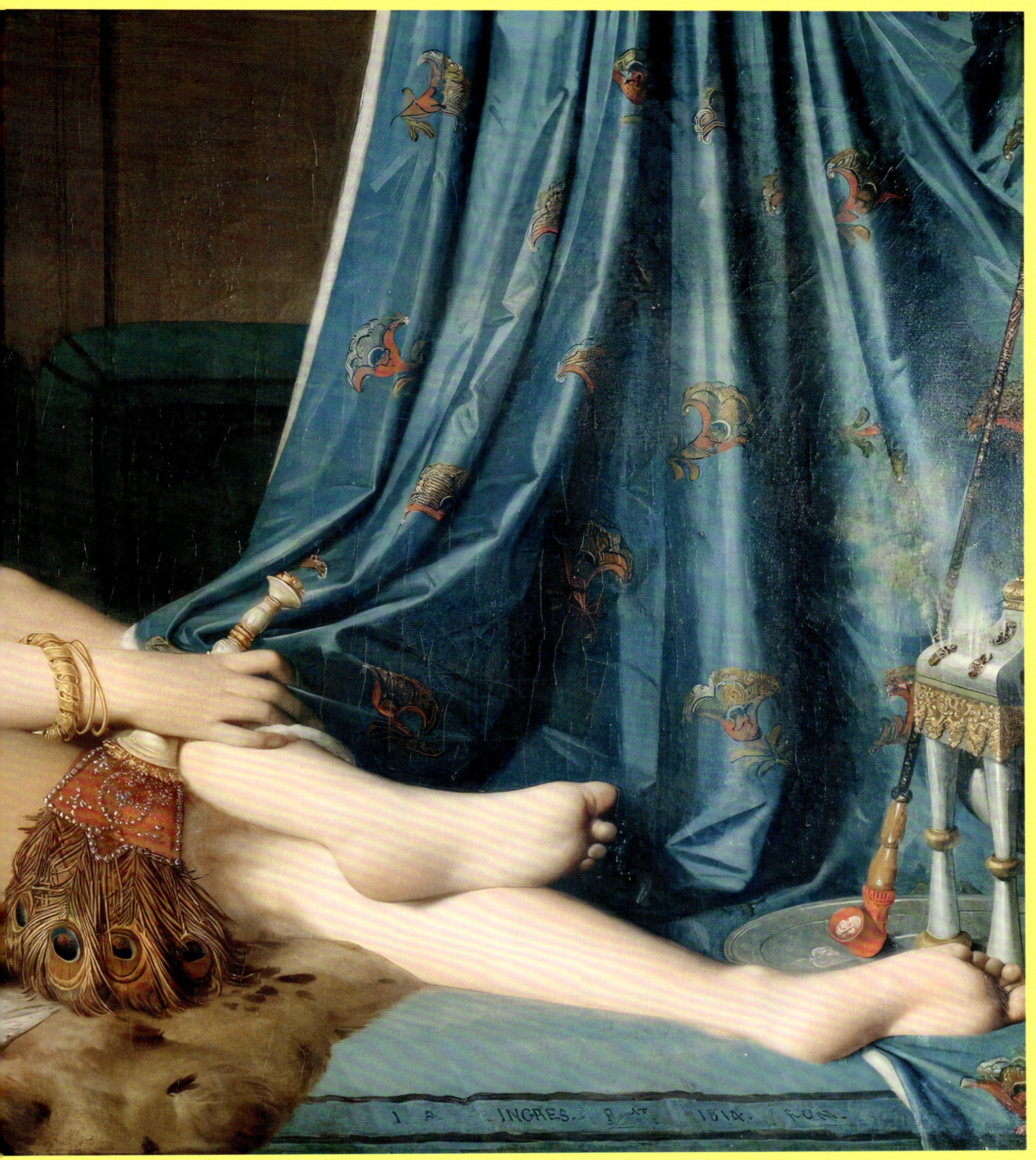
J. A. INGRES. Pxt. 1814. ROM.

THE GREEK SLAVE *Modelled 1841–1843*

Hiram Powers was an American sculptor working in Italy in the 19th century. *The Greek Slave* was his first idealized figure carved in marble, and the one that made the sculptor's name. Calling his female nude in chains *The Greek Slave* not only referenced the classical *Medici Venus* sculpture from which she was adapted, but it also presented her as a Christian woman being sold at a Turkish slave market during the Greek War of Independence (1821–1832).

The first version of *The Greek Slave* was exhibited in London in 1845 to some 40,000 people, while two later versions of the sculpture were viewed by more than 100,000 visitors when they toured America between 1847 and 1851. In an accompanying text, Powers successfully sold the sculpture's nudity to the American public (and clergy) by explaining that the woman's nakedness was not her fault, but that of her captors. This allowed conservative American audiences to see her as a symbol of Christian virtue and permitted them to look at – and admire – the female nude from a moral high ground.

Powers's reputation as America's most famous sculptor was cemented when *The Greek Slave* was exhibited in London again, at the Great Exhibition of 1851. Given the historical moment at which it was exhibited – pre-Civil War America and post-abolition Britain – it was impossible not to see the sculpture in terms of ongoing debates about slavery. Exhibited almost simultaneously on both sides of the Atlantic, it became the most reproduced, collected and talked about work of art in the world.

In all, six full-sized marble versions of *The Greek Slave* were made, each slightly different, as well as porcelain statuettes and prints for domestic environments. Small-scale reproductions were collected by many to show their support for the abolitionist cause, with the subject's lofty historical and contemporary moral credentials allowing conservative American and Victorian British audiences alike to own and display a female nude within a domestic setting.[15]

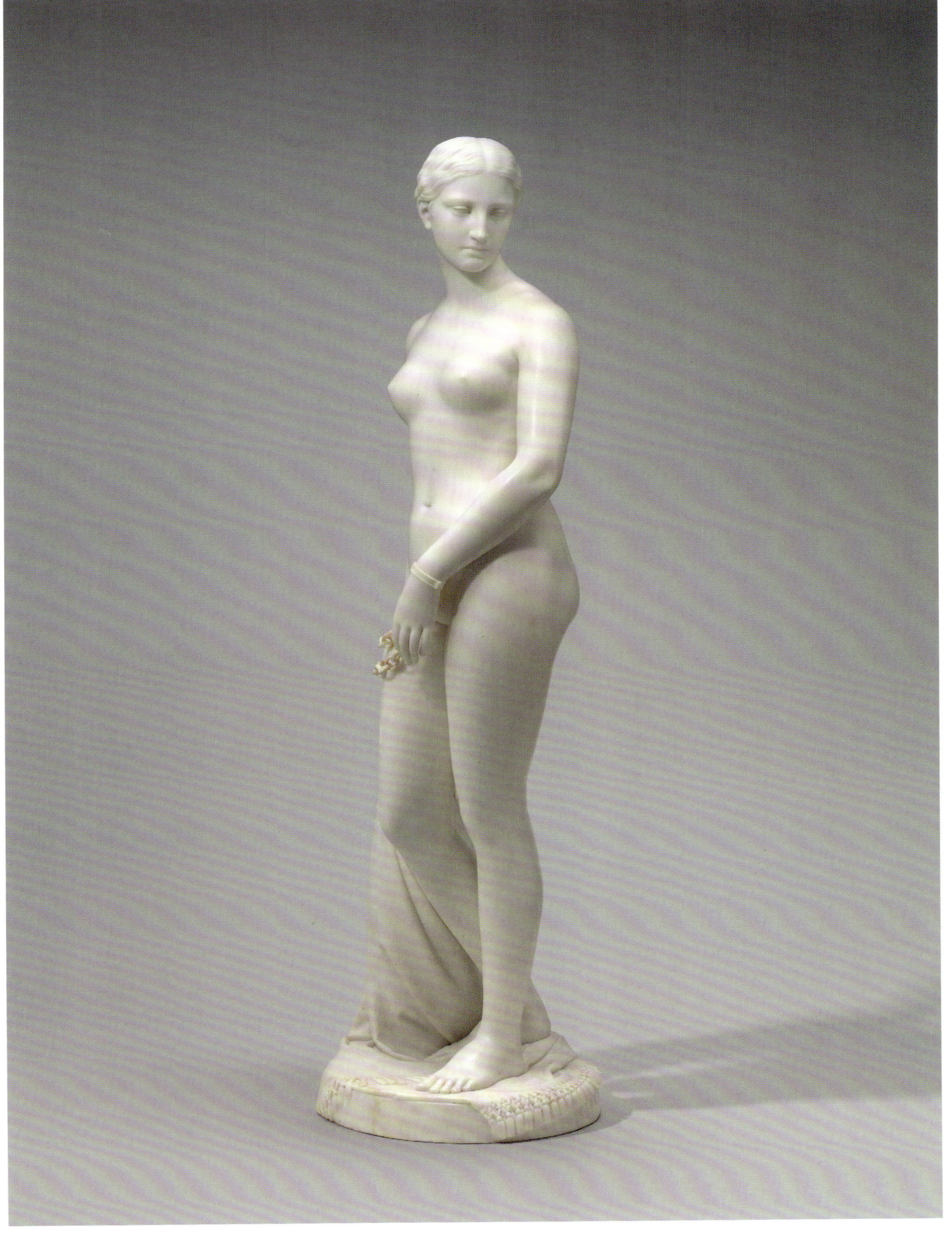

FOUND DROWNED *1848–1850*

Found Drowned is a painting by the British artist, George Frederic Watts, which depicts the popular Victorian theme of the 'fallen woman', brought down by poverty, prostitution or pregnancy out of marriage, whether through adultery, abandonment or abuse. It was inspired by Thomas Hood's famous poem, *The Bridge of Sighs* (1844), which tells the story of a young woman who committed suicide by jumping off Waterloo Bridge into the River Thames in London. It suggests that she was homeless, possibly shunned by her family for being pregnant.

Watts believed that art had the power to stimulate social change and was horrified by the plight of the urban poor and the unfair treatment of Victorian women. With this painting, the artist does not pass judgement on his subject, but on the hypocrisy of Victorian society. His large-scale rendition of the tragedy of a woman 'found drowned' – a term used in courts and newspapers to avoid the stigma of suicide, which was illegal at the time and would prevent a Christian burial – does not let us look away from or ignore the issue.

Watts positions the life-sized figure of the woman holding a heart-shaped locket in her hand in the shape of a cross, having been washed to shore and washed of any sin. A single star lights the night sky.

———

'Watts believed that art had the power to stimulate social change and was horrified by the plight of the urban poor and the unfair treatment of Victorian women. With this painting, he does not pass judgement on his subject, but on the hypocrisy of Victorian society'

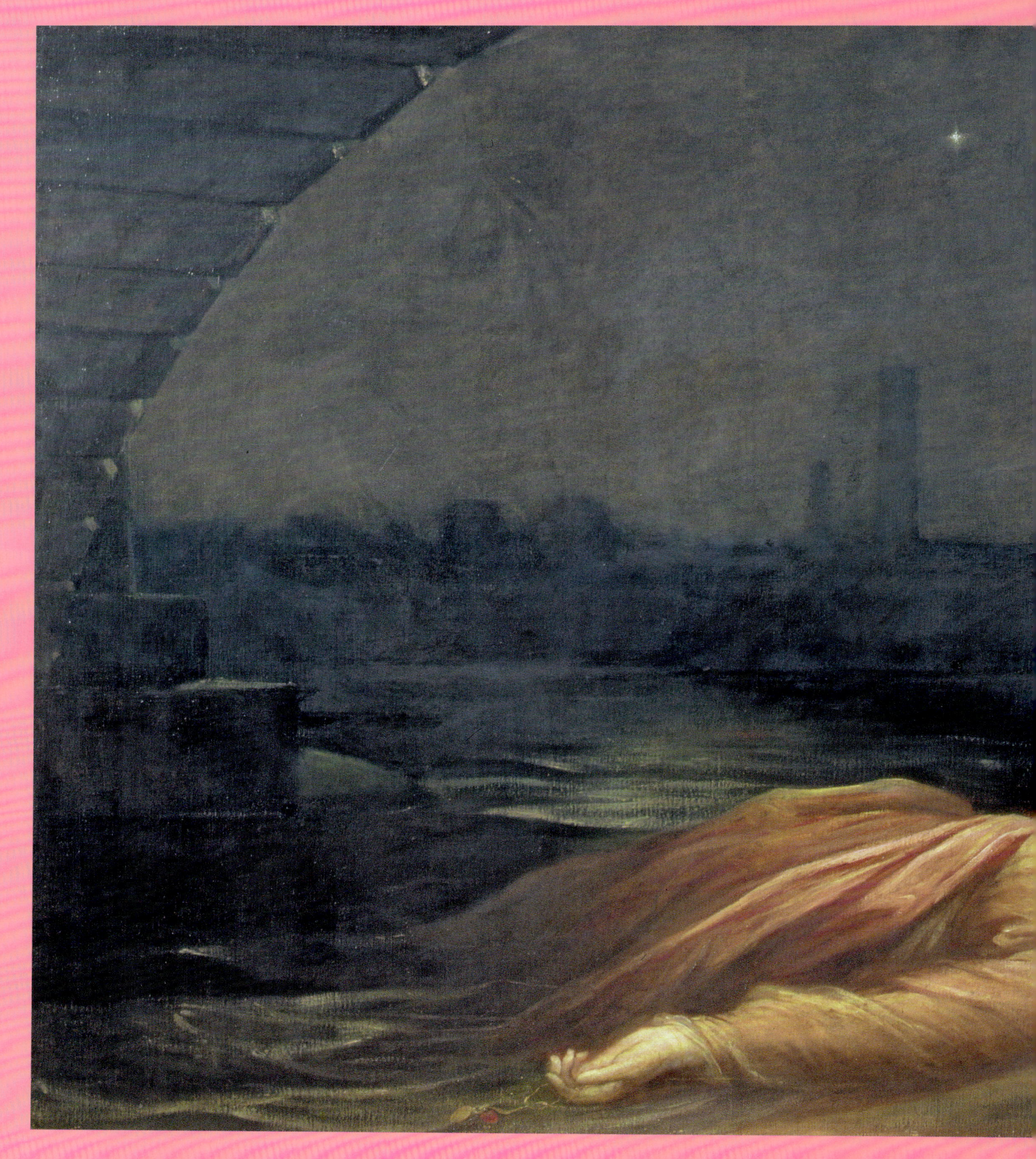

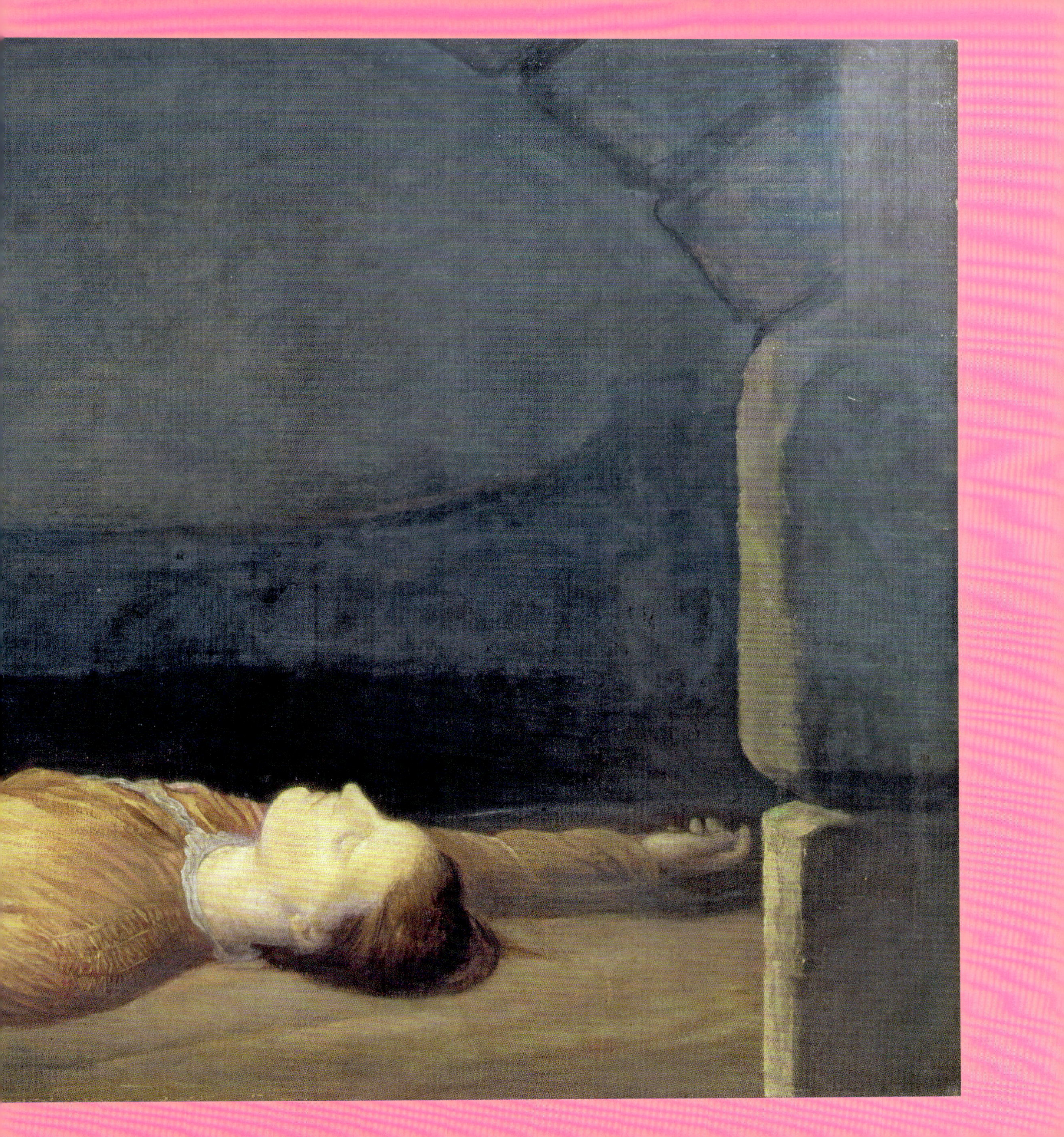

John Bell
(British, 1811–1895)

A DAUGHTER OF EVE *1853*

Among those who saw *The Greek Slave* by Hiram Powers (p. 70) at the Great Exhibition in London in 1851 was the British sculptor, John Bell. *A Daughter of Eve – A Scene on the Shore of the Atlantic* is his abolitionist response to Powers's sculpture, executed in a similar style and scale. However, Bell's sculpture of an enslaved African woman is not cloaked in allegory or references to the past, and although idealized, she appears to be more 'real'. Her earrings and the cloth around her waist are more contemporary and the silver manacles that are attached to the figure (rather than carved into it) add to the effect of this being a real person who has been shackled.

In the first half of the 19th century, Britain had transformed itself from being the leading slave-trading nation to the nation most opposed to it, with the Royal Navy patrolling the Atlantic to look for and capture illegal slave traders. Made and viewed in post-abolition Britain, the anti-slavery message of Bell's sculpture was clear for all to see. While *The Greek Slave* is more of an abstract depiction of slavery, Bell's work is a more specific representation that pointed a finger at the very real, ongoing condition of slavery that was still legal in the United States, as his African woman is on the cusp of becoming a slave in America.

A plaster version of the work was first exhibited in Dublin, Manchester and London in 1853, but when a bronze version was included in the International Exhibition in London in 1862 – while the American Civil War was raging across the Atlantic – it was truly seen and appreciated for its strong anti-slavery message. A smaller ceramic version was also exhibited that year under a more pointed title: *The American Slave*.[16]

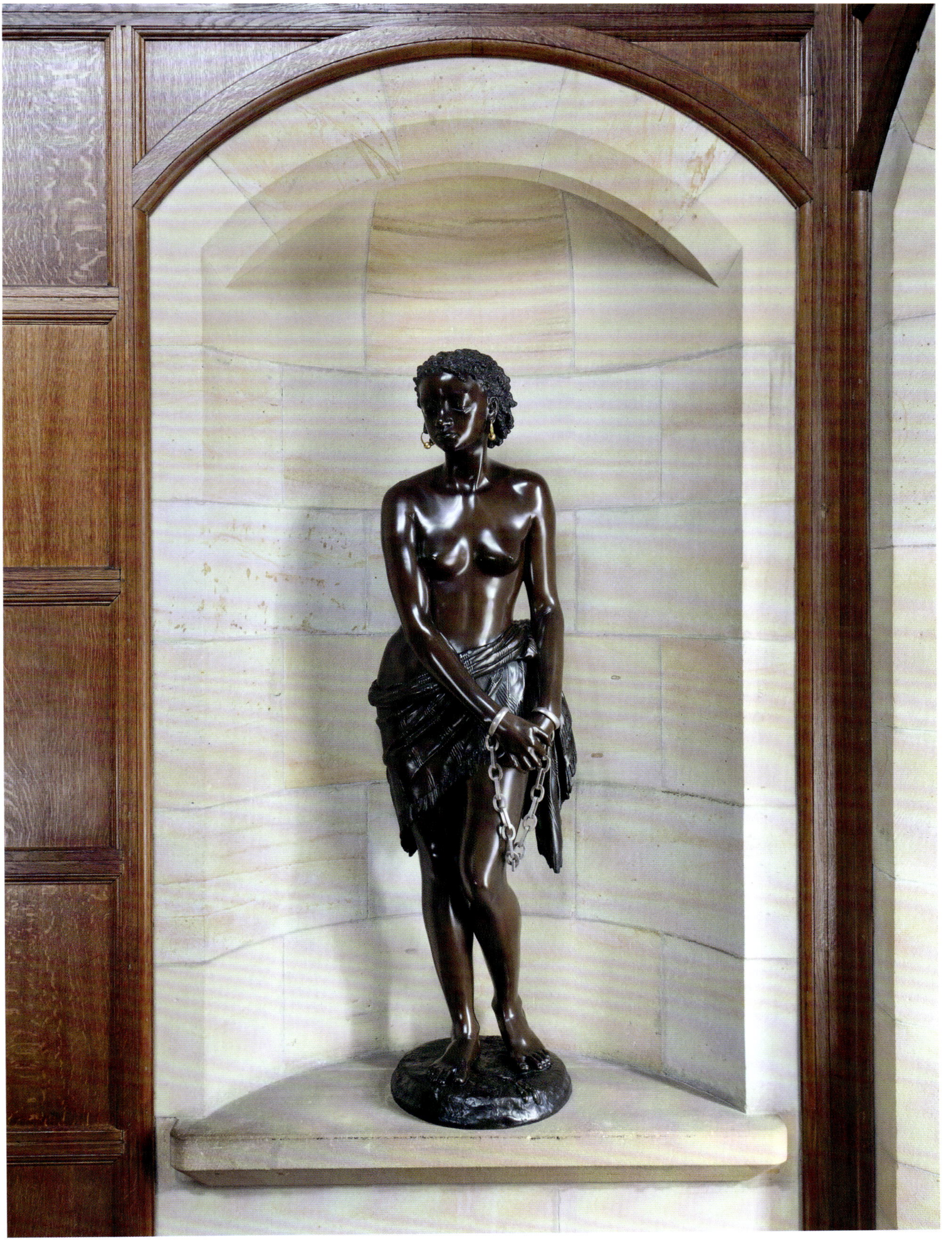

Alexandre Cabanel
(French, 1823–1889)

LA NAISSANCE DE VÉNUS

(The Birth of Venus) <u>1863</u>

In France in the 1860s, during the Second Empire of Napoleon III, there was a renewal of interest in the 'nude' in art. The nude allowed the artist and viewer to look at and examine the female body, while the use of themes from classical mythology enabled artists to produce erotic scenes without offending public morality.

Venus, the goddess of love and beauty, was a particularly popular subject and the Paris Salon of 1863 was nicknamed 'Salon of the Venuses' because of the sheer number exhibited. Among these was Alexandre Cabanel's *The Birth of Venus*, which proved to be the hit of the Salon and was purchased by Napoleon III for his collection.

It is a prime example of the type of nude that was expected, admired and deemed acceptable. Cabanel's idealized figure was painted in his signature slick, polished style, which means that his nude does not look like real flesh and blood. She appears without any particular facial features or expression to suggest sexual desire or pleasure, and there is no clothing or accessory to tie her to contemporary society or real life. She has a profusion of long, unruly tresses, but certainly no body hair, which would definitely turn her into a real woman. These conventions allow Cabanel (and the viewer) to get away with his voluptuous Venus reclining suggestively in a bed of sea foam on the crest of a wave.

‘Cabanel's Venus is a prime example of the type of nude that was expected, admired and deemed acceptable. The idealized figure was painted in his signature slick, polished style, which means that his nude does not look like real flesh and blood’

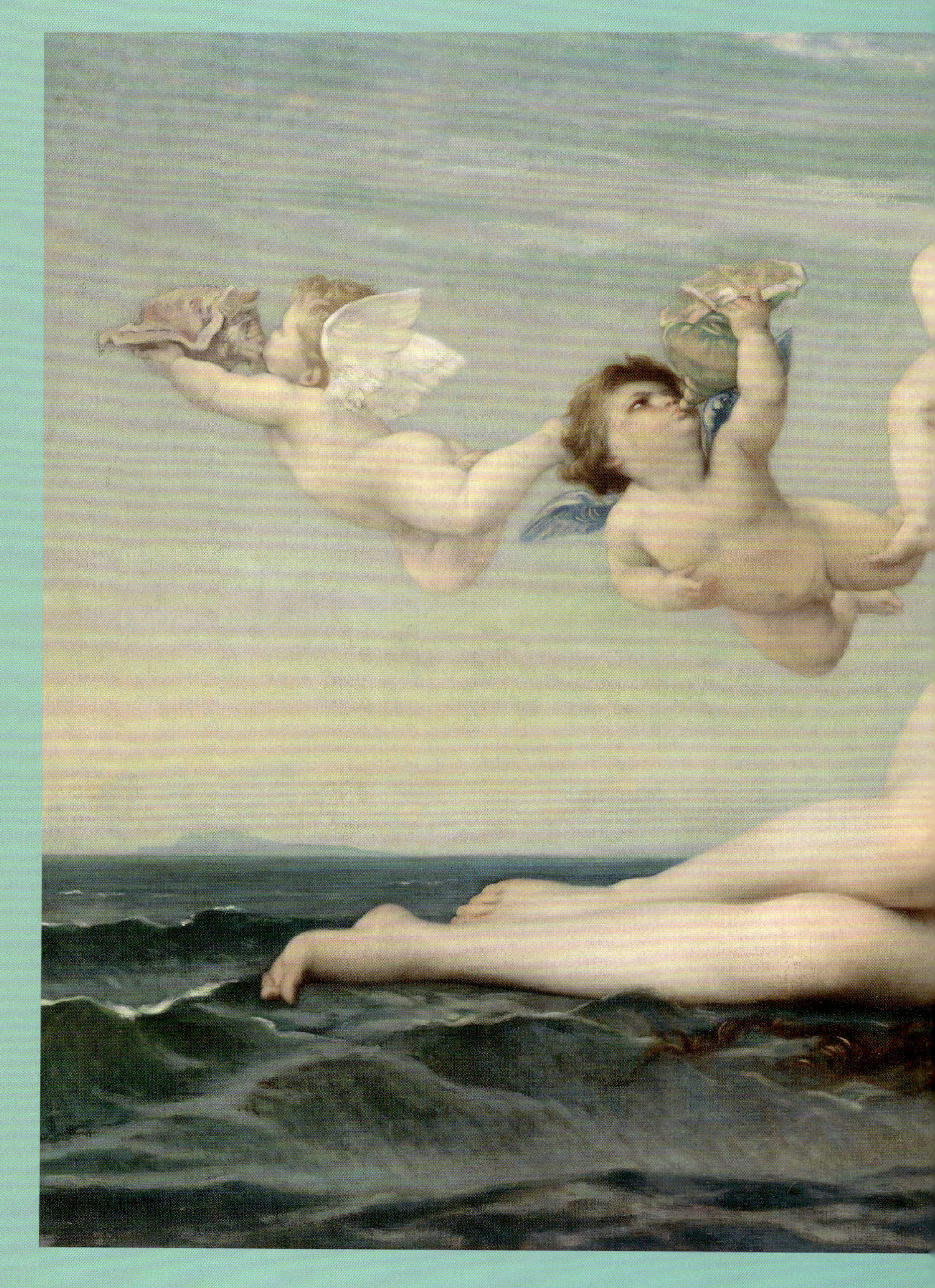

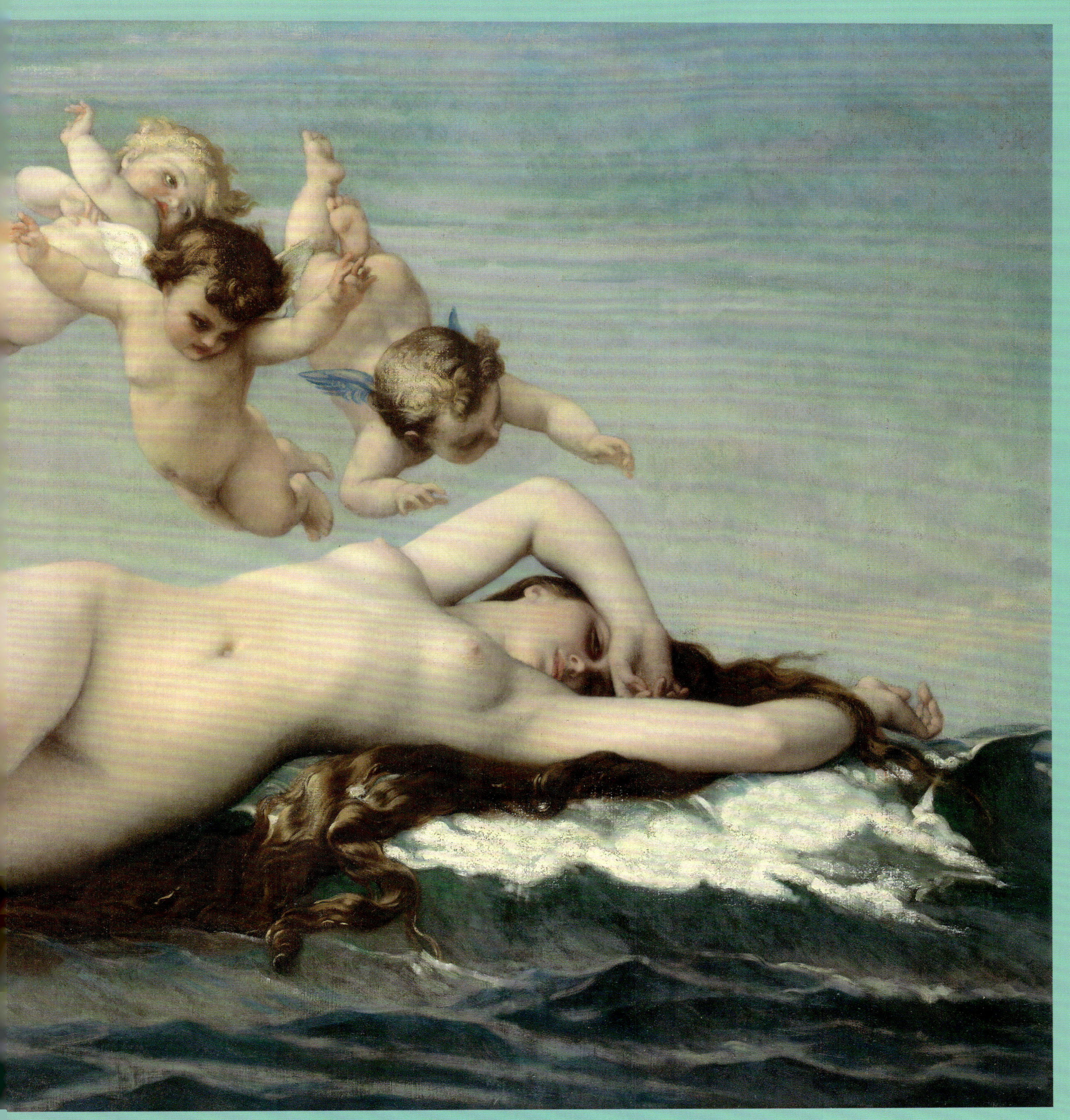

OLYMPIA *1863*

When it was exhibited in Paris in 1865, Édouard Manet's *Olympia* caused a scandal. Although it drew on and referenced a long tradition of reclining female nudes, such as Titian's *Venus d' Urbino* (p. 24) and Ingres's *Grande Odalisque* (p. 66), and it acknowledged the contemporary fashion for nudes, Manet did not follow the accepted conventions that allowed Salon audiences to comfortably ogle the nude female body. Unlike Cabanel's *The Birth of Venus* (p. 78), which was painted the same year as *Olympia*, there are no allegorical trappings to hide Olympia's eroticism. Her choker, jewellery, dangling shoe and the robe that she is lying on all signal that she is in a state of undress: she is *naked*, not nude, and therefore sexual.

Audiences found her overt sexuality unnerving. All the devices that were usually employed to maintain a safe distance between the subject and the viewer – distance in time and space (classical, allegorical, mythological, exotic 'other') – were absent, leaving the viewer face to face with a real woman in modern, urban Paris. Manet's nude is not sacred, but profane, and she was read as a prostitute. Indeed, at the time, 'Olympia' was a nickname for high-class prostitutes known as courtesans.[17]

Manet had also painted from a model, rather than a statue, which increased the impact of his subject being a real woman. Moreover, his model – Victorine Meurent – was a popular artist's model who was recognizable to Parisian audiences, which helped place the scene in contemporary Paris. Equally disturbing for the audience is the fact that there is no moralizing in the painting. Manet does not pass judgement on the woman – if anything he calls out the viewer and the hypocrisy of society with his portrayal of a woman who is very definitely 'naked'.

——

'All the devices that were usually employed to maintain a safe distance between the subject and the viewer were absent, leaving the viewer face to face with a real woman in modern, urban Paris'

With his depiction of a Parisian courtesan being brought flowers by her maid, Manet completely modernized the tradition of the female nude. His subject seems to ignore the bouquet, as if it is neither special nor meaningful – as presumably they would be from a client. The arching cat signals that someone has entered the room (us?), and Olympia is meeting that person's gaze head on. Her confrontational gaze makes the viewer a part of the scene, implicating us as either client or voyeur.

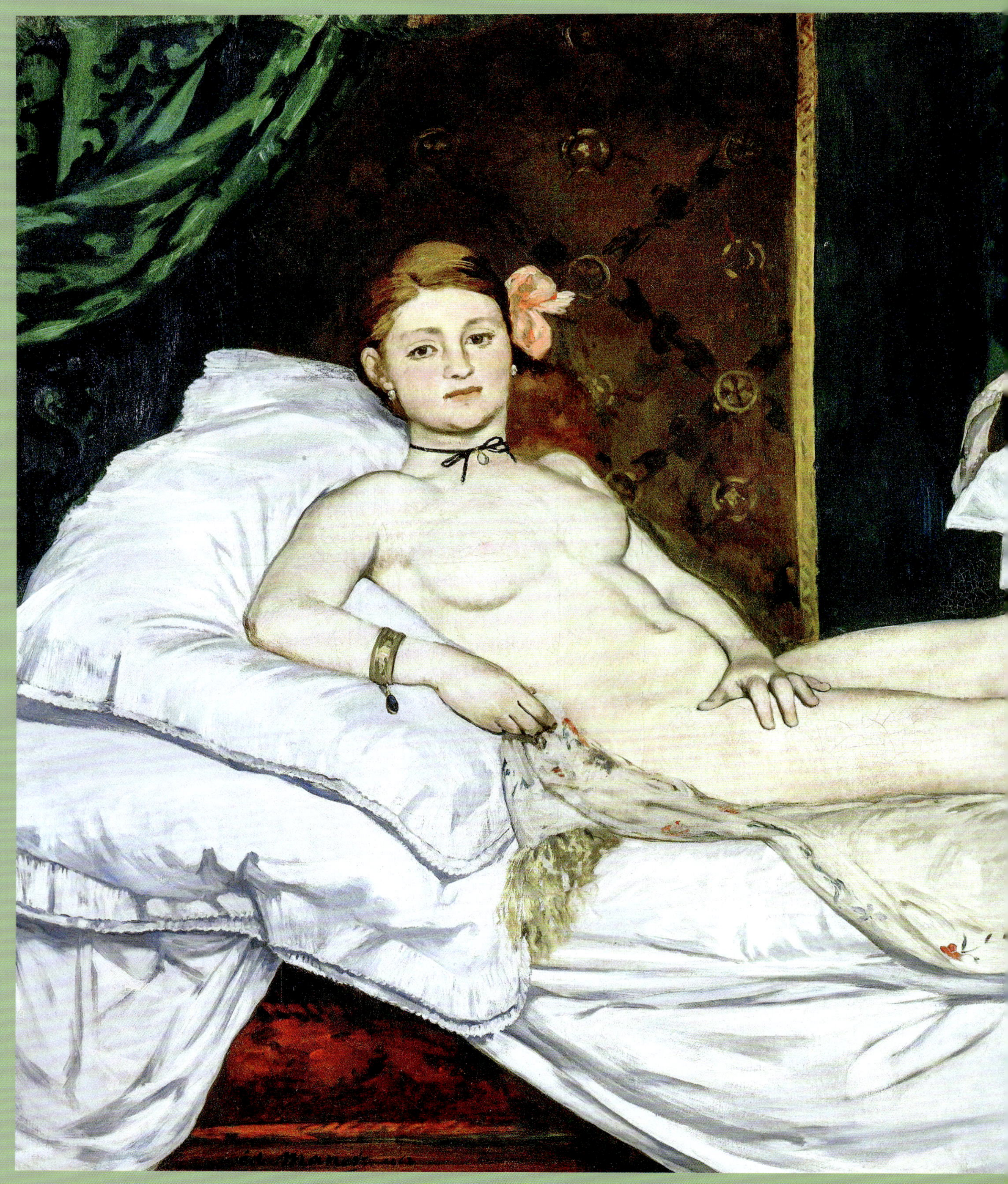

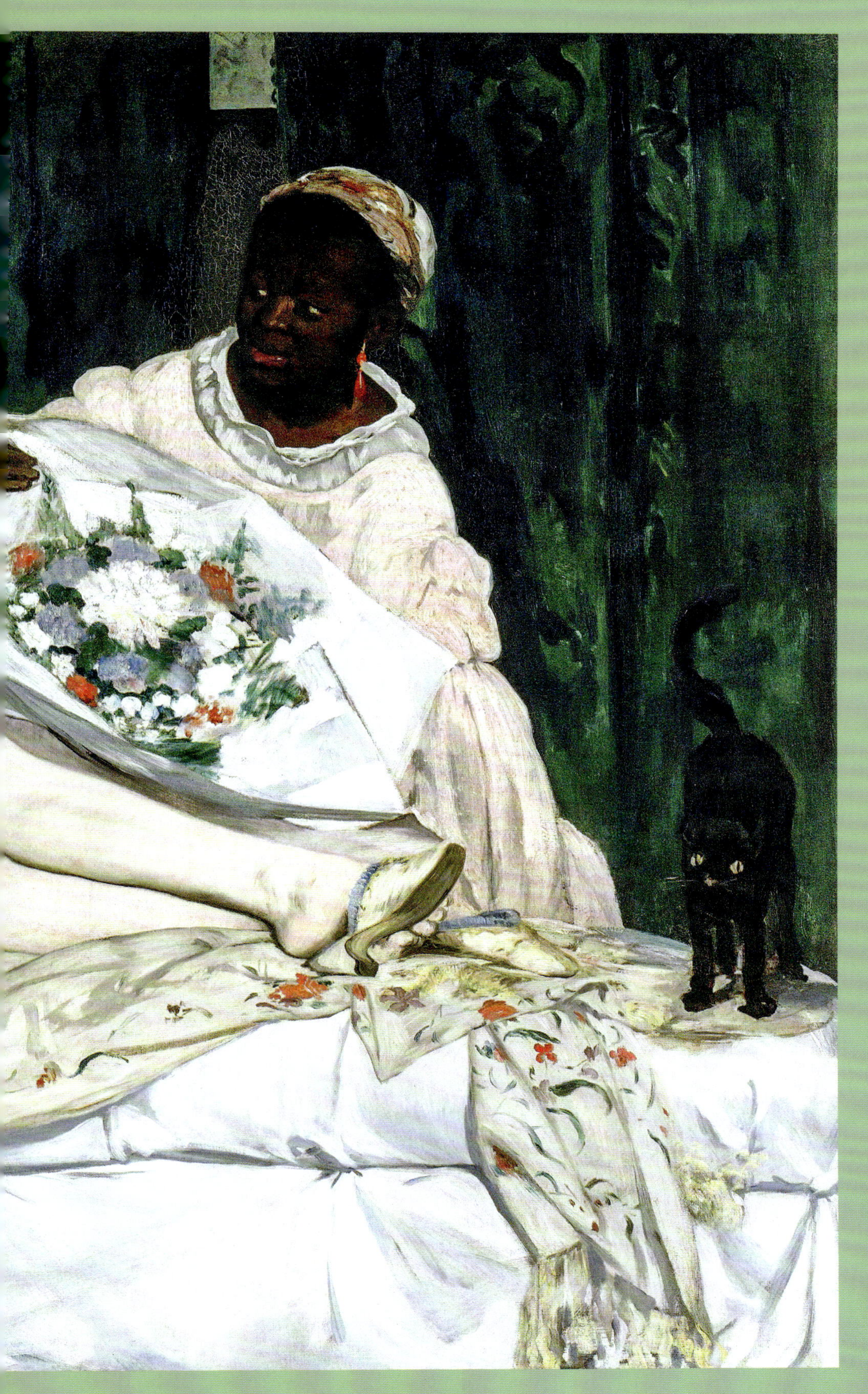

THE DEATH OF CLEOPATRA *1876*

Edmonia Lewis's mixed heritage – part Black, part Native American – drew attention, curiosity and prejudice in the 19th century. Despite the racism, sexism and discrimination that she faced in society and the arts, she became the first North American sculptor of colour (of any gender) to achieve international recognition and fame.

Lewis started working as a sculptor in Boston, Massachusetts, while the Civil War raged. There, she made enough money from plaster portrait busts and medallions of famous abolitionists to move to Italy in 1865. After a spell in Florence, where she was welcomed by America's most famous sculptor, Hiram Powers (p. 70), she set up a studio in Rome in 1866. She became part of a circle of expatriate sculptors that included a number of women, all striving for the same recognition afforded to male artists. Lewis began working in marble, creating a sensation with her portrait busts of famous Americans and sculptures of African American and Native American figures that expressed universal themes of courage, love, liberty and freedom. Her Neoclassical style, mixed with naturalism, suited her subject matter and the American taste for heroic historical and literary figures.

Lewis was drawn to strong female characters from the Bible and the past, such as Cleopatra, the legendary Egyptian queen who committed suicide rather than being taken captive. Lewis's *The Death of Cleopatra* was a triumph when it was exhibited at the Philadelphia Centennial Exhibition of 1876. Although Cleopatra was a popular figure for Neoclassical artists, Lewis's more realistic, expressive depiction of death both unnerved and garnered praise, with her stylized monumental sculpture praised as the 'most remarkable piece of sculpture in the American section'.[18]

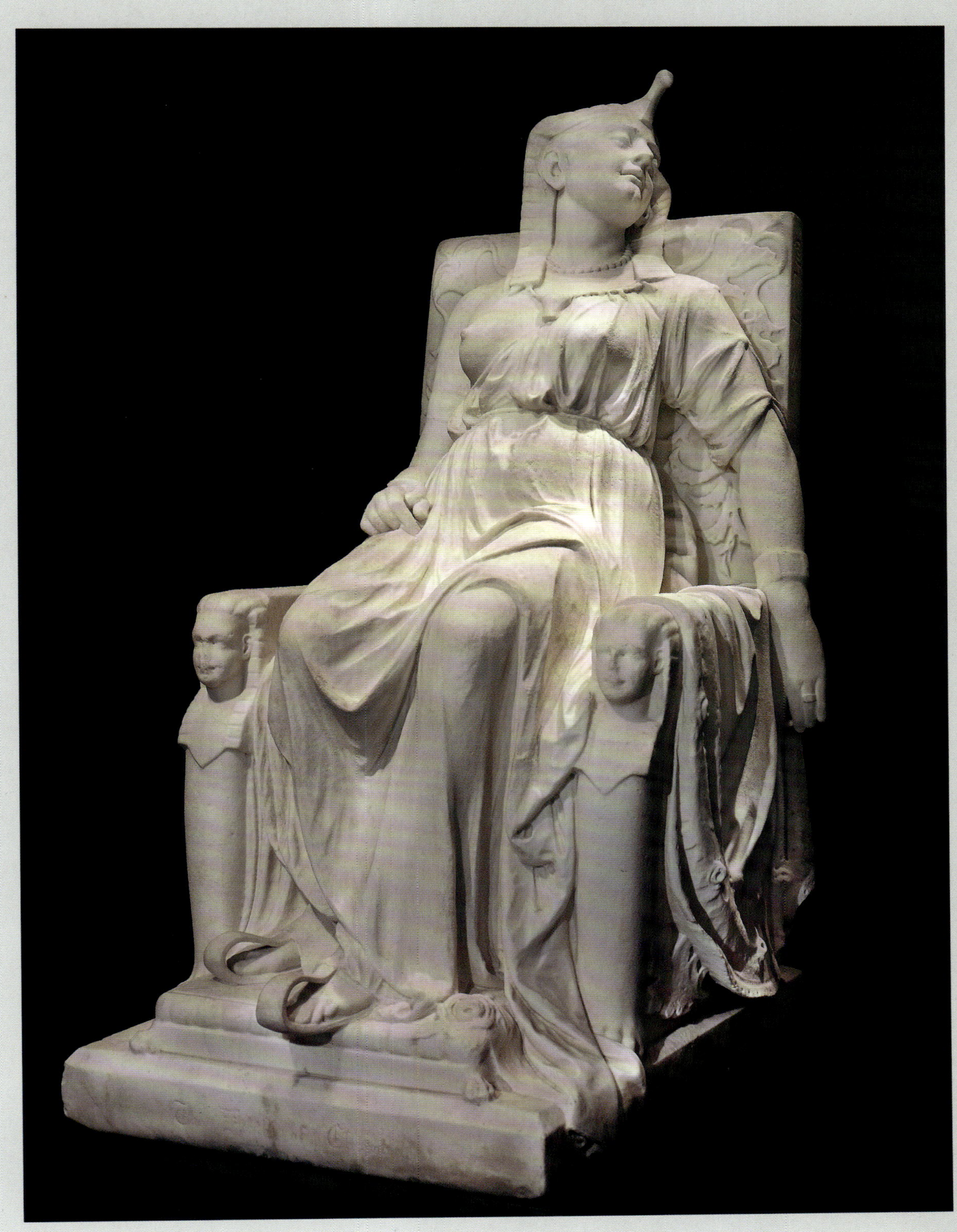

MADAME X *1883–1884*

John Singer Sargent's portrait of the American socialite Virginie Gautreau was first exhibited at the Paris Salon of 1884, where it was ridiculed for the 'indecency' of her dress and the pallor of her skin. Although exhibited as *Madame X*, Gautreau was such a well-known society figure that she was recognized immediately. The trend-setting Gautreau was known for her signature artful look – using dramatic make-up and lavender powder to exaggerate her pale complexion and wearing glamorous gowns with plunging necklines to highlight her sculptural beauty.

Sargent's striking portrait of her in a fashionable black dress shows her in a statuesque pose, recalling classical sculpture, as well as showing off her perfect Gibson Girl[19] figure. In his original painting, Sargent showed one of the jewelled straps of the dress slipping off her shoulder. Some of the scandal surrounding the painting had to do with Gautreau's own reputation, as her affairs were less than discreet; Sargent's portrait, with its hint of undressing and the subject's haughty, sensual demeanour, was seen to be flaunting Gautreau's femme fatale lifestyle in polite society.

Gautreau herself thought it was a masterpiece when it was finished, but the scandal caused such negative publicity that she and her mother asked Sargent to remove the painting from the Salon. He refused, pointing out that it was painted 'exactly as she was dressed', although he later repainted the strap so that it was now on her shoulder. Sargent kept the painting until Gautreau died in 1915, then sold it to the Metropolitan Museum of Art in 1916, writing 'I suppose it is the best thing I have done.'[20]

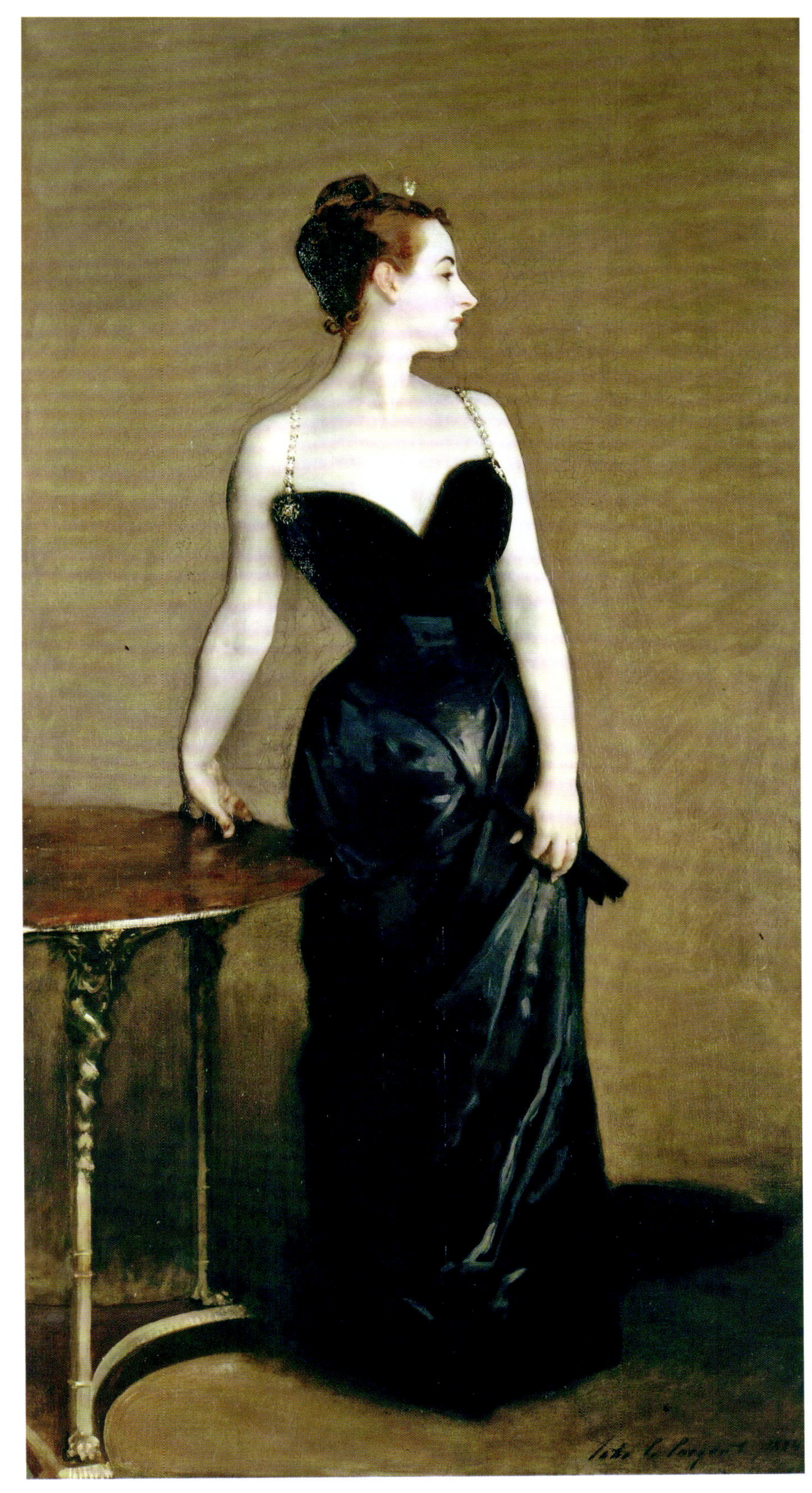

WOMAN COMBING HER HAIR *1885*

A major part of the Impressionist artist Edgar Degas's output is his paintings of women in their activities and worlds, and above all, their bodies in motion. At the ballet and circus, or working in a laundry, Degas could see women at work and observe their movements, both natural and performed. In these active, physical professions, he could see interesting body shapes and movements, and, of course, more of the body itself in different positions, unencumbered by long dresses or other restrictive clothing. In these situations, the women were not hindered by the social conventions that meant most middle-class women were either unseen or only seen in highly circumscribed behaviours and settings. Inspired by the new photography, Degas tried to capture passing moments of modern life and fix them in time. He would sketch in front of a scene, but then continue in the studio, working and reworking ideas to arrive at his very carefully composed and constructed images of 'real', off-guard moments.

In the last Impressionist exhibition in 1886, Degas exhibited 10 pastels of women in natural, intimate poses, which was unprecedented in the history of art. Described in the catalogue as 'a series of nudes of women bathing, washing, drying, rubbing down, combing their hair or having it combed',[21] the pastels were layered, reworked and burnished, with the paper often becoming fluffed up and mixed with the pigment, creating a surface texture like hair on skin. These nudes were not Venuses or odalisques, but something more real and universal. As Degas explained: 'The nude has always been represented in poses which presuppose an audience, but these women of mine are honest, simple folk, unconcerned by any other interest than those involved in their physical condition … It is as if you looked through a keyhole.'[22]

While the phrase 'keyhole aesthetic' might sound a bit suspect to our contemporary ears, it does not actually mean that Degas was sneaking a peek at an unsuspecting woman. He worked with models posed in his studio to create these realistic-looking scenes of 'glimpsed moments' of women absorbed in their private ablutions, oblivious to our presence or gaze. Degas imbued his women performing unremarkable activities common to us all with a grandeur that implored his audience to look not to an idealized past or an imagined exotic elsewhere for beauty, but to find it in contemporary life and the real people around them.

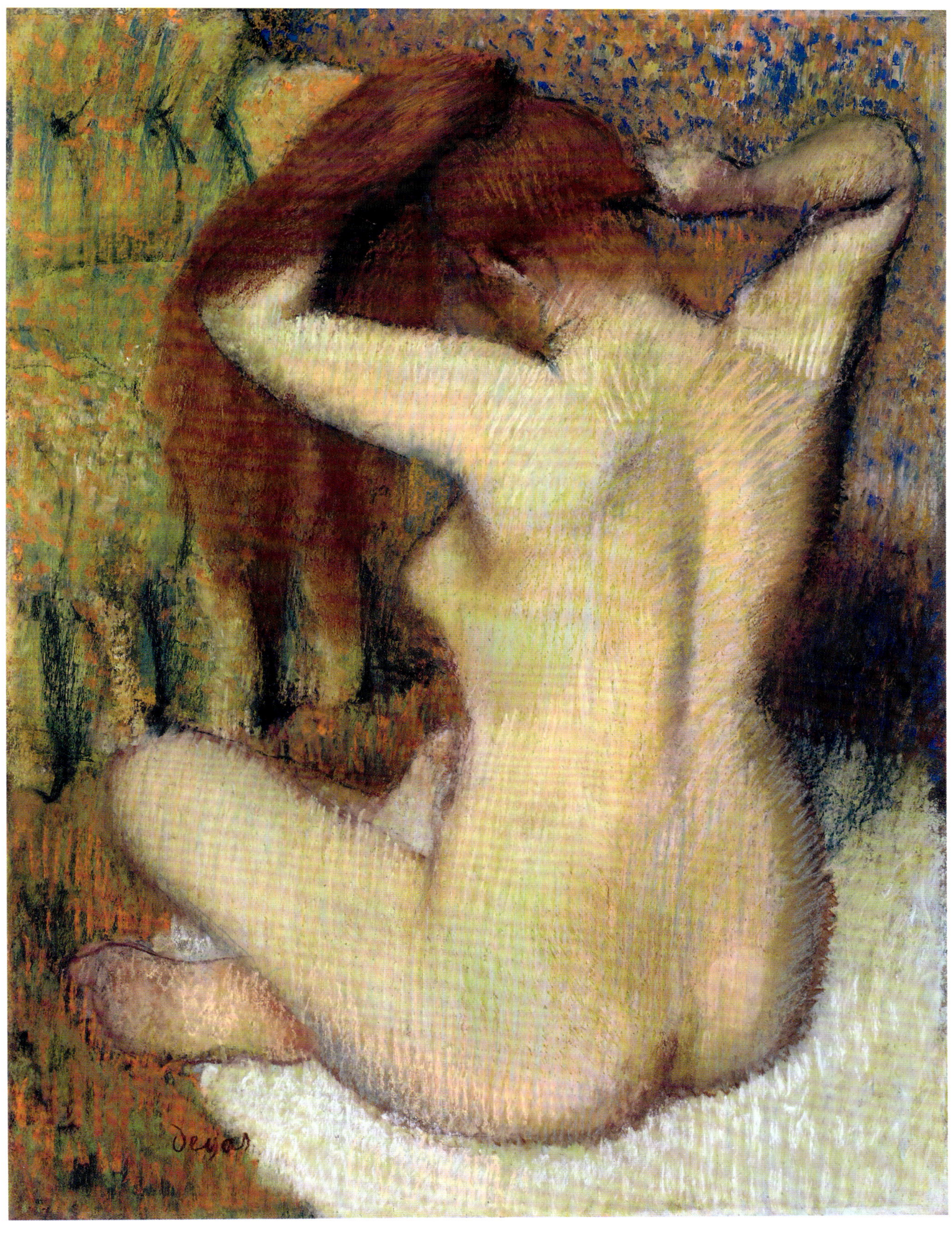

THE BATH *1891*

Like her friend and mentor, Edgar Degas (p. 90), who invited her to exhibit with the French Impressionists in Paris, Mary Cassatt was interested in portraying aspects of real contemporary life. The American artist shared with Degas a desire to capture fleeting moments that were not usually seen by others, where her characters sit, stand and act unselfconsciously, apparently unaware of a viewer. However, while Degas's models were often performers of some sort, Cassatt's were respectable women like herself, depicted in unguarded moments of their private lives.

In 1890, Cassatt saw an incredibly influential exhibition of Japanese prints in Paris. She was drawn to their style as well as their subject matter, particularly those featuring women's intimate lives, such as the prints of Utamaro (p. 60). She began to collect Japanese prints and this became the inspiration for a series of 10 colour aquatints for her first solo exhibition in 1891. The series centred on moments from the daily lives of modern, upper-middle-class women: taking care of children, getting dressed, having tea with friends, writing letters, riding an omnibus and so on.

The Bath is the first of this series. While it is a lovely image, it is not a sentimentalized vision of motherhood, as in conventional art of the Gilded Age/Victorian era, but a matter-of-fact one. The woman appears more resigned (or tired) than beatific, a much more recognizable expression to anyone who has had to catch and contain a squirmy toddler to bathe them! Here, the mundane is deemed worthy of representation and activities from ordinary women's lives become the focus of vanguard art.

Cassatt soon became known for her tender, intimate views of mothers and children rendered in a unique style that draws on the love of line seen in Japanese prints, the bright colours of Impressionism, and the skewed perspectives and photographic cropping of Degas. Cassatt went on to make more than 200 prints, believing that art should not just be the preserve of the wealthy.

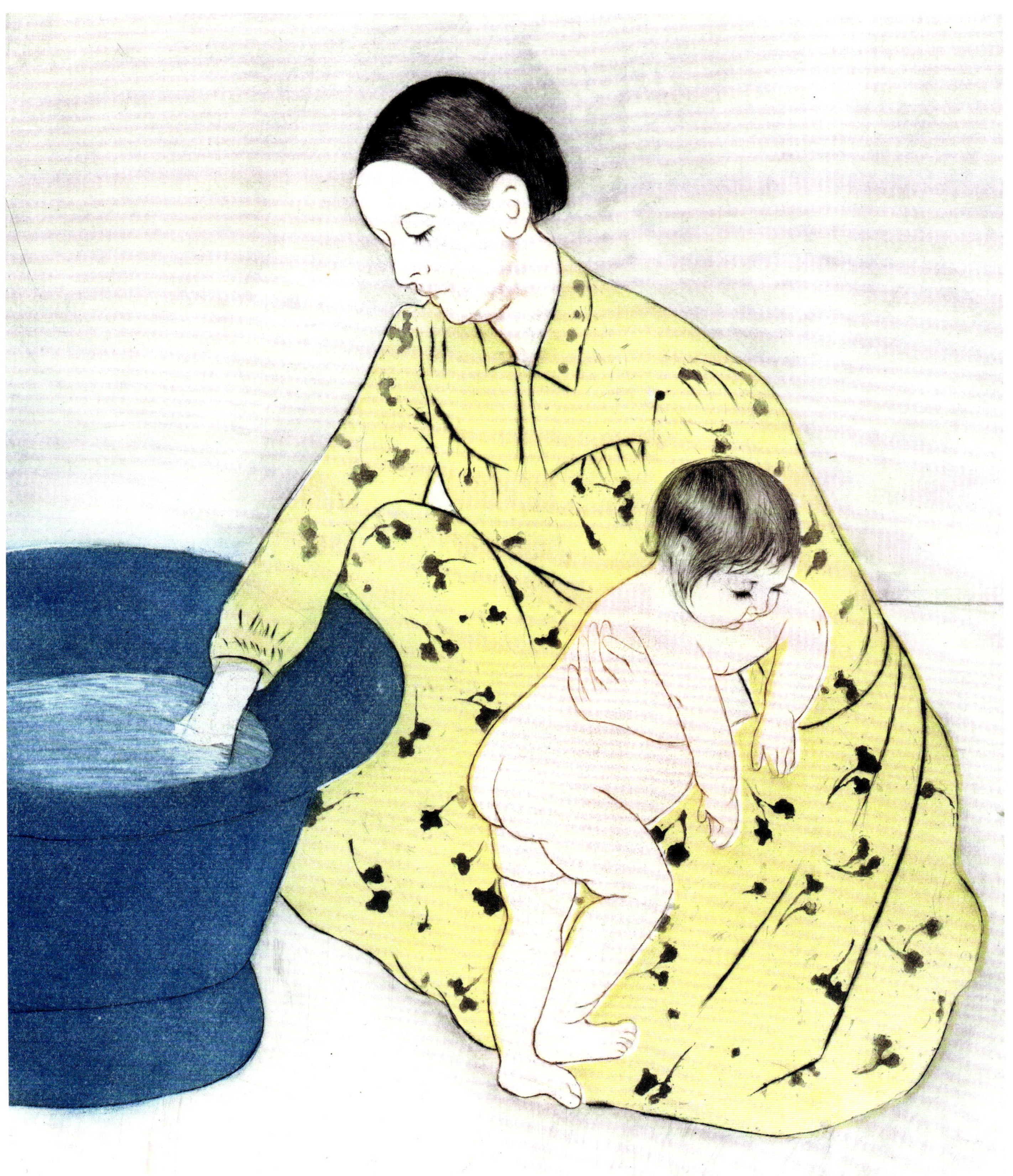

NAFEA FAA IPOIPO?
(When Will You Marry?) <u>*1892*</u>

While Degas (p. 90), Cassatt (p. 92) and Lautrec (p. 96) depicted aspects of the lives of real women of modern Paris, Paul Gauguin provided visions of exotic women from other cultures, tailored to his European audience. He called his style 'synthetism' (from the French, *synthétiser*, 'to synthesize') and his aim was to paint not so much what he saw, but what he felt, using colour for dramatic, emotional or expressive effect.

Gauguin travelled around the globe collecting influences, styles and ideas that he synthesized into a unique approach that drew on an eclectic mix of Western and non-Western art forms and cultures. These included medieval tapestries for their boldness and drama, Japanese woodcuts for their line and spatial composition, prehistoric art, Egyptian sculpture, Greek friezes, Easter Island statues, statues of Buddhas and the folk art of Brittany for their authenticity, the folklore and myths of the Caribbean and Polynesia, as well as contemporary developments in modern European art.

In 1891, Gauguin left France and went to Tahiti to escape 'the disease of civilization'. In the first two years he was there he created 66 paintings, including *Nafea faa ipoipo? (When Will You Marry?)*, which depicts two Tahitian women, one in native dress, the other in the European style worn by missionaries. His dazzling paintings combine exotic colours, landscapes and people, Tahitian myths and Christian rites, presenting a fantasy of idyllic island life unspoiled by modern civilization. While the paradise that he portrayed might have been a romanticized fantasy, his interest in non-Western civilizations and the careful portrayal of the 'distinctive characteristics of the Tahitian face' was genuine – and influential.

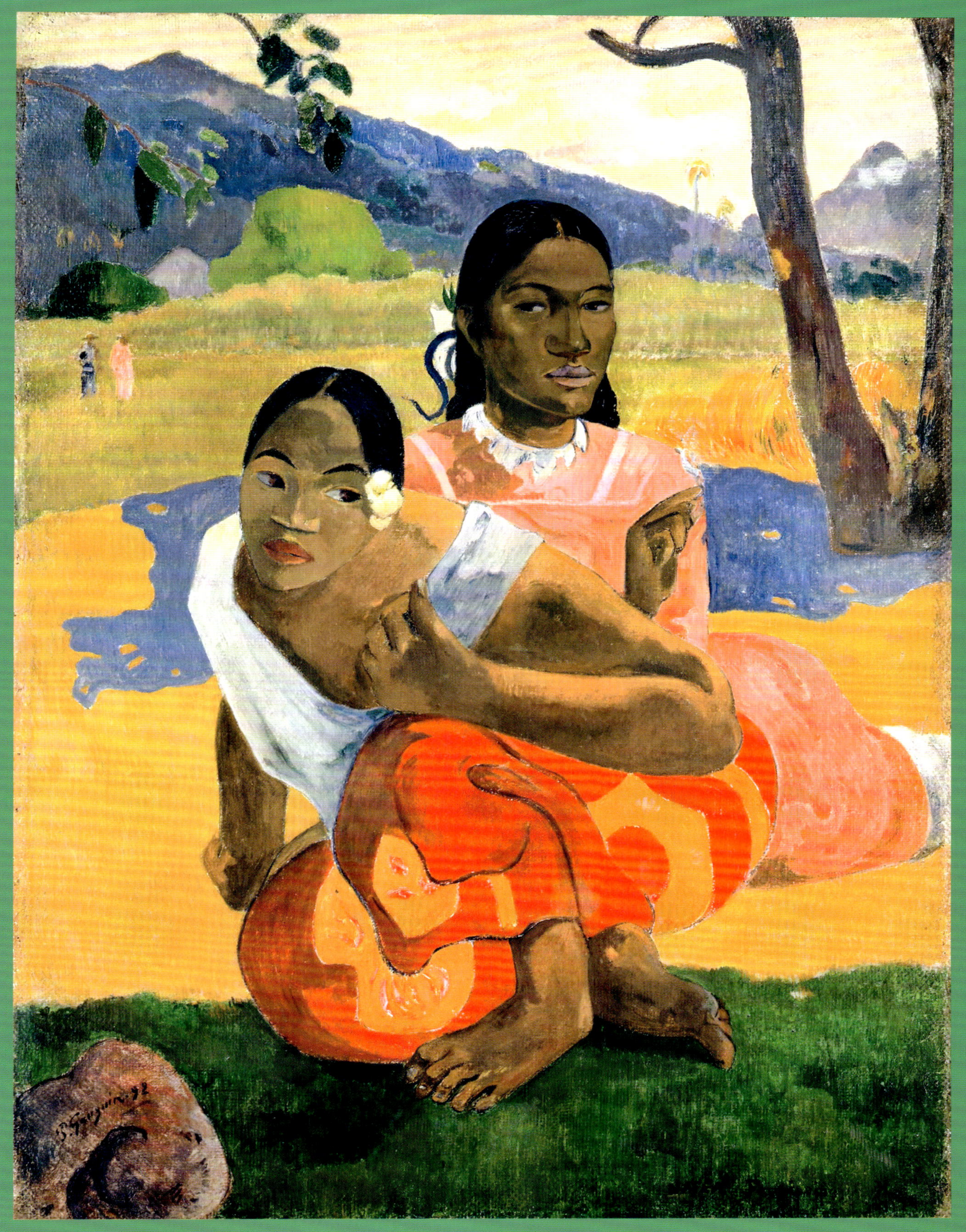

AU SALON DE LA RUE DES MOULINS

(The Salon on the Rue Des Moulins) <u>*1894*</u>

Like Edgar Degas (p. 90) and Mary Cassatt (p. 92), Henri de Toulouse-Lautrec was obsessed with capturing the essence and atmosphere of *fin de siècle* Paris. All three artists were engaged in portraying aspects of the real women of modern Paris: Degas through his backstage scenes of performers and images of the everyday rituals of the 'everywoman', Cassatt with her scenes of the private lives of middle-class women and Lautrec with the women of Paris's bohemian nightlife (sex workers and performers). Japanese prints (p. 60) were even more of an influence on Lautrec than they were on the other two, as he developed his distinctive style with its flat, bold patterns and calligraphic line.

Around 1888, Lautrec began painting the themes for which he is best known – theatres, music-halls (especially the Moulin Rouge), cafes, circuses and brothels. Although the subject matter and interest in figures in motion is similar to that of Degas, Lautrec's figures are not representative types, but identifiable people – mostly his friends – painted or drawn from direct observation.

—

'Although the subject matter and interest in figures in motion is similar to that of Degas, Lautrec's figures are not representative types, but identifiable people – mostly his friends – painted or drawn from direct observation'

Lautrec became famous for a poster advertising a cabaret at the Moulin Rouge dance hall and *The Salon on the Rue des Moulins* was painted at the height of his fame. The setting is a famous Parisian brothel that Lautrec not only frequented, but also lived in for a while as he immersed himself in the everyday lives of prostitutes (the woman at the centre is one of his favourite prostitutes, Mireille). There are no customers, nudity or judgement in the painting; the women are neither shamed nor romanticized, they just 'are', as they sit bored and wait, be it for medical checks or clients.

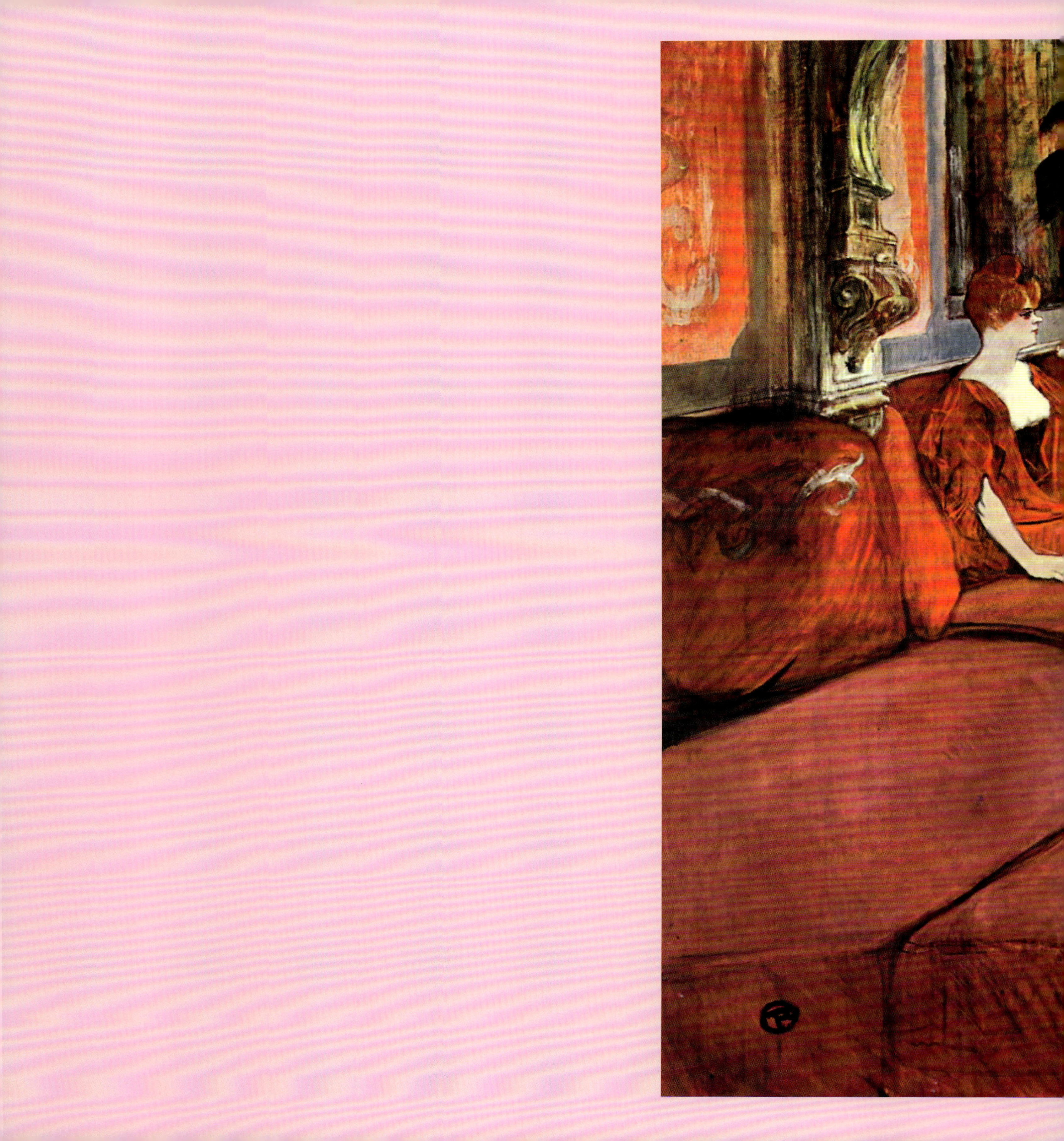

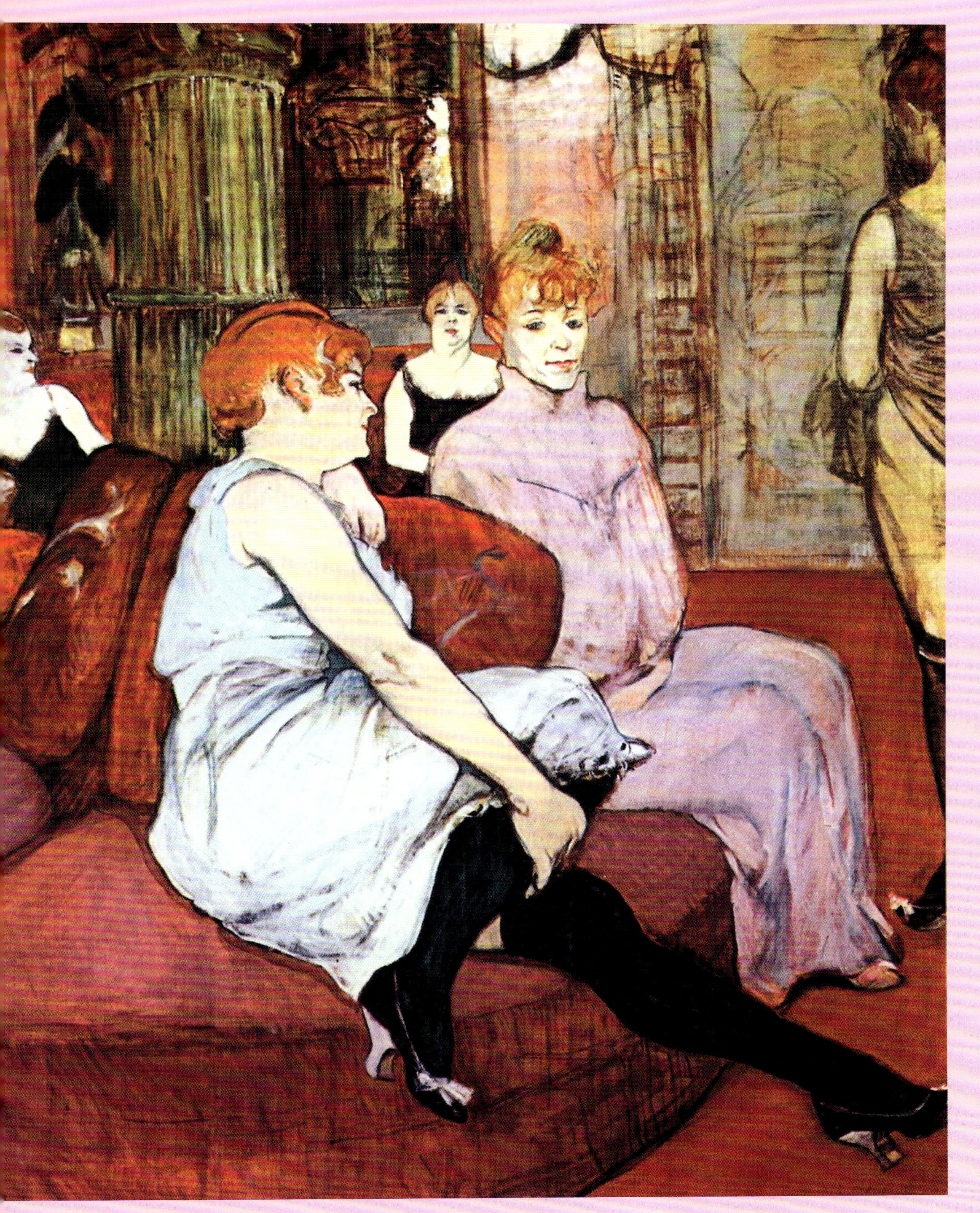

Edvard Munch
(Norwegian, 1863–1944)

MADONNA *1894*

Women were a recurrent theme in much of the art of the 1890s, and were usually shown as either virginal and angelic, or sexual and threatening; they were either Madonna or whore. The Norwegian artist Edvard Munch confused matters with his provocative images of an erotic female nude flaunting her sexuality and radiating with expressive pleasure. Originally entitled *Woman Making Love*, it could have been read as a straightforward declaration of female liberation and sexual freedom, especially as red berets like the one she is wearing were worn by the women of Kristiania Bohème, an avant-garde group of artists and writers in Norway who believed in free love.

Munch's radically modern expressive style and subject were enough to cause a scandal when the painting was exhibited in Norway in 1895, as female nudes were not commonplace in the Norwegian art of the time. This was exacerbated by the fact that the title of the painting was now *Madonna*, so the image and its interpretation became more complicated – and blasphemous.

All of a sudden, this wasn't just any woman in the throes of passion, but the mother of baby Jesus, and she was not serene, pure and clothed, but sensual, sexual and naked. You can call her Madonna and put her in a red, halo-like hat, but there is no disguising that this woman is no virgin: she is most definitely enjoying the pleasures of the flesh – her flesh, in fact.

Or, perhaps even more shockingly, she is a Madonna/mother/saint and a woman who enjoys sex. By conflating notions of the Virgin Mary with the femme fatale and the women of Bohemia, perhaps Munch is suggesting that a woman at the turn of the century doesn't (or shouldn't) have to be saint or sinner, mother or whore. Maybe she can be both – or neither?

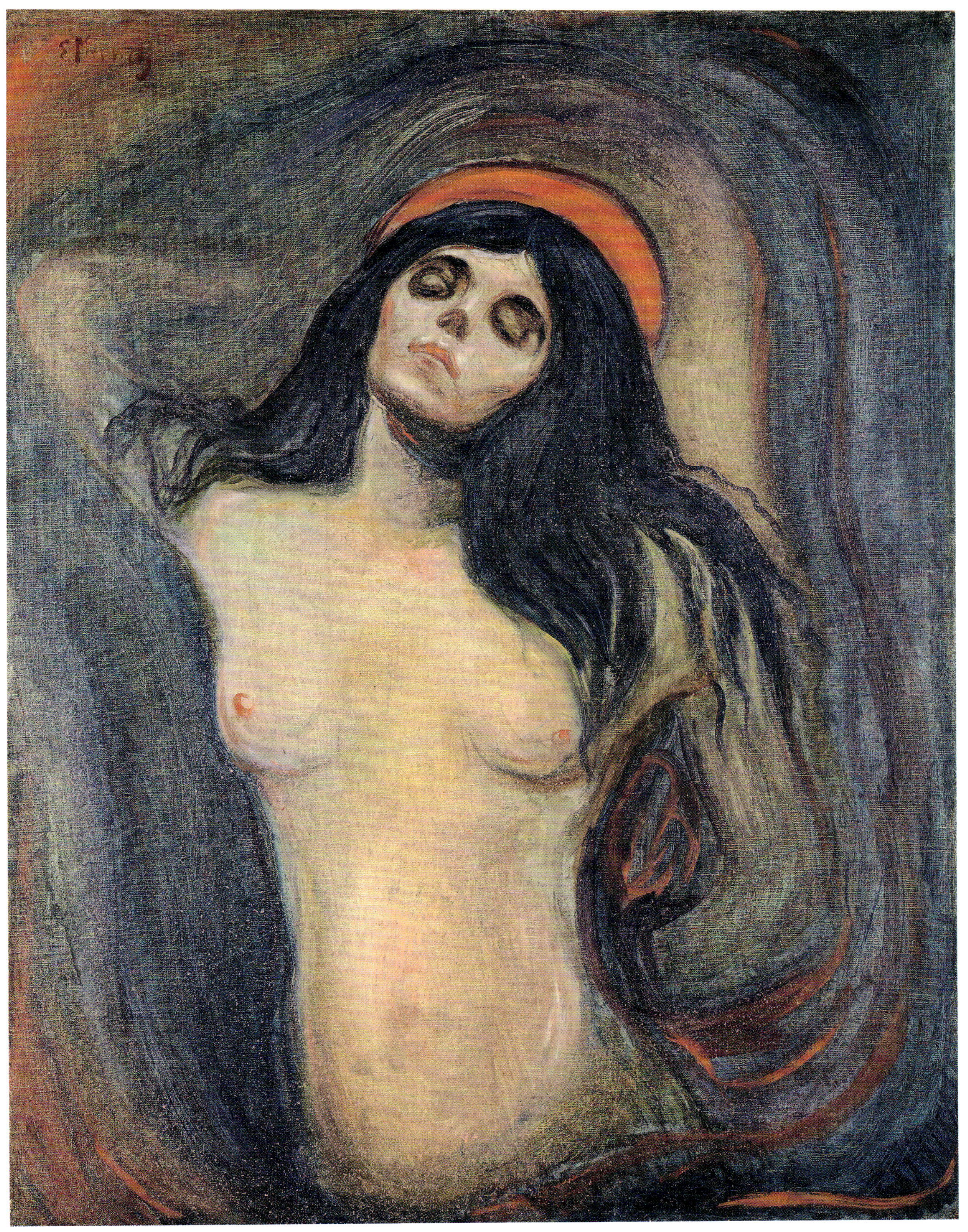

FLAMING JUNE *1895*

Frederic Leighton was one of the most celebrated British painters of the late Victorian era. He specialized in depictions of beautiful women in allegorical or mythological guises, their eroticism clothed in flowing drapery, gorgeous colours and elegant surroundings. However, this 'sleeping beauty', curled up in the summer sunshine, is not tied to a particular date, place, or moralizing or uplifting story. The sleeper's vivid orange gown is just sheer enough to allow a titillating glimpse of her beautiful body without seeming lewd, and the monumental, sensuous figure fills the canvas, its dazzling opulence heightened by the splendid golden frame that Leighton designed for it.

In contrast to Walter Crane's 'woman on a mission' of the same year (p. 104), Leighton's flamboyant painting embodies the 'art for art's sake' ideals of the Aesthetic Movement, insisting that creating beautiful objects is not only enough, but that heightening pleasure in beauty was the true purpose of art.

Flaming June was the hit of the Summer Exhibition at the Royal Academy in London in 1895, but soon fell out of fashion, seeming like a remnant of an outmoded, sentimental style. This would change in the 1960s, however, when *Flaming June* became one of the treasures of Puerto Rico's Museo de Arte de Ponce, her fame and popularity earning the ethereal beauty the nickname 'The Mona Lisa of the Southern Hemisphere'.

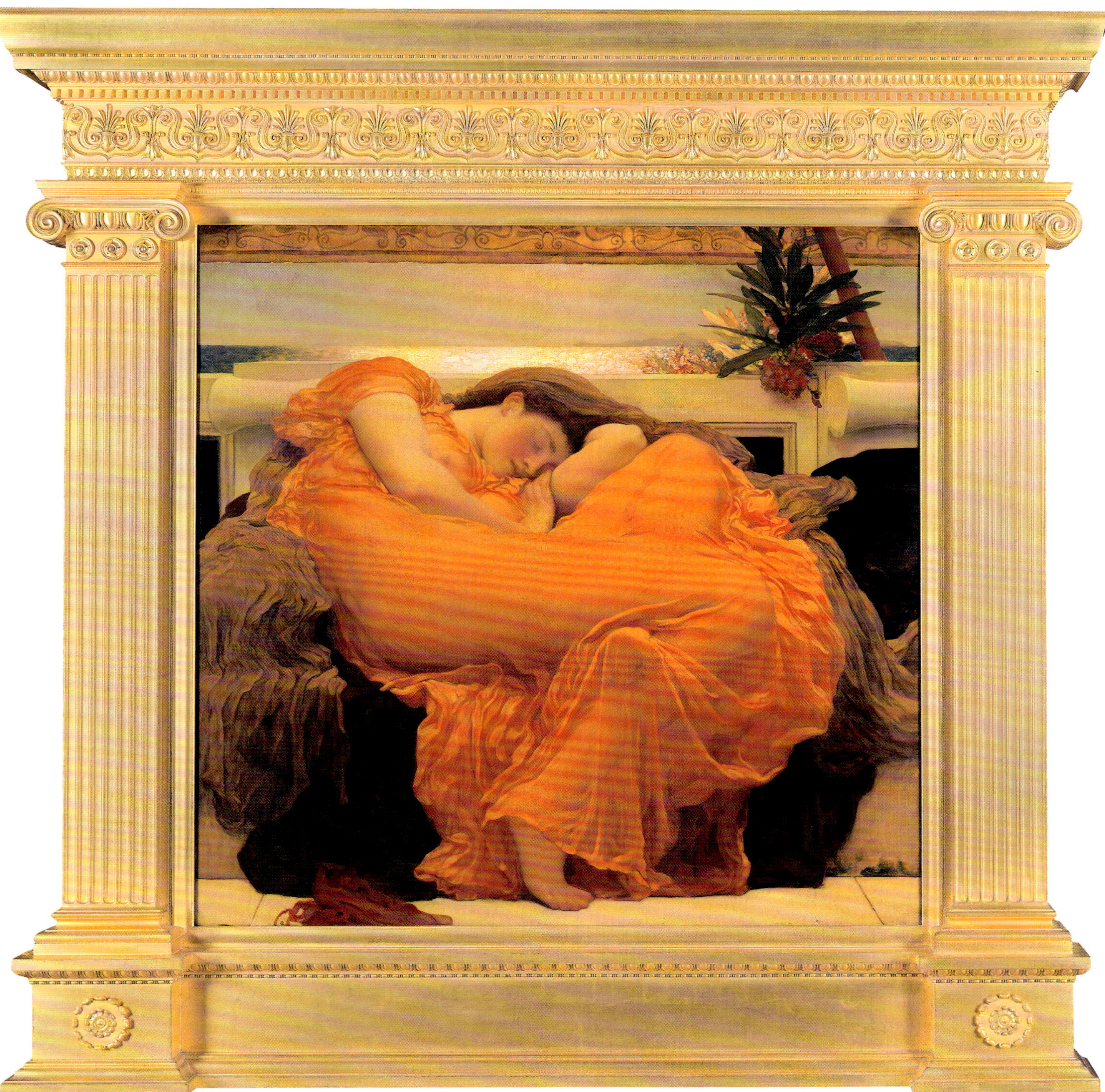

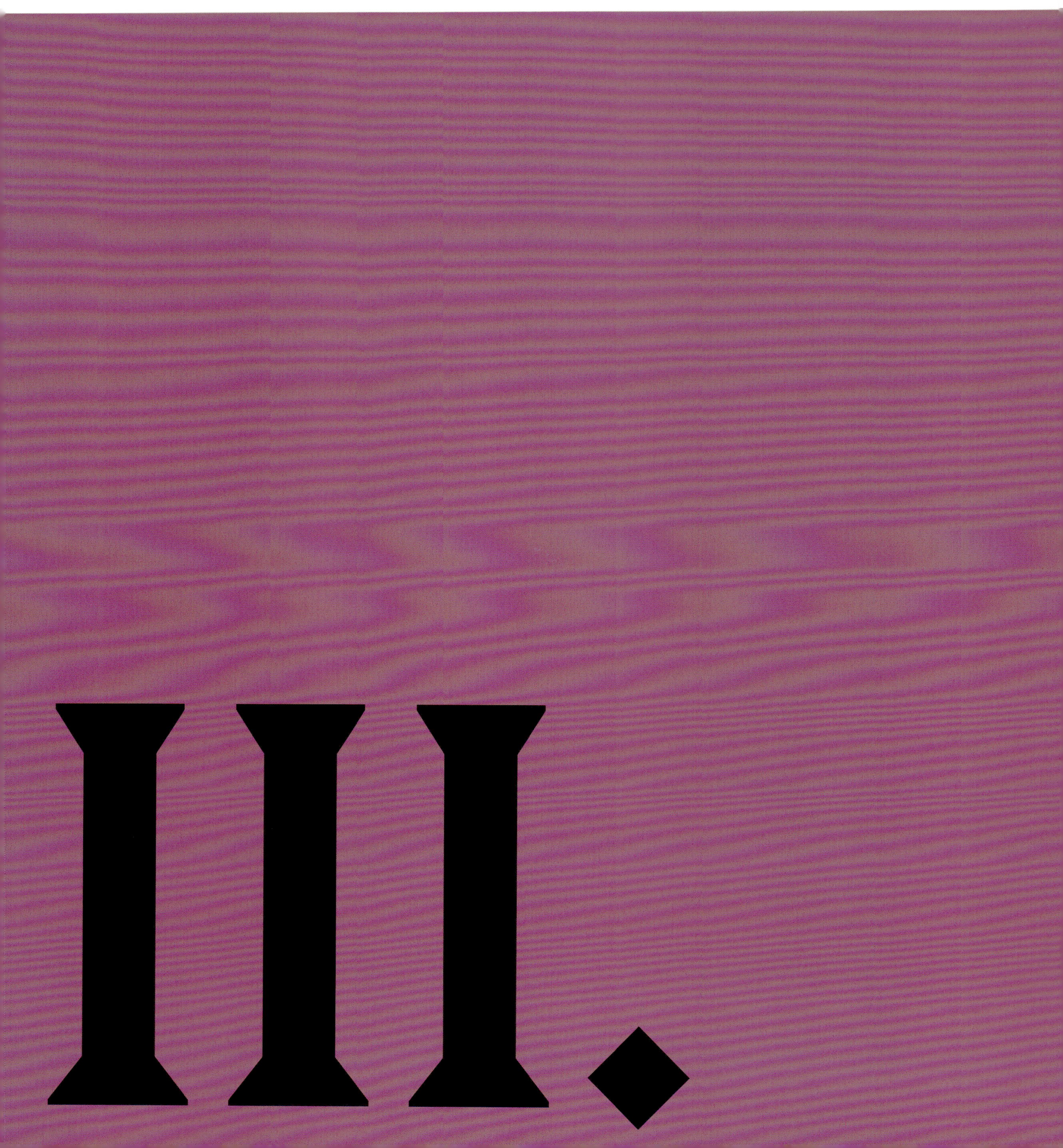

III.

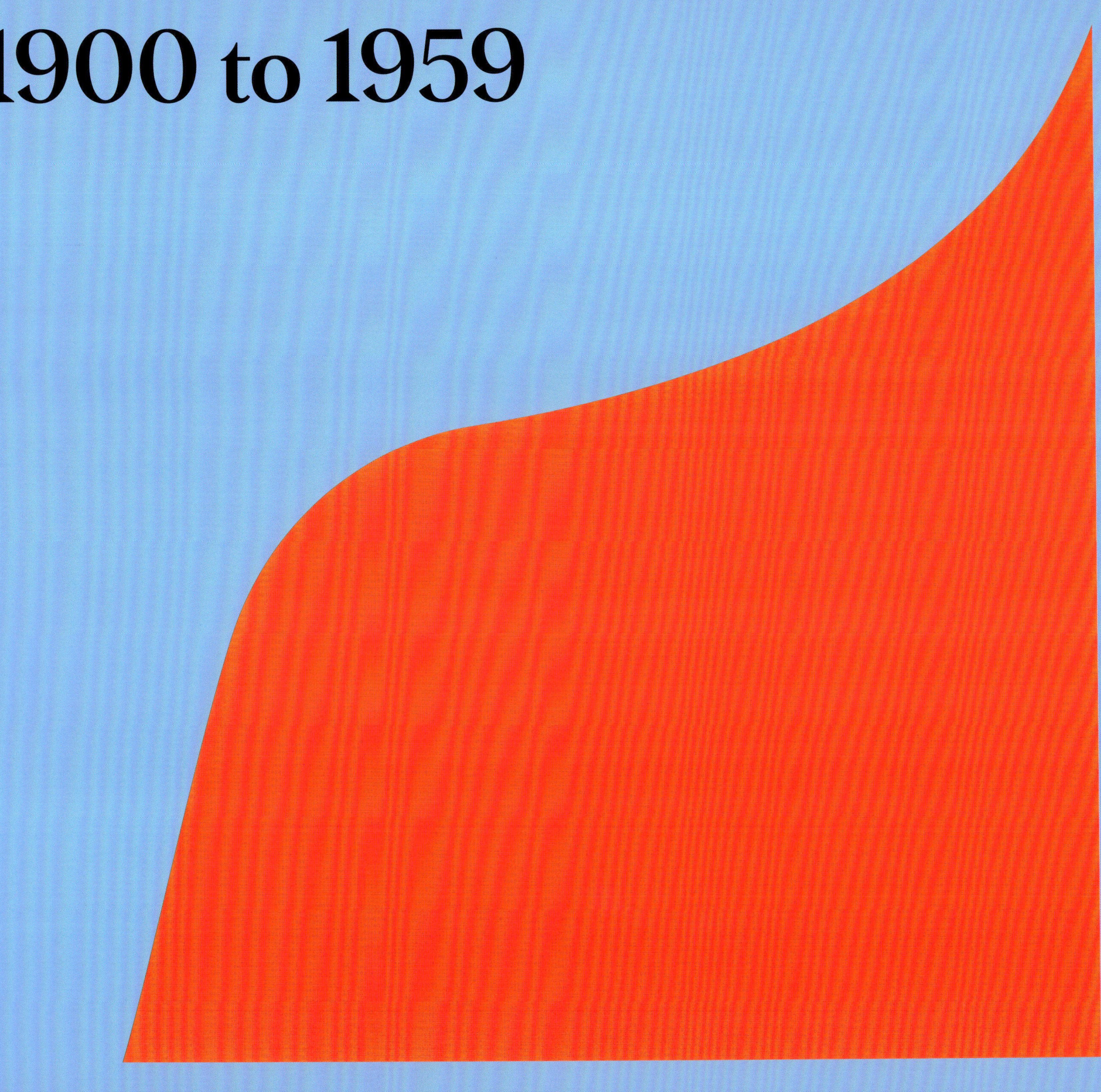

1900 to 1959

ADELE BLOCH-BAUER I _1907_

Art Nouveau was an international art movement that swept through Europe and the USA from the late 1880s until World War I. It was a determined and successful attempt to create a thoroughly modern art, typified by an emphasis on lines that were rendered boldly and simply. The female form was a central motif for many Art Nouveau artists and designers, including Gustav Klimt. Klimt was the leading artistic figure in Vienna, Austria, at the turn of the century, and the co-founder and first president of the Vienna Secession, a breakaway group of freethinking young artists in the city at the end of the 19th century. They favoured a broader definition of art that included applied arts and believed that art could play a central role in social improvement.

The quintessential Art Nouveau artist, Klimt is known for his celebration of female beauty through sumptuous portraits rendered in his distinctive style, which combines a naturalistic treatment of human skin with exquisite patterning and lavish ornamentation. Adele Bloch-Bauer, the wife of a wealthy Jewish industrialist, was one of Klimt's key subjects and the only person that he painted twice.

While working on _Adele Bloch-Bauer I_, Klimt visited Ravenna, Italy. There, he saw early Byzantine mosaics, which inspired him to incorporate gold and silver leaf into his paintings. Adele is presented here as a precious jewel in a box of gems, with a halo behind her that gives her an air of the divine, like a goddess or saint. The visual decadence of the opulent portrait with its flowing curves, rich colours, mixture of realism and abstraction, and shimmering, glittering all-over gold abstract design make it unmistakably Klimt and one of the highlights of his 'golden style'.

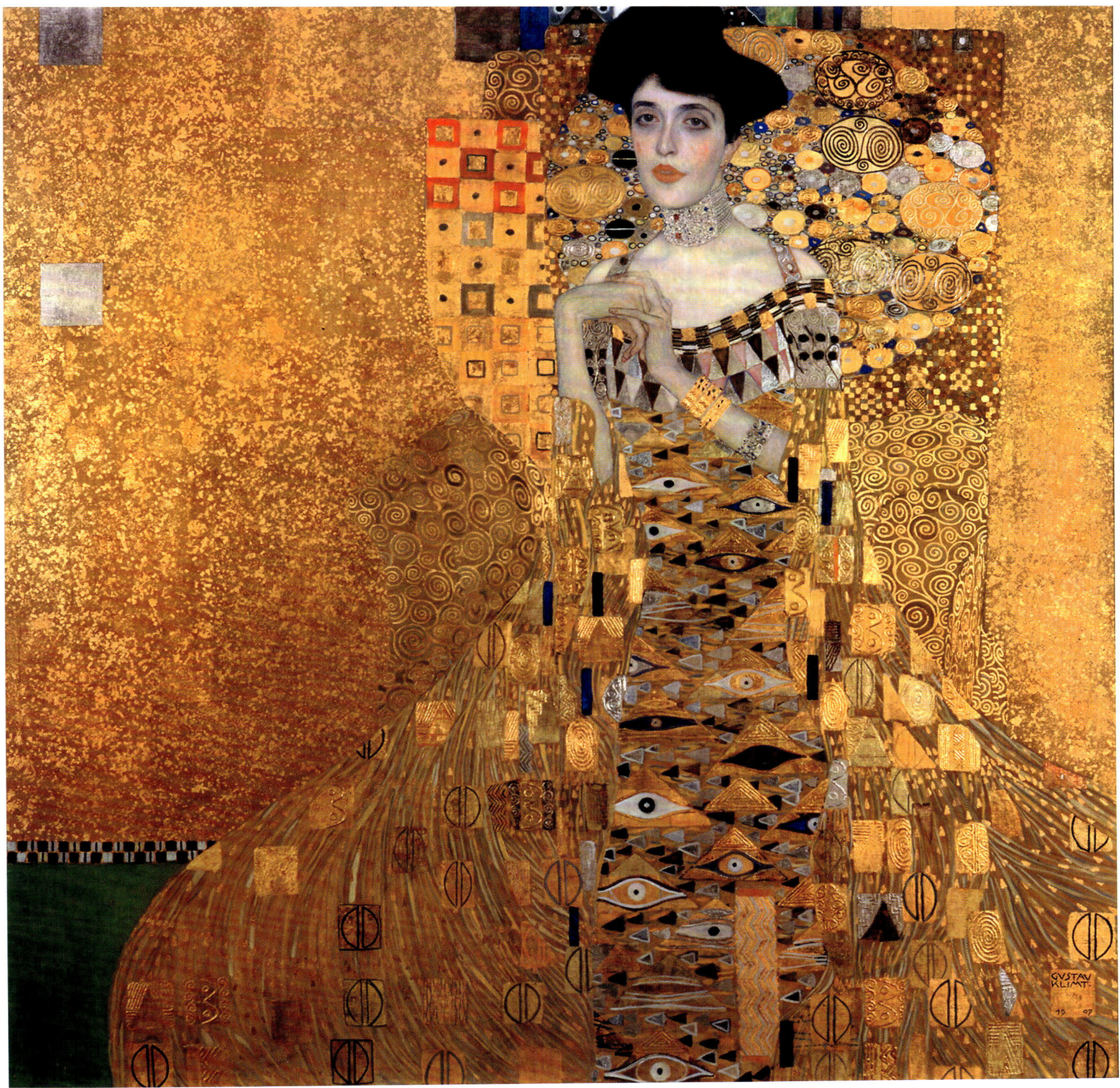

NUDE IN BLACK STOCKINGS *1917*

Expressionist artists use colour and line symbolically and emotively. Instead of recording an impression of the world around them (like the Impressionists), they impress their own temperament on their view of the world. This concept of art was so revolutionary in the early 20th century that 'Expressionism' became a synonym for 'modern' art in general.

The most famous exponent of Austrian Expressionism was Egon Schiele, who made the nude modern by making it explicitly erotic. He took the linear quality of his mentor, Gustav Klimt (p. 108), and transformed it into an aggressive, nervous line to create pictures of twisted, anguished figures and unashamedly erotic female nudes.

Schiele's works powerfully express emotional aspects of the human condition – despair, passion, loneliness and eroticism. The blatant sexuality and lack of idealization of his female figures outraged Viennese public sensibilities, leading to his imprisonment for 24 days in 1912 for exhibiting a 'pornographic' drawing in a place where it could be seen by children. More than 100 of his drawings were confiscated and many burned.

Schiele was aware of the innovative nature of his work and relished the role of the tortured artist. In 1931, he wrote to his mother: 'I shall be the fruit which will leave eternal vitality behind even after its decay. How great must be your joy therefore, to have given birth to me.'[24] Schiele did decay quite quickly – he died in the Spanish flu pandemic of 1918 at the age of 28 – but his radical, edgy portraits of the human psyche and raw sexuality went on to be an important touchstone for many artists who followed.

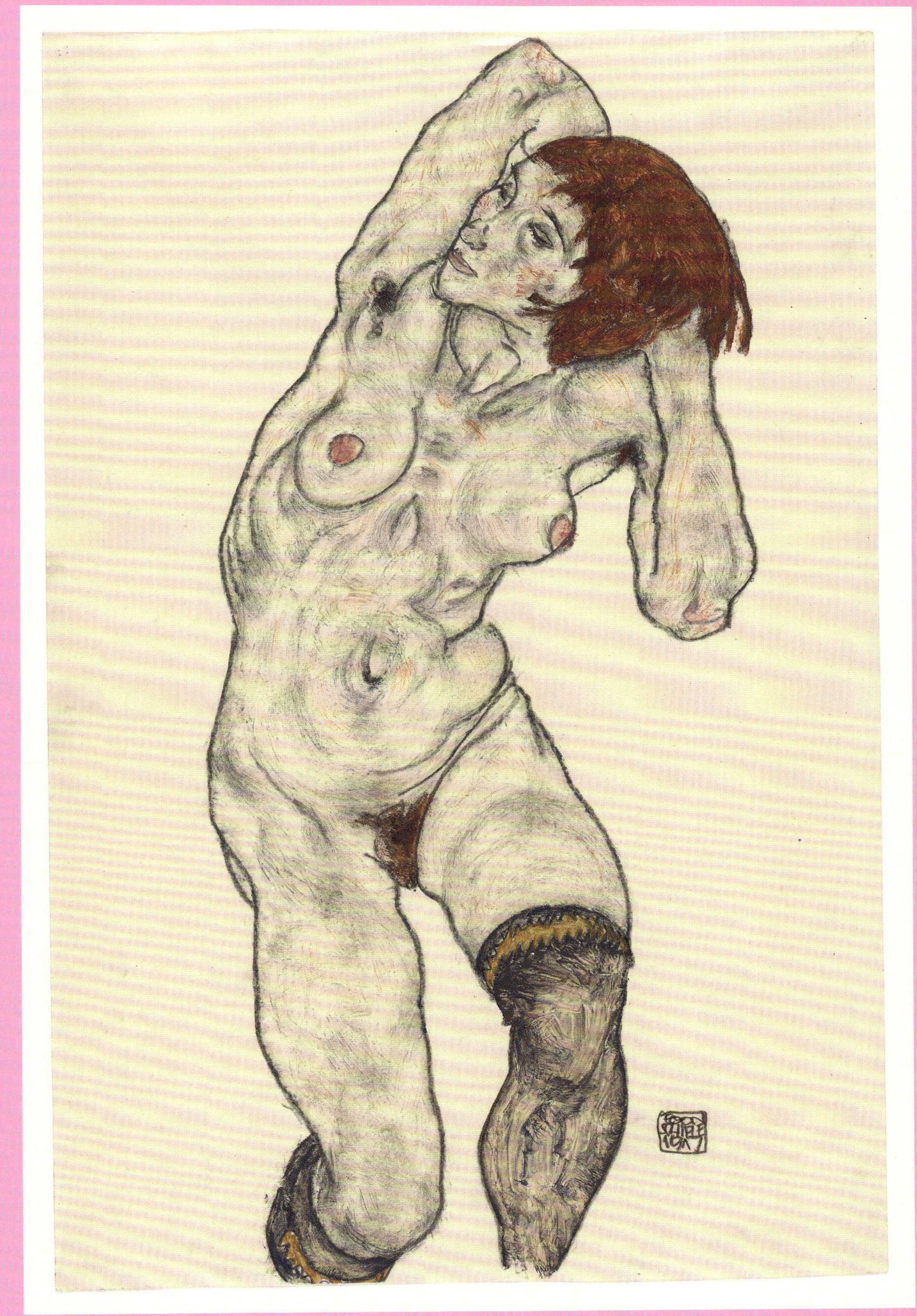

RECLINING NUDE *1917*

In the early 20th century, Paris was the centre of the art world and home to a large international community of modernist artists. Among them was Amedeo Modigliani, an archetypal bohemian artist whose life was the stuff of legend. The Italian's good looks, poverty and illness (exacerbated by drugs and alcohol), his drunken exhibitionism and his fights with his girlfriends are almost as well-known as his elegant, hypnotic, elongated portraits and sensual nudes.

Modigliani's large-format reclining and seated nudes of 1916–1919 draw on Italian Renaissance depictions of idealized female bodies, but they are not clothed in mythology or allegory. Unlike the Venus prototypes that preceded them, these beauties do not look like statues or goddesses, but like the real women of the day that they were. Even though they are somewhat abstracted through Modigliani's unique, recognizable style, the women retain their individual features – fashionable hairdos, body hair, seductive looks.

The blatant eroticism of the nudes caused a scandal when they were exhibited in 1917, and the police closed the show on the grounds of indecency. Yet while they were provocative in 1917, Modigliani's distinctive style makes his modern nudes seem much more like 'Modiglianis' than actual women, and they are now some of the best-known and most loved works of the 20th century.

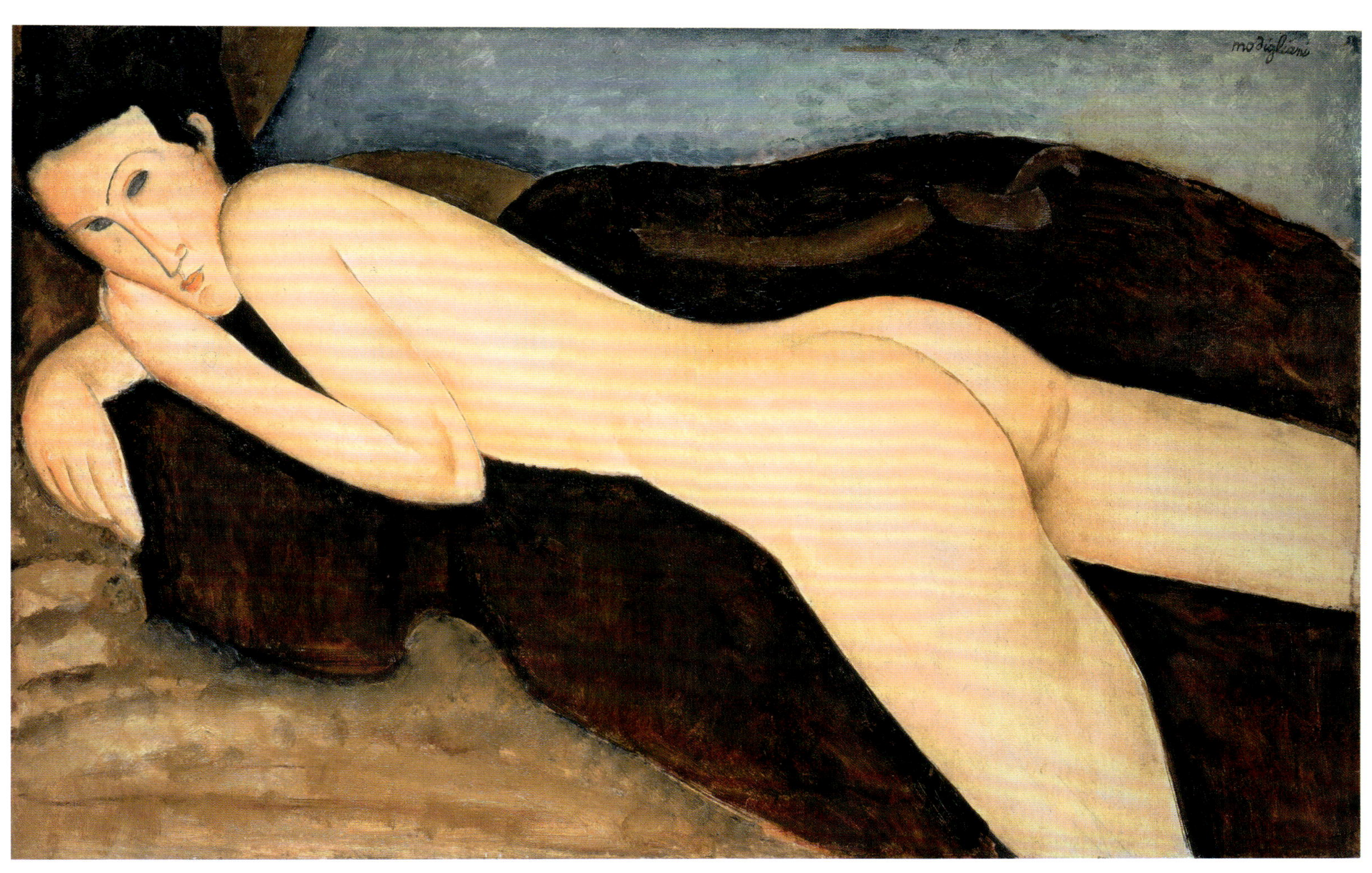

modigliani

DADA–ERNST *1920–1921*

Hannah Höch was the sole female member of the revolutionary Dada art group in Berlin, Germany, after World War I. While she was an important figure in Berlin Dada, Höch was still very much an outsider, kept on the periphery of the 'boys club'; she was both a part of the movement and distanced from it by her gender.

Höch's work is preoccupied with gender roles in general and with the various social roles and media images of women in particular. A sense of frustration, anger and helplessness is effectively conveyed in her photomontages, in which she 'corrects' the image of women portrayed by the media and society to present a more truthful, complicated version.

In *Dada-Ernst* (*Dada-Serious*, and perhaps a reference to fellow Dadaist, Max Ernst) we see themes that recur in Höch's work, such as dance (as female pleasure), woman as commodity and an enthusiasm for machines. We also see her working method, which involved cutting up images and text from the mass media and reassembling them in open-ended narratives. The photographs of women that Höch used are of those she admired – dancers, actresses and artists – and women associated with Dada, revolution, liberation and the new. While addressing the turbulent political climate of post-war Berlin, the overriding concern is that of the 'New Woman' and the desire for a legitimate female public sphere; issues that were pertinent to Höch as she tried to establish her identity.

Höch's relationship with fellow Dada artist Raoul Haussman at the time was perhaps another source of frustration, particularly in the disjunction between his 'feminist' theories – in which he called for a sexual revolution as well as an economic and political one – and the reality of the often psychologically and physically violent nature of their relationship. *Dada-Ernst*, with its violent juxtapositions, provides a powerful image of the fears and hopes of Weimar women.[25]

Many of Höch's images transcend their era and speak of issues that are still relevant today: representations of women and sexuality; issues of spectatorship; and visibility. They also anticipate the work of artists working later in the century, such as Barbara Kruger (p. 182) and the Guerrilla Girls (p. 180).[26]

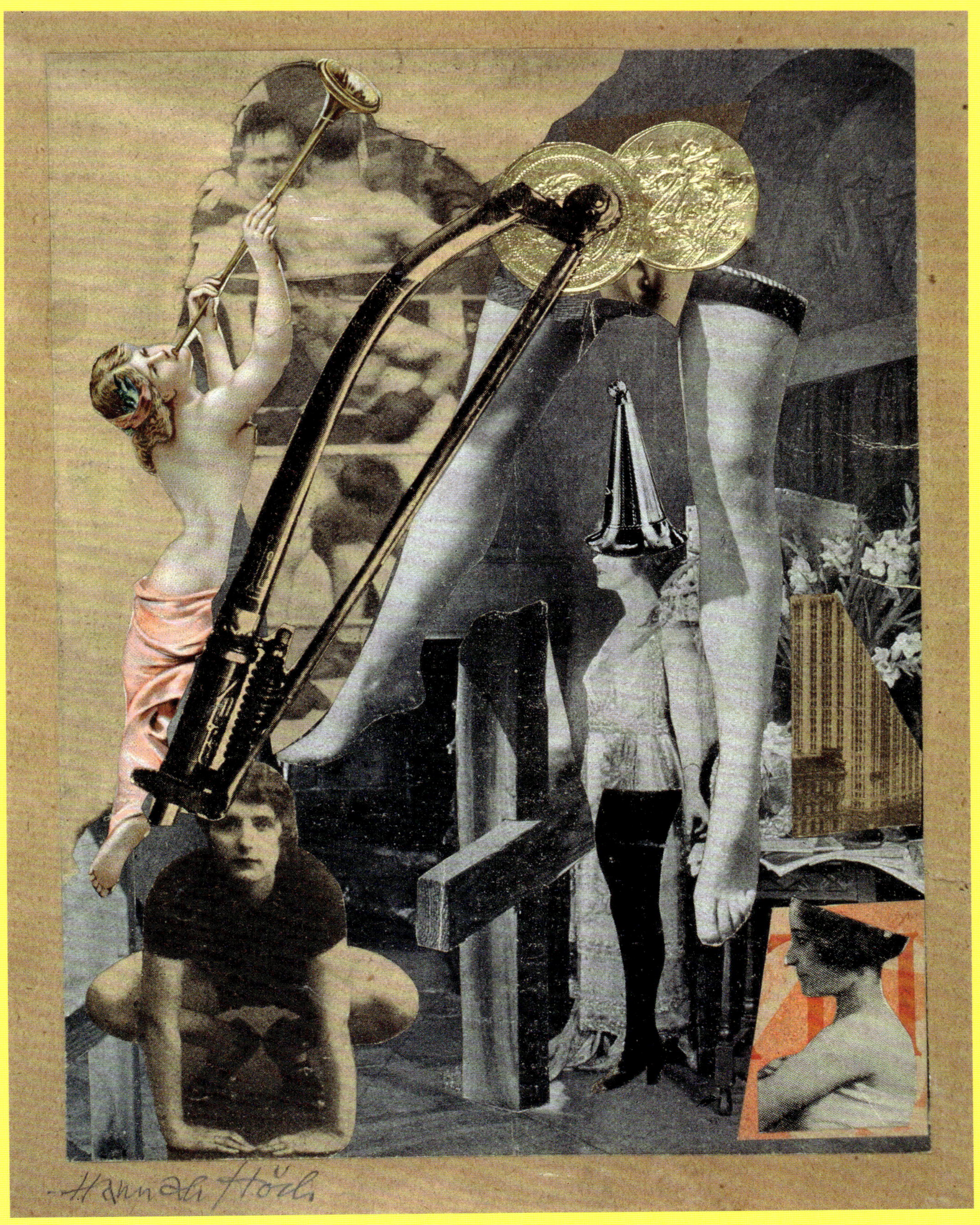

Hannah Höch

NOIRE ET BLANCHE

(Black and White) <u>1926</u>

Man Ray was a multidisciplinary artist who moved with ease between the seemingly incompatible worlds of the Parisian avant garde of the 1920s and 30s and commercial photography. His photographs were featured in a wide range of periodicals in Europe and America, helping to break down the distinctions between high and popular art, fashion and culture.

Man Ray's photographs are not character studies, but object studies, and his women – whether terrifying or ideal – are always sensual and exotic. *Black and White* (1926) shows Kiki de Montparnasse's[27] head laid on a table next to an upright African mask and is a good example of how Man Ray's work was presented to different audiences. In May 1926, it was published in French *Vogue* and in July 1928 it appeared in the avant-garde Belgian art journal *Variétés* (in *Variétés* the image was also published with its negative print, reversing the black and white of the heads).

Images that present the female as an 'object' play to a different gaze, depending on their context. High-fashion photographs, such as those in *Vogue*, are intended as objects of female desire and pleasure; they are recipients of the female gaze. However, when the same photograph is displayed in a different context, the woman becomes an eroticized, fetishized object of the male gaze.

———

In fashion and Surrealism – the art movement with which Man Ray was associated – the mannequin and the mask symbolize woman as object; as constructed, as manipulated, as violating the boundaries of alive and not alive. Both Man Ray's photographs and Hannah Höch's photomontages (p. 114) often contain masks, fragmented female bodies and disembodied heads, and yet they illicit very different responses from the viewer. While Höch's are harrowing, angry commentaries on the representation of women and their roles in society, Man Ray's are more a meditation on art than life – here the play of black and white, light and shadow, form and pattern.

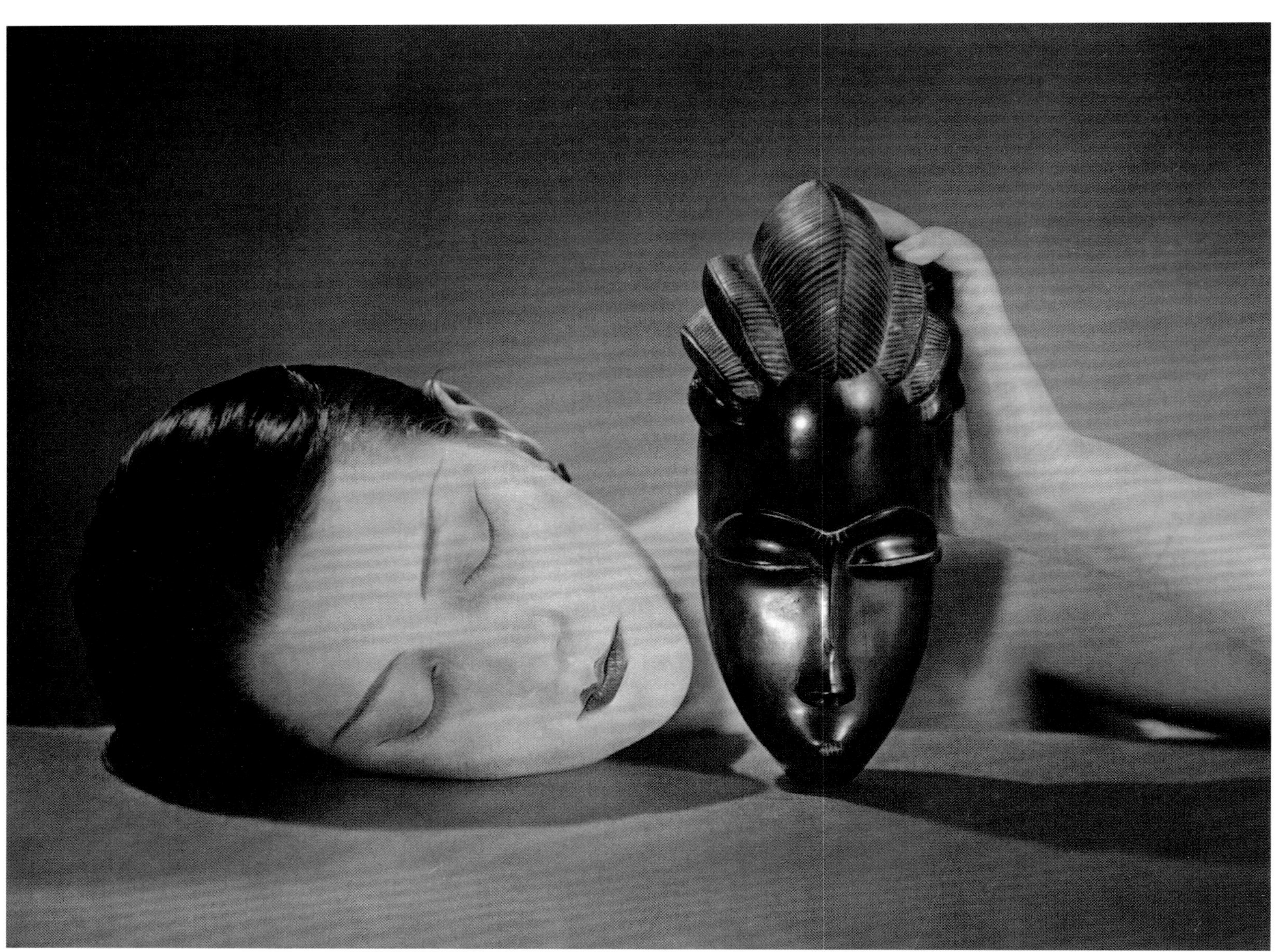

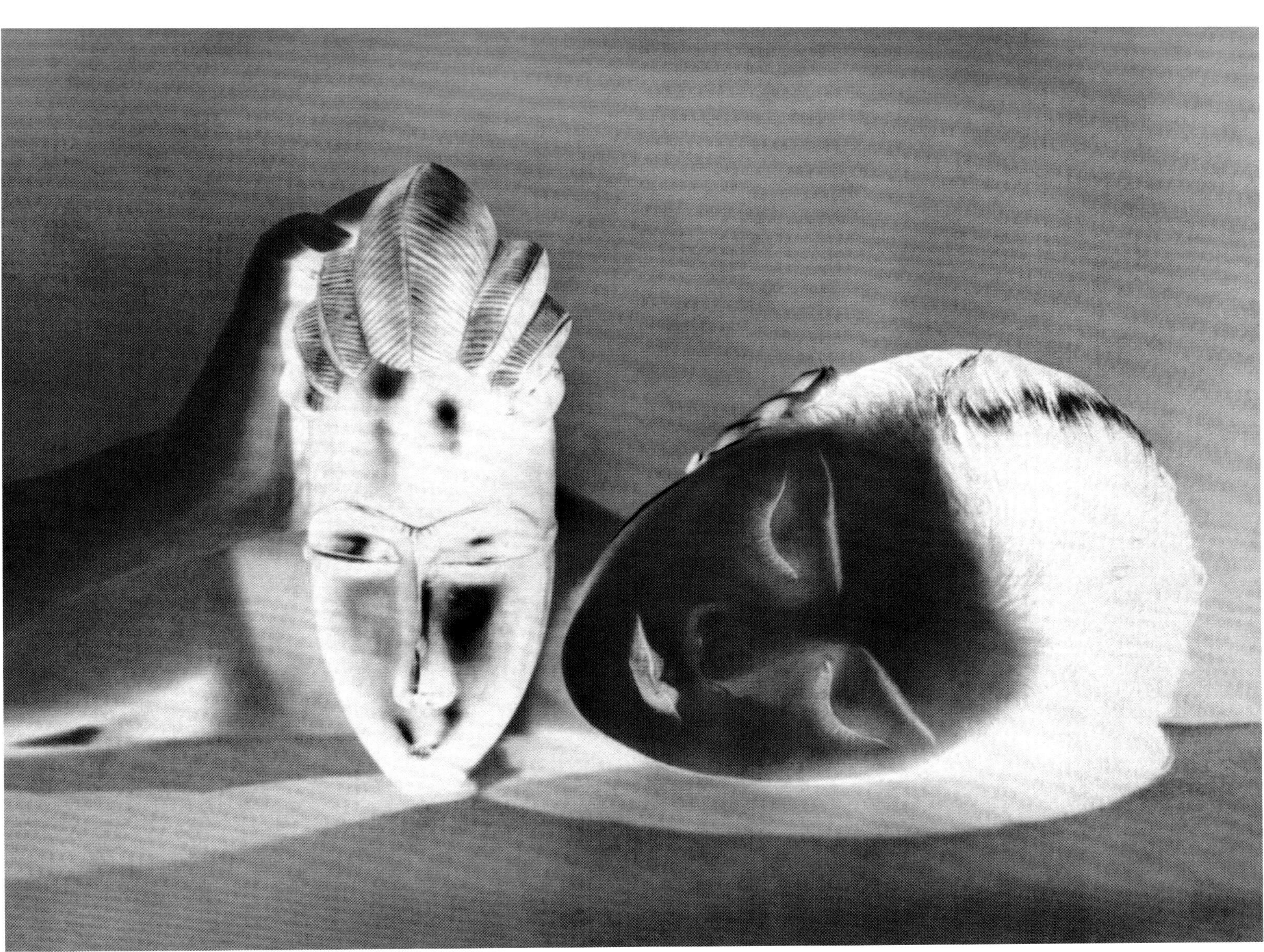

Gerda Wegener
(Danish, 1886–1940)

QUEEN OF HEARTS (LILI) *1928*

Gerda Wegener was a prominent exponent of the early style of Art Deco, in its luxurious, highly decorative phase, which can be seen in her illustrations of elongated, fashionable, modern women. She is also known for portraying gender-fluid characters and same-sex desire, exploring gender and sexual identity. In 1904, she began painting her husband, the Danish artist Einar Wegener, as a woman when one of her models failed to show up. He soon became Gerda's favourite model, adopting the alter-ego of Lili Elbe. Soon after, Einar began to identify as male-to-female transgender. The couple moved to Paris in 1912 where they lived together as two women and were embraced by the avant-garde community.

In Paris, Wegener was acclaimed for her portraits of Lili, fashion illustrations, illustrations of lesbian erotica, advertisements and glass mosaics, winning two gold medals and a bronze at the Paris World's Fair in 1925. Elbe, meanwhile, gave up painting to become an artist's model – mainly her wife's – and in 1930 became one of the world's first patients to undergo gender reassignment surgery.

Like her contemporary in Paris, Tamara de Lempicka (p. 122), Wegener painted strong, beautiful, confident women. In her many portraits of Lili, there is an element of role-play and a sense of two people collaborating on an image or look, rather than it being imposed upon the sitter, as in traditional portraits of women by male artists. Here, the artist identifies with the sitter – lover, friend, partner, muse – who is not being subjected to the male gaze, but is part of something more complicated, or at least less easy to define. In life and art, the two created Lili as a chic, confident, sassy modern woman of the 1920s. In *Queen of Hearts (Lili)*, Lili inhabits the persona of the archetypal flapper with her short dress, bobbed hair and insouciant gaze as she smokes and plays cards.

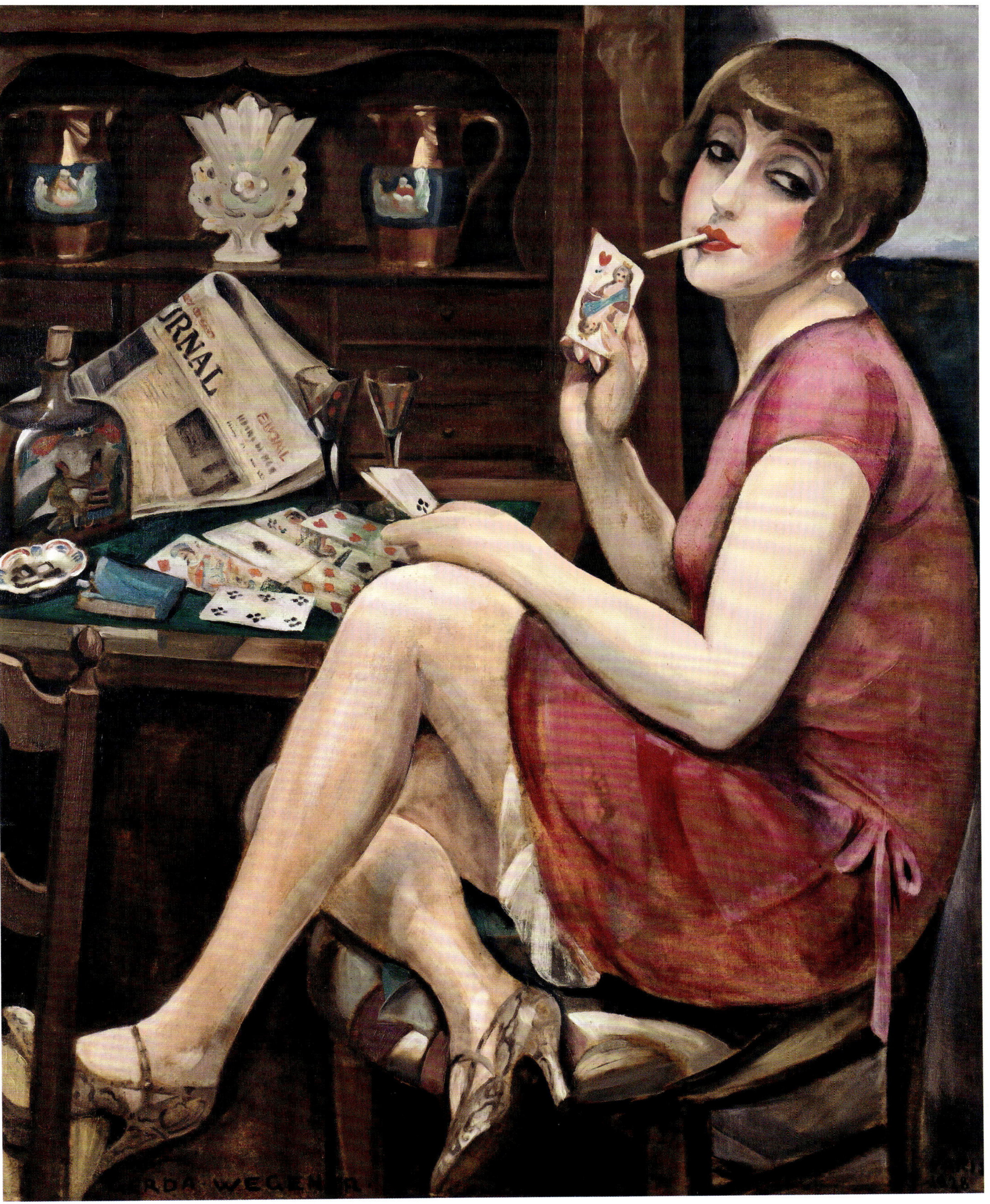
RDA WEGENER

LA MUSICIENNE
(The Musician) <u>1929</u>

The Jazz Age of F. Scott Fitzgerald's 1925 novel, *The Great Gatsby*, conjures up an era of flappers, the Charleston and the tango; a time when people wanted to forget the traumas of the Great War, enjoy themselves and look to the future. Speed, travel, luxury, leisure and modernity were what this fashion-conscious culture craved, and Art Deco gave them the images and objects that reflected their desires.

Events outside the art world were particularly influential. The exotic sets and costumes of Sergei Diaghilev's Ballets Russes started a craze for Oriental and Arabian dress, while the discovery of Tutankhamen's tomb in 1922 sparked a vogue for Egyptian motifs and shimmering metallic colours. American jazz culture and dancers such as Josephine Baker captured the imagination, as did 'primitive' African sculpture.

Polish artist Tamara de Lempicka was a prominent figure in the Paris of the Roaring Twenties, noted for her glamorous, decadent lifestyle and parties, as well as her paintings of sleek young men and women at ease in their ultra-stylish surroundings. Lempicka cultivated her image as an exotic aristocrat-émigré, declaring 'I live life in the margins of society, and the rules of normal society don't apply to those who live on the fringe.'[28] Fiercely independent, she was openly bisexual and extremely hard-working, known for painting all day, stopping only for 'baths and champagne'.[29]

Lempicka successfully projected herself as the modern woman through both her life and art. Portraits of herself and others were made in her instantly recognizable style, which was characterized by bold, angular forms and metallic colours, capturing the later, more streamlined Art Deco look. In *La Musicienne*, we see Lempicka's friend and lover – Ira Perrot – also a married woman, appearing as the epitome of modern sexy female beauty set against the architecture of the new metropolis – the skyscrapers of New York City.

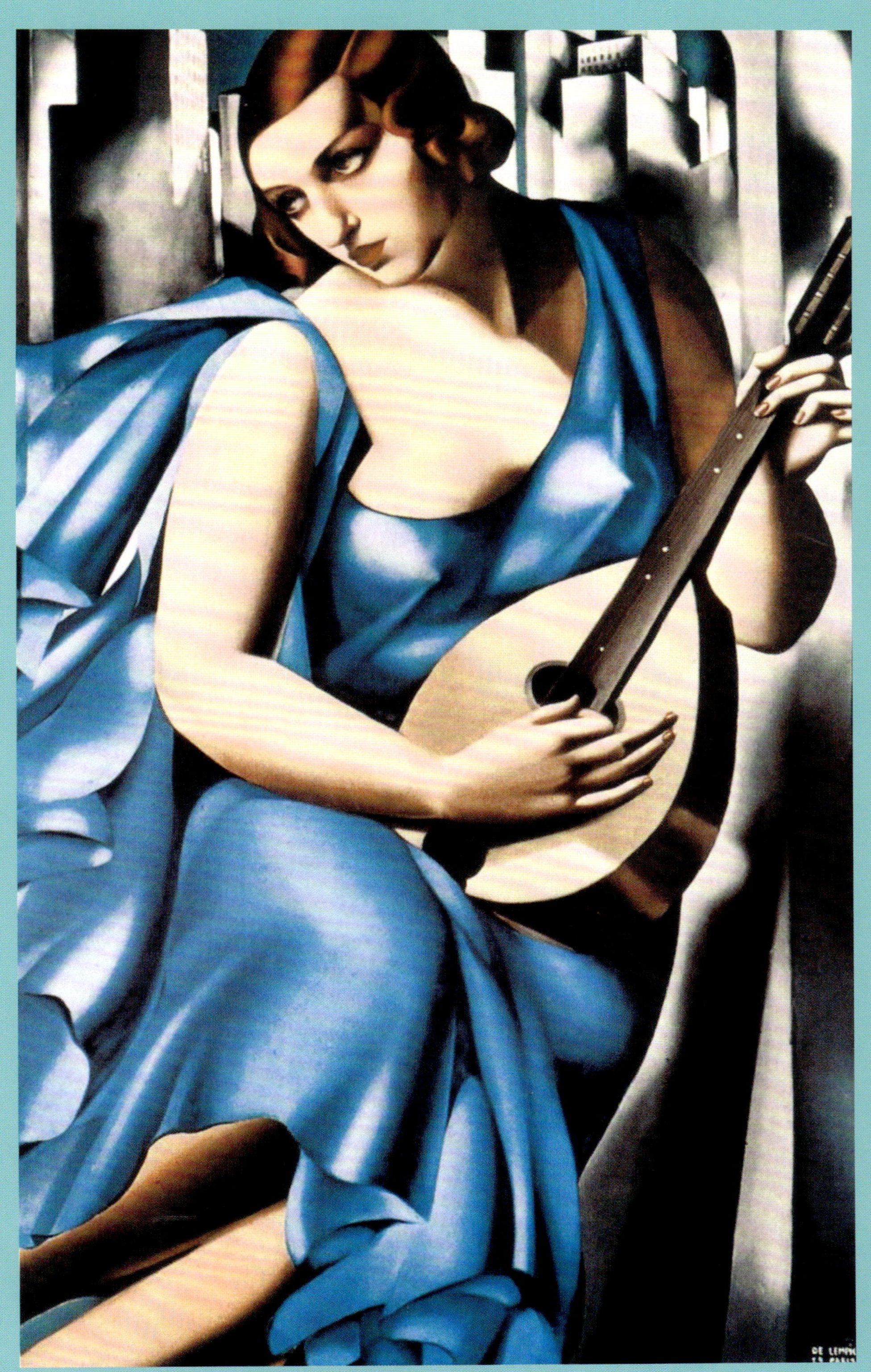

HILL WOMEN *1935*

Amrita Sher-Gil was born in Hungary and raised in India. From 1929 to 1932 she studied at the École des Beaux-Arts in Paris, immersing herself in the bohemian lifestyle of the city and experimenting with the ideas and techniques of modern European artists such as Paul Gauguin (p. 94) and Amedeo Modigliani (p. 112). In 1934, she returned to India, writing to her father that 'I can only paint in India. Europe belongs to Picasso, Matisse, Braque and the rest. But India belongs only to me.'[30]

On a quest to introduce modern art to India and to create a style of her own that would be both distinctly Indian and definitely modern, Sher-Gil travelled around the country studying traditional Indian art forms, from cave paintings to miniatures. Her mature style is a fusion of modern European techniques and Indigenous styles, using simplified forms and expressive, vibrant colour and line to portray real people in real-life activities.

Sher-Gil is known for her scenes of domestic life in India, particularly those of women from all walks of life, including poor rural women such as those in *Hill Women*. However, the women and their everyday lives, which are the focus of her attention, are not romanticized visions. Sher-Gil's women are bored and sad, but also resolved and dignified. As Sher-Gil wrote: 'I am personally trying to be, through the medium of line, colour and design, an interpreter of the life of the people, particularly the life of the poor and sad.'[31]

Women are front and centre in her art: the separate worlds that they inhabit and the work they do is elevated by being deemed worthy of representation. In 1976, Sher-Gil was declared one of nine National Art Treasure Artists of India, meaning that her work cannot be exported; in 1978, *Hill Women* featured on a stamp, taking her Indian modern art around the country.

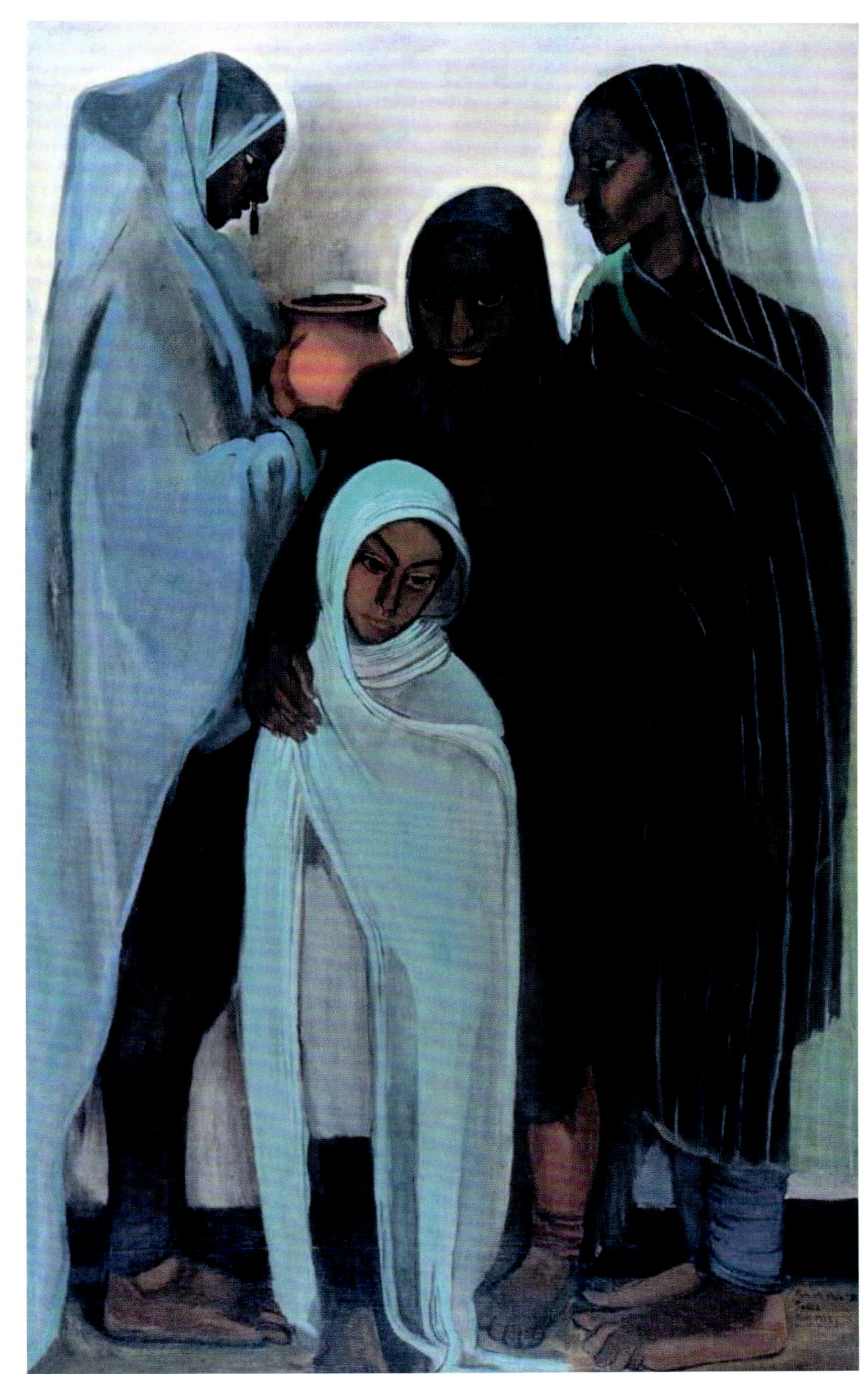

MIGRANT MOTHER *1936*

From the moment it first appeared in print, *Migrant Mother* became the face of the Great Depression, the poignant image of a worried mother and her children capturing the human cost of the worst economic downturn in the Western world. The photograph was taken by Dorothea Lange, who was working for the US government's Resettlement Administration, a federal agency created to record the conditions of the urban and rural poor as a means to agitate for federal assistance. In 1936, Lange was in California documenting the plight of farmers and migrant workers in the state. She came across a pea picker's camp of 2,500 agricultural workers, hungry and destitute because of the failure of the early pea crop.

Lange recounted her experience later: 'I saw and approached the hungry and desperate mother, as if drawn by a magnet. I do not remember how I explained my presence or my camera to her, but I do remember she asked me no questions. I made five exposures, working closer and closer from the same direction. I did not ask her name or her history. She told me her age, that she was thirty-two. She said that they had been living on frozen vegetables from the surrounding fields, and birds that the children killed ... There she sat in that lean-to tent with her children huddled around her, and seemed to know that my pictures might help her, and so she helped me.'[32]

Lange meant for her work to be socially and politically useful. In her striking images she helped humanize the economic crisis by focusing on individuals made homeless and unemployed. The people in her photographs are proud and independent, in need of help but unlikely to ask for it. The intimate photograph of Florence Owens Thompson, *Migrant Mother*, is her most famous image and one of the most enduring images of Depression-era America. Quickly picked up by newspapers around the country, the haunting image of the extreme hardships that people were facing helped prompt the government to send food to the pea picker's camp. However, by then, this migrant mother and her family had moved on.

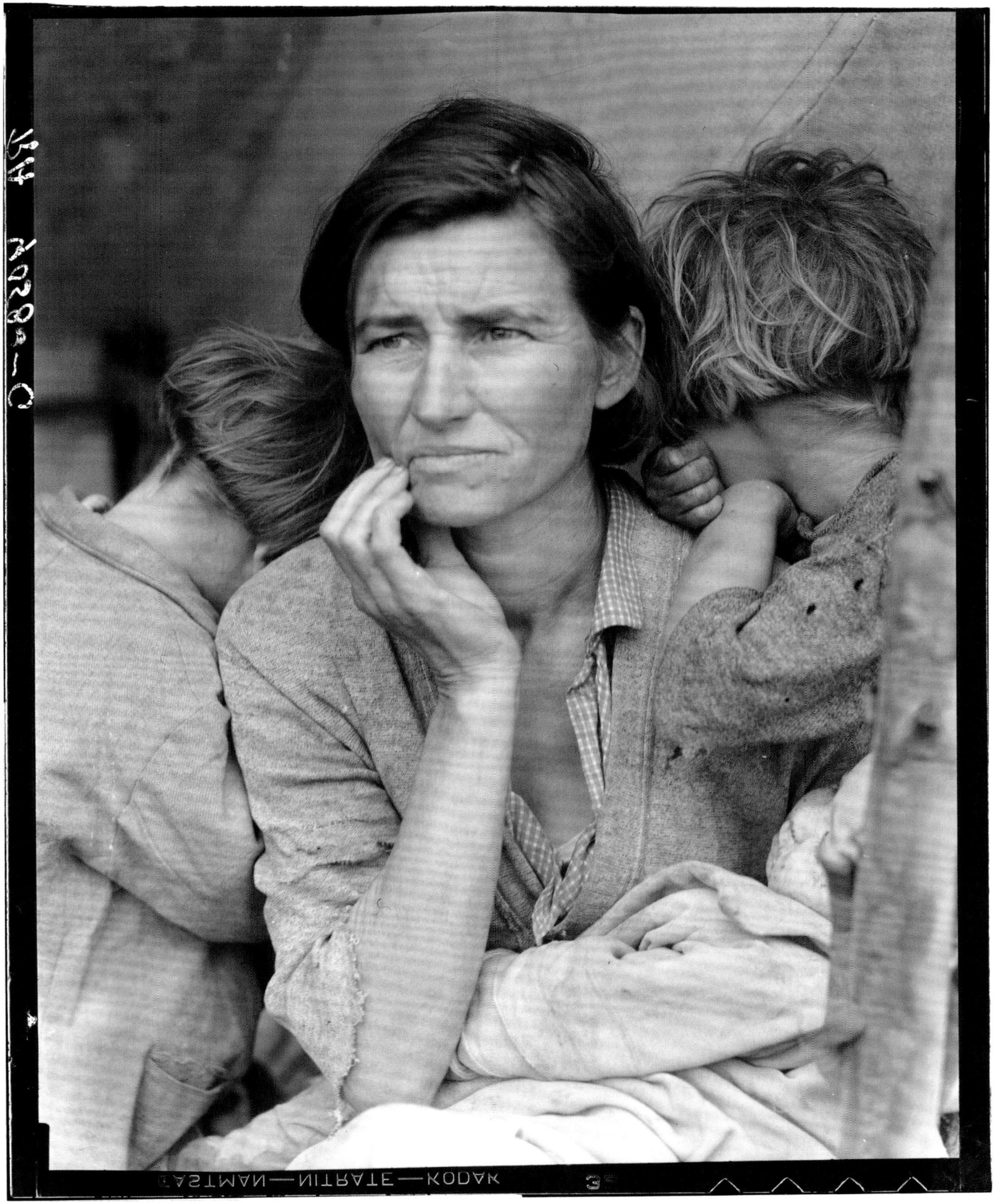

EASTMAN — NITRATE — KODAK

WORKER AND COLLECTIVE FARM GIRL *1937*

In 1934, Socialist Realism was declared the official artistic style of the Soviet Union. All artists had to join the state-controlled Union of Soviet Artists and produce work in the accepted mode, under the three guiding principles of party loyalty, presentation of correct ideology and accessibility. The style of choice was Realism, which was most easily understood by the masses.

However, this was not a critical social realism, such as Dorothea Lange's (p. 126), but an inspirational and educational one. Socialist Realism was to glorify the state and celebrate the superiority of the new classless society being built by the Soviets. Paintings and sculptures approved by the state typically showed men and women at work or playing sports, political assemblies, political leaders and the achievements of Soviet technology. These were portrayed in a naturalistic, idealized fashion, in which the people are young, muscular, happy members of a progressive, classless society, and its leaders are heroes.

Internationally, *Worker and Collective Farm Girl* by Vera Mukhina is probably the most striking and best-known sculpture of the Soviet era. The sculpture features a male industrial worker and a female agricultural worker brandishing a hammer and sickle aloft. Fusing her love of Greco-Roman sculpture with a touch of Art Deco modernity, Mukhina created a dynamic, monumental Social Realist sculpture. This is not a romantic sculpture of a man and woman in love, but an urban man and a rural woman – comrades – striding confidently into their Communist future. The piece was made for the top of the Soviet Pavilion at the Paris World's Fair of 1937, and at almost 25 metres (80 feet) tall the stainless steel sculpture dominated the Paris skyline, facing off against the pavilion of Nazi Germany.

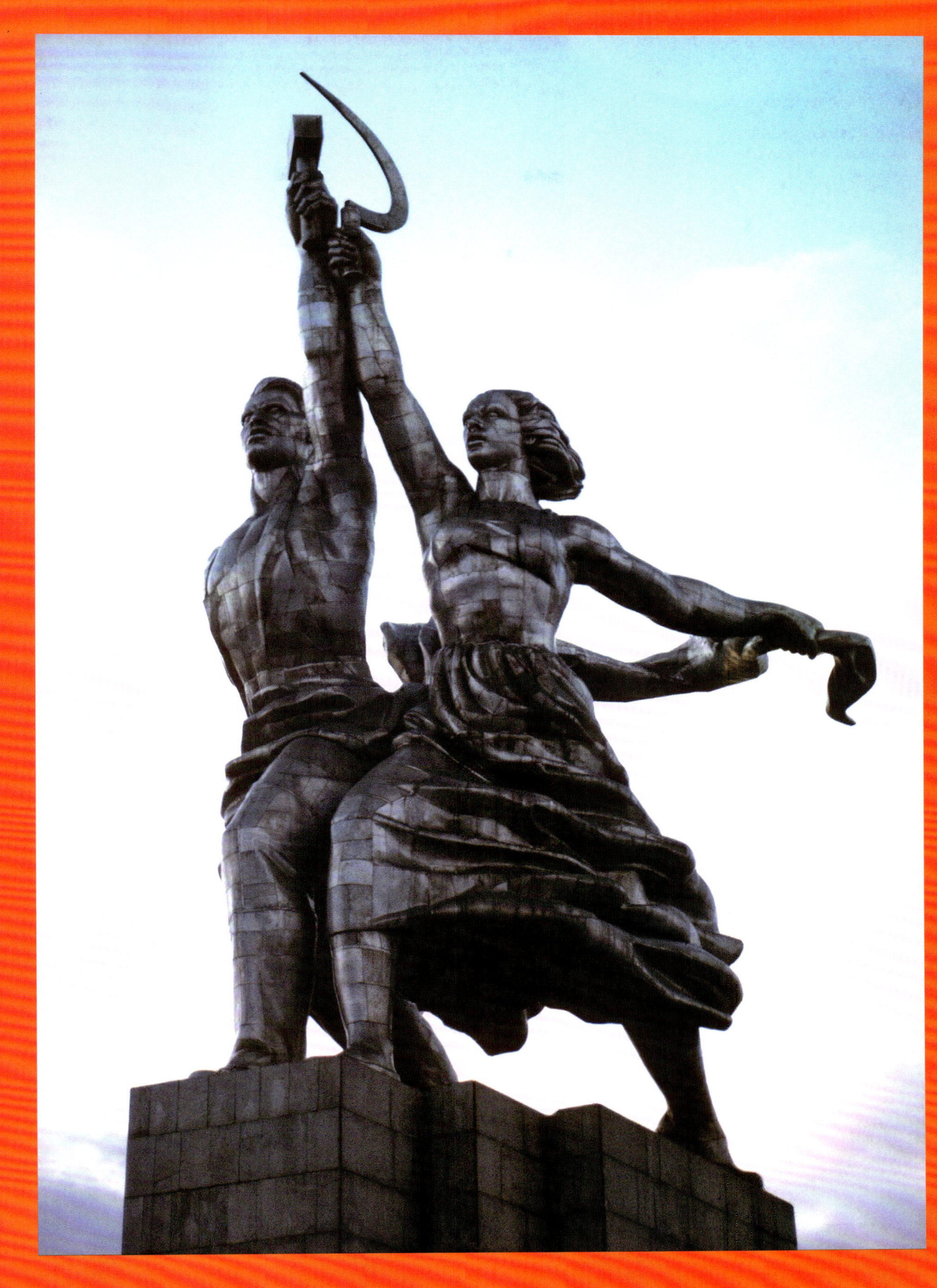

DESERTED DEN *1937*

Surrealism, meaning 'above realism' or 'more than real', was one of the 20th century's most popular and pervasive art movements. Launched by the French poet André Breton in 1924, it affected all branches of the arts and spread to all corners of the globe. Despite the misogyny implicit in much Surrealist philosophy and work, there were a number of important female Surrealists, including the Czech artist Toyen, who was a founding member of the Surrealist Group in Czechoslovakia, which formed in Prague in 1934.

Like many Surrealists, Toyen was interested in the ideas of the Austrian psychoanalyst Sigmund Freud, and absent figures, ghostly apparitions, crumbling walls, animals and erotic imagery are typical of her dreamlike, often nightmarish, paintings and illustrations of the 1930s. For Breton, a close friend and supporter, Toyen's work was 'as luminous as her own heart yet streaked through by dark forebodings.'[33]

The female body in this artwork is conspicuous by its absence, as is knowledge of the gender of its maker to a viewer by the signature alone. Haunting, beautiful and thought-provoking, Toyen's *Deserted Den* could stand for her personal rejection of gender stereotypes. The artist symbolically abandoned the 'corset' and constraints of her gender in 1923, when she changed her name – Marie Čermínová – to rid it of gender specificity (in Czech, the ending of surnames indicates gender). Čermínová became 'Toyen', an ungendered pseudonym adapted from the French word *citoyen* (citizen). Now she could be known as an artist, and not a 'female artist'.

The boldness of such a move or stance can be liberating and exciting, but such a leap into the unknown can also be frightening and unnerving. This is captured for me in the use of the word 'den' in the title. A den is a cosy, familiar, protective place, whereas nature and the outside world appear ominous in this image, rather than welcoming.

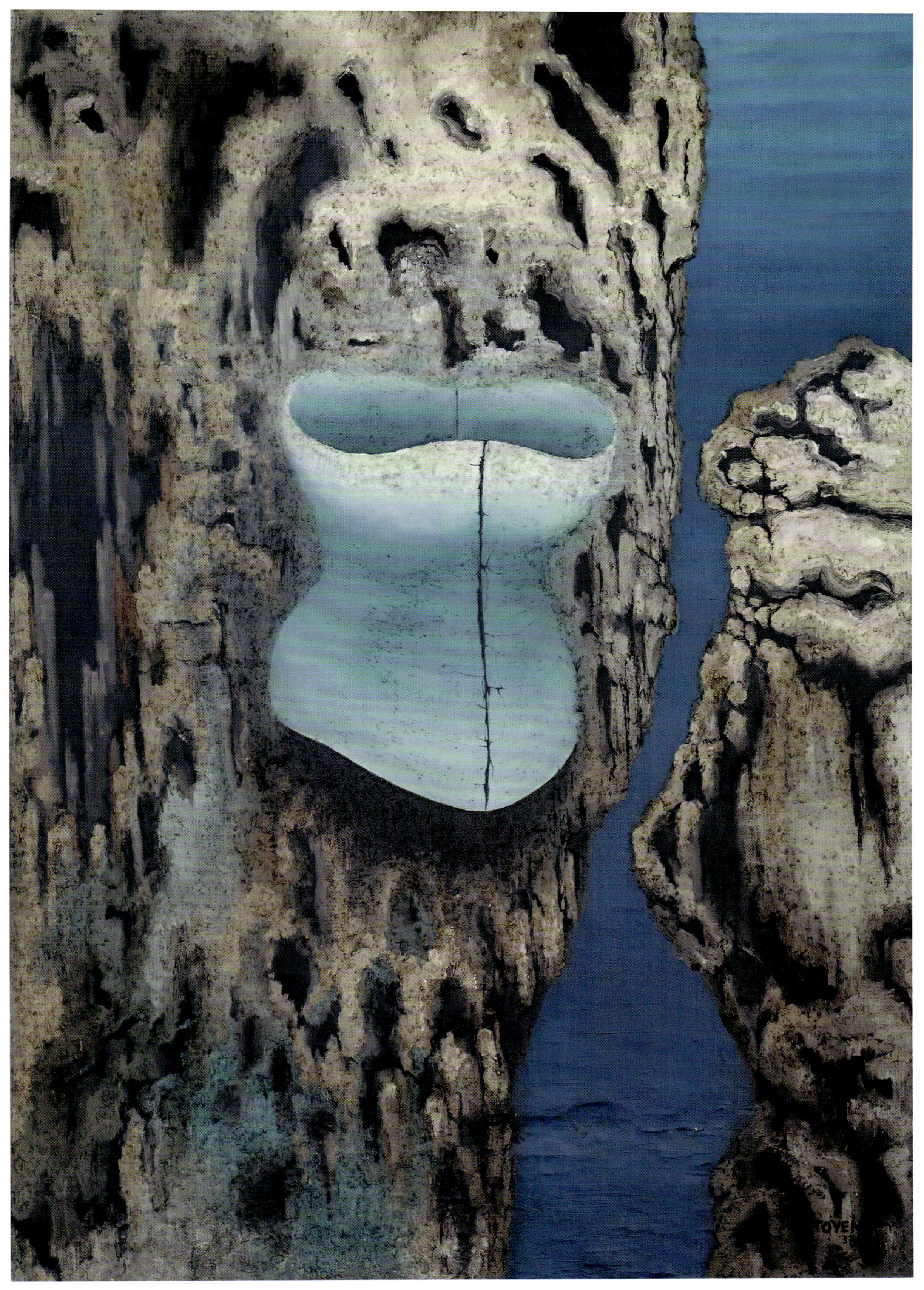

SELF-PORTRAIT WITH CROPPED HAIR *1940*

Known for her fiery personality, independent spirit, bawdy humour and alluring sexuality, Frida Kahlo became a celebrity in her own lifetime. Most of her art focuses on her life and her personal reality as a woman: a woman living with illness and injury, a woman who wished to have children but failed to, a strong woman, a seductive woman, a woman in love, a woman heartbroken, a woman depressed. Through more than 50 self-portraits and other semi-auto-biographical paintings, Kahlo shows us how incidents, events and emotions from her life are written on her body, all delivered to the viewer with an unflinching, unapologetic gaze.

While her paintings function as conversations with her inner self, many of the experiences and raw emotions that she shares are common to us all. In *Self-Portrait with Cropped Hair*, we see the aftermath of a broken relationship, namely Kahlo's divorce from her famous husband, the Mexican muralist Diego Rivera. Theirs was a passionate, turbulent relationship, which saw them married in 1929, divorced in 1939 and remarried a year later.

With an expression that seems both sad and defiant, Kahlo sits on a lone yellow chair surrounded by swirling locks of hair that look alive, sharing her heartbreak with us, as well as her resilience and fierce determination to be taken seriously as an artist. Handwritten across the top of the painting are lyrics from a Mexican folk song, which read: 'Mira que si te quise, fué por el pelo, Ahora que estás pelona, ya no te quiero.' ('Look, if I loved you, it was because of your hair. Now that you are without hair, I don't love you anymore.')

You don't need to be familiar with the song to appreciate the sentiment, which can be found in many break-up/country songs. How often do people change their look after a relationship ends? Kahlo has cut off her hair because Rivera loved it so, and is also wearing what looks like one of Rivera's suits – a memento of him. This is an image of transformation. The artist has cast off the long, embroidered Mexican dresses that she was known for and the flowers in her long hair (but retained her signature make-up and jewellery), in favour of a more androgynous look. It is a bold assertion that she is her own person, not someone's wife, and I also think it says 'I am my own independent artist; a force to be reckoned with. I will make it on my own.'

Mira que si te quise, fué por el pelo,
Ahora que estás pelona, ya no te quiero.
1940. Frida Kahlo.

THE SHEPHERDESS OF THE SPHINXES *1941*

Born in Buenos Aires, Argentina, Leonor Fini arrived in Paris in the early 1930s and quickly became known as a glamorous, mercurial, fiercely independent female celebrity, surrounded by cats and a bewitched entourage of past, present and would-be lovers of both genders. An artist, designer and writer, Fini was known for her dramatic theatrical paintings of female power and female sexuality and the exotic personas that she adopted to present herself and her artwork to the world. In 1936, one of her many lovers, the American art dealer Julien Levy, described her as having the 'head of a lioness, mind of a man, bust of a woman, torso of a child, grace of an angel, and discourse of the devil ...'[34]

In Fini's erotic dreamworld, men are unthreatening, delicate, androgynous – or absent – and women are strong, sexy beauties. Throughout her work, there is almost always Fini herself, as well as other strong female characters, based on friends such as the Surrealist artists Leonora Carrington, Meret Oppenheim and Dora Maar, who I imagine to be making up her bevy of beauties in *The Shepherdess of the Sphinxes*.

The wartime painting shows a magnificent shepherdess (Fini) in an apocalyptic land-scape, surrounded by an army of sphinxes. Fini is calling on the mythical creatures of knowledge and beauty to help her right the wrongs being committed all around them, as the world is under attack. Every time I look at this painting of the 'shepherdess with big hair', I can't help but think of Wonder Woman (who was created the same year in the USA). There were obviously many around the world at the same time who thought that women should be sorting things out; that the world was in need of new superheroes, and they should be female ones who could be strong and beautiful, dropping love bombs instead of fire power.

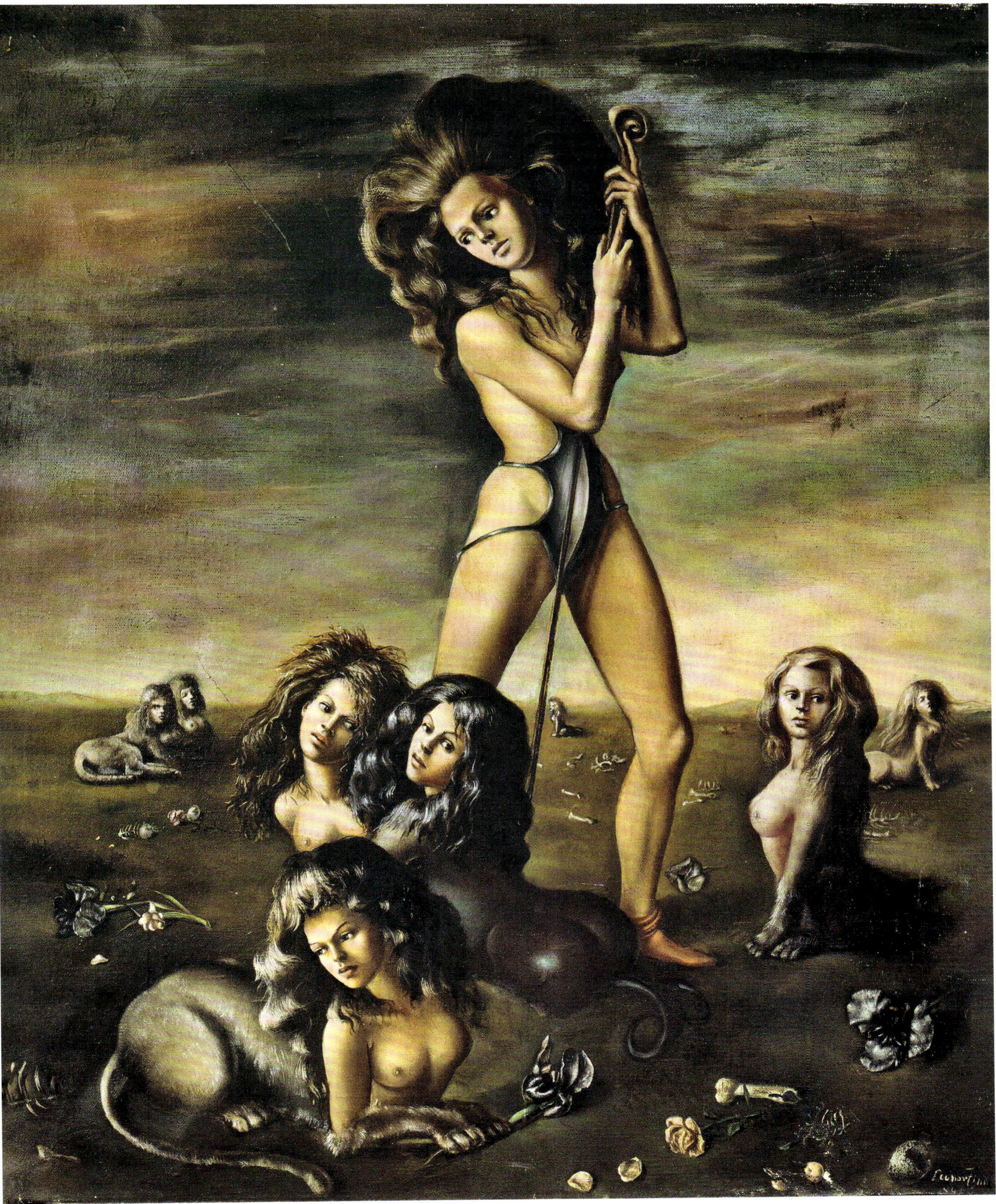

FFI WORKER, PARIS, FRANCE *1944*

Lee Miller began her relationship with photography as a fashion model in New York in the late 1920s, before transforming herself into a Surrealist muse and artist in Paris in the late 1920s and 1930s, working as an assistant and inventor with Man Ray (p. 116).

During World War II, she worked for British *Vogue* as a photographer, creating photo-essays about women's contributions to the war effort in England, and then became an official war correspondent in the field with the US army. She arrived in Normandy in July 1944 and accompanied the Allied forces through France and then into Germany in 1945, where she helped document the atrocities of the Dachau and Buchenwald concentration camps. Her harrowing death camp photos were published in American *Vogue* from June 1945 with a direct message from Miller to a disbelieving public: 'Believe It.'

While in France in 1944, Miller documented key aspects of the Occupation and liberation of the country. Her photograph of a French Resistance worker may look like a fashion shoot but it speaks of serious issues facing women in France during and after the war. This woman's elaborate hairstyle, lipstick and 'girly' dress are a deliberate contrast to the feminine ideals promoted by the occupying Nazis, which were that an Aryan woman should be young and physically fit, ideally blond and blue-eyed, and wear practical clothing, sensible hair and no make-up. Consequently, dressing nicely and wearing red lipstick became an act of patriotism and resistance for French women during the Occupation.

After France had been liberated, a woman's hair could also show which side they had been on. Women accused of collaborating with the Nazis – especially of 'horizontal collaboration' – had their heads shaved and were paraded through the streets to be publicly shamed and abused by local residents. Miller was also witness to this.

Miller's images give cause to think about the way that hair has been – and continues to be – a way to express identity and pleasure, resistance and 'attitude'. Throughout time and across cultures hair can also be a signifier of femininity, class and sexuality; a site of celebration but also of gendered punishment.

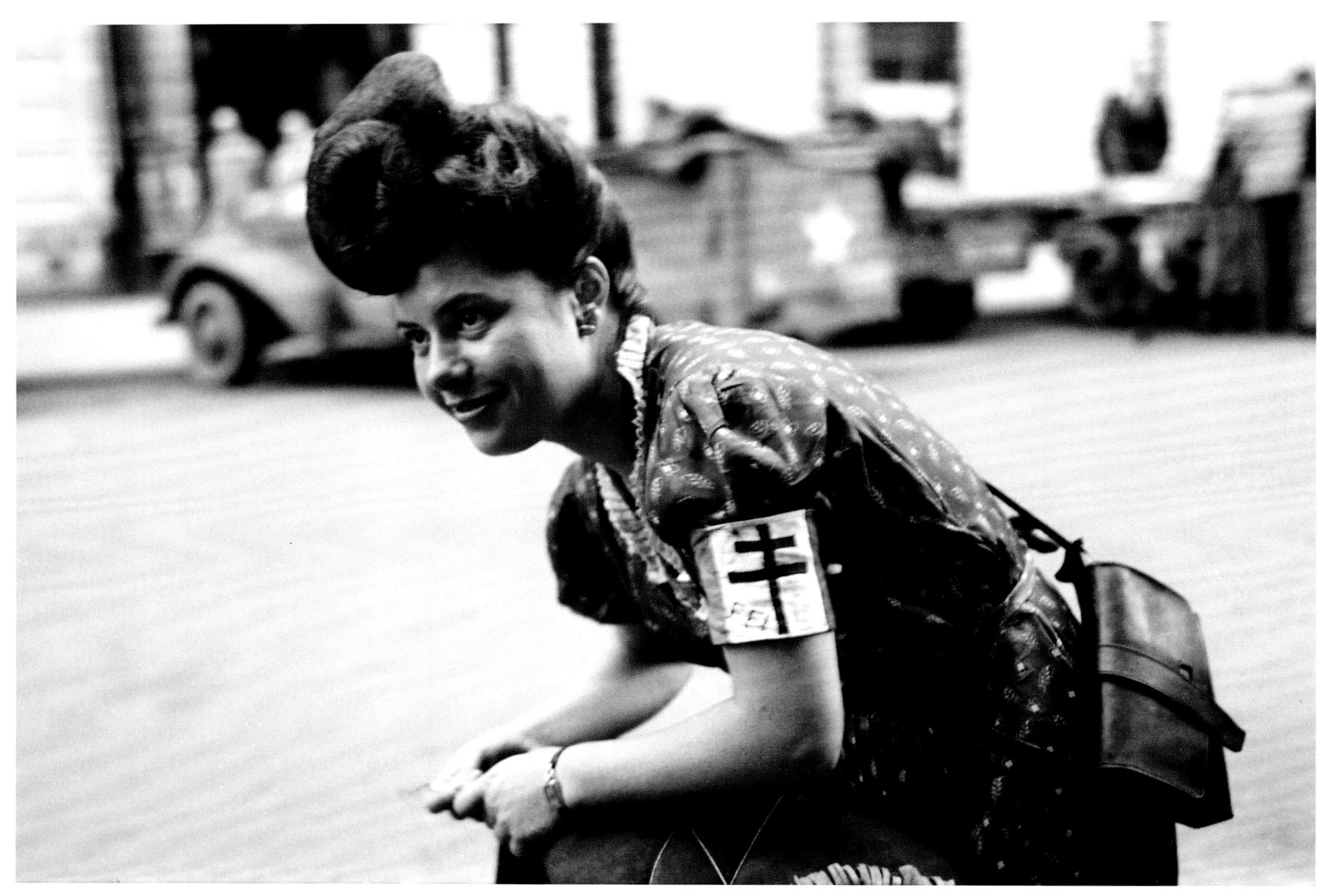

FFI (Forces Française de l'interior)
Worker, Paris, France,
1944

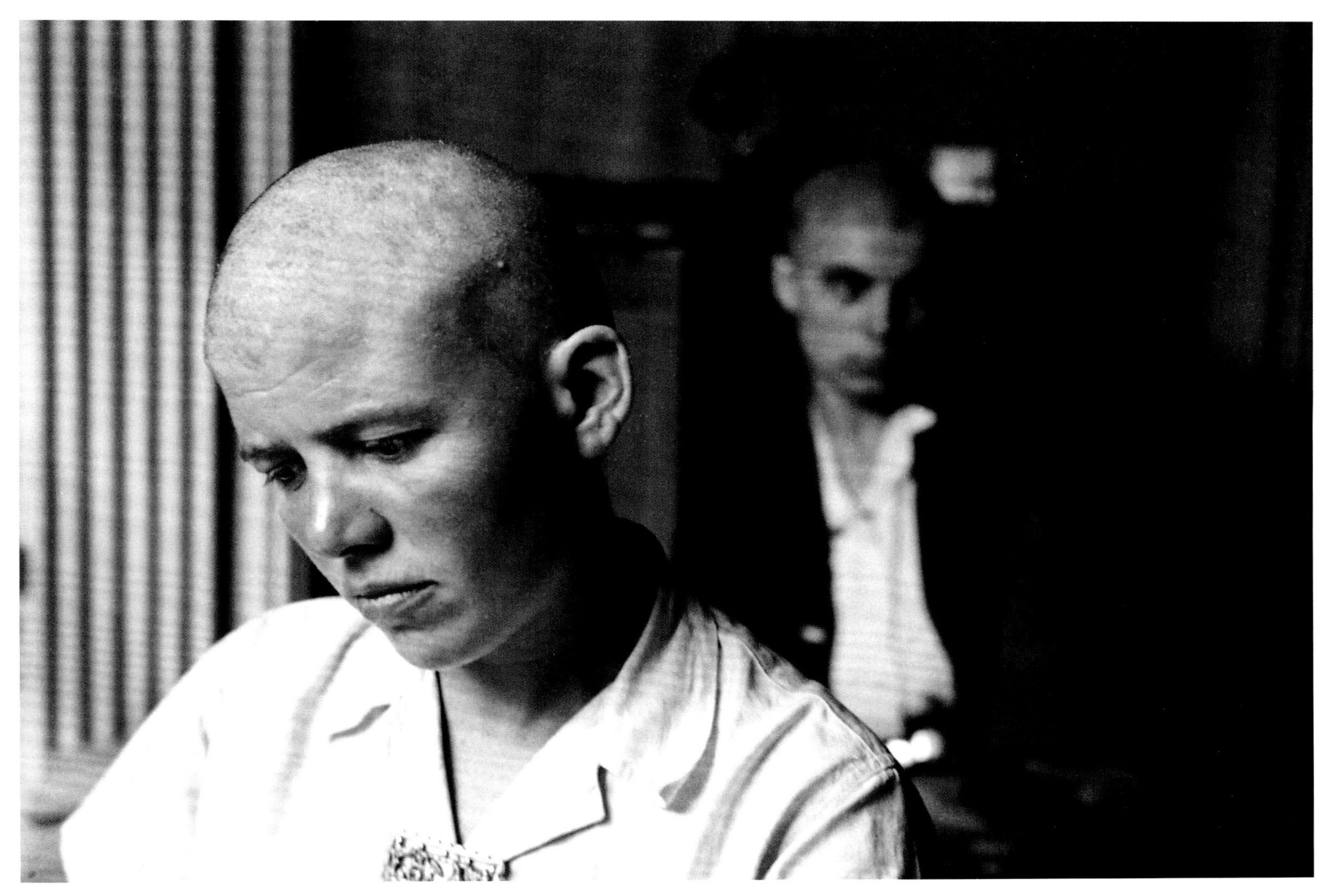

*Woman accused of collaborating
with the Germans, Rennes, France,*
1944

HURRICANE WOMAN *1948–1949*

Germaine Richier was one of the most important female artists working in France after World War II. She combined the expressive violence of Expressionism with the mystery and magic of Surrealism to create powerful sculptures whose corroded surfaces and sheer physicality captured the despair and hope of the era in which she lived.

Hurricane Woman is a life-sized, middle-aged, heavy, lumbering woman with a roughly scarred surface. She is not a figure of youth and physical perfection, but one who has been ravaged by time, experience and the elements. However, her intact facial features seem to imply a sense of hope and determination, lending the monumental figure a certain dignity and sense of life. As Richier explained: 'All their slashed, torn shapes were conceived full and complete. Only afterward did I hollow them out and tear them to make them look varied on every side and to impart a changing, alive appearance to them. I love life, I love everything that moves.'[35]

Richier's work was praised by critics for its 'authenticity', a key tenet of the existential philosophy that was popular in post-war Paris. *Hurricane Woman* can simultaneously seem like a symbol of the horrors of war or a post-apocalyptic survivor, emerging from the devastation to take on the challenge of creating a new society. That this was a job for someone weathered and toughened by life and its traumas – and not the pristine, idealized females of classical sculpture – comes across forcefully in *Hurricane Woman*. For Richier, this was an integral feature of her work: 'A form lives to the extent to which it does not withdraw from expression. And we decidedly cannot conceal human expression in the drama of our time.'[36]

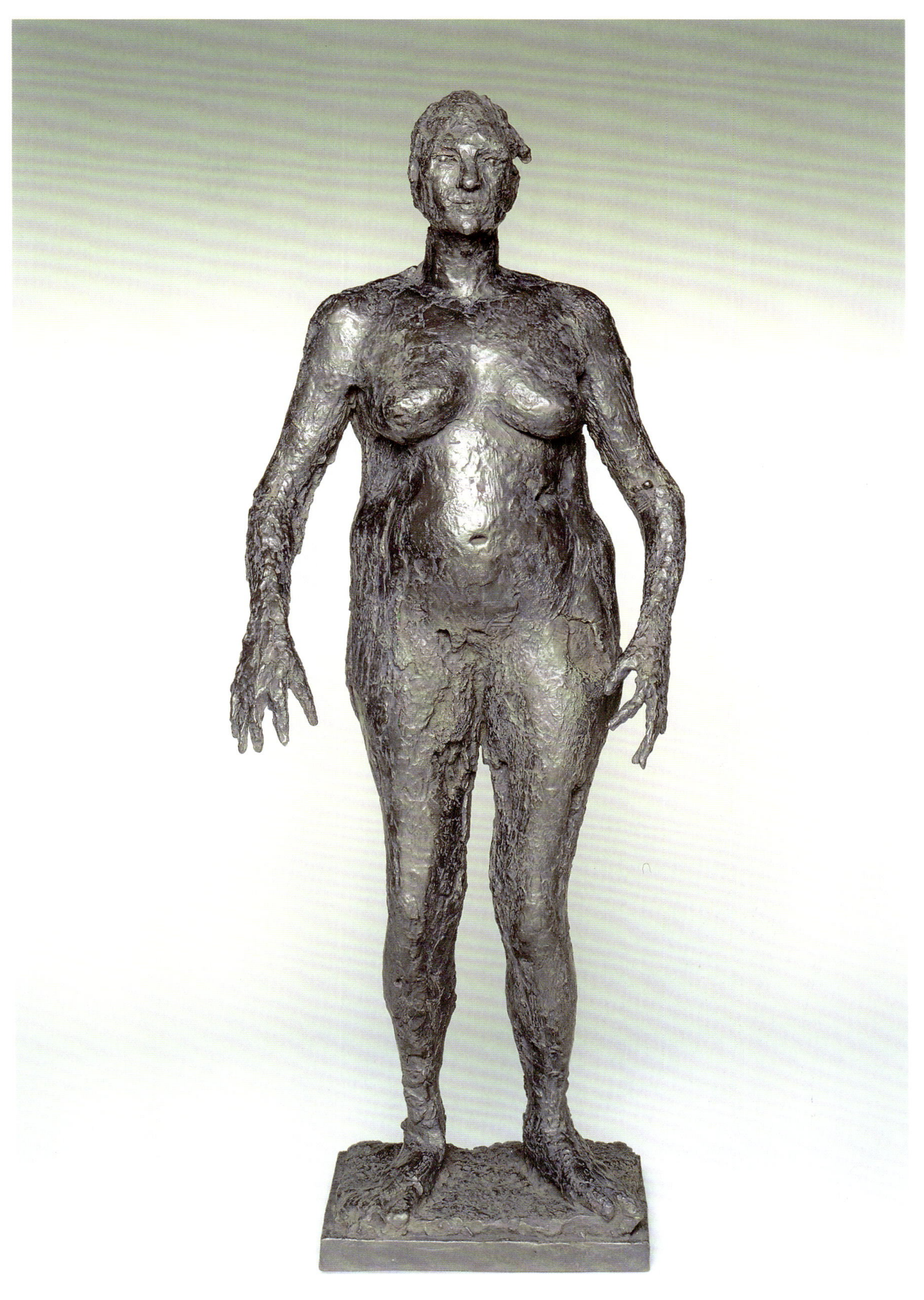

Eve Arnold
(American, 1912–2012)

BAR GIRL IN A BROTHEL IN THE RED LIGHT DISTRICT, HAVANA *1954*

The pioneering American photographer, Eve Arnold, began her exploration of the world in all its diversity in the 1950s. At a time when fashion photography, celebrity photography and portrait photography were posed, staged and retouched, Arnold's natural, candid images were unusual. Her images tell the stories behind the people, introducing the human beings behind the personas of public figures, whether they were movie stars, politicians or fashion models in Harlem.

She is particularly known for her photographs of the lives and conditions of women from all walks of life in different parts of the world, portrayed with sensitivity, compassion and respect. There is a sort of levelling effect, where bar workers and migrant workers are given the same treatment and respect as the rich and famous, who are in turn humanized in her work. The results of her insatiable curiosity about the world around her and the people in it were shared via magazines, newspapers, exhibitions and books.

'At a time when fashion photography, celebrity photography and portrait photography were posed, staged and retouched, Arnold's natural, candid images were unusual'

Arnold published many of her images about women in a photobook in 1976, where she also explained her motivation and method: 'This is a book about how it feels to be a woman, seen through the eyes and the camera of one woman – images unretouched, for the most part unposed, and unembellished ... There were the known and the unknown – and always those marvellous faces ... Each had her own story to tell — uniquely female but also uniquely human ... I have been poor and I wanted to document poverty; I had lost a child and I was obsessed with birth; I was interested in politics and I wanted to know how it affected our lives; I am a woman and I wanted to know about women.'[37]

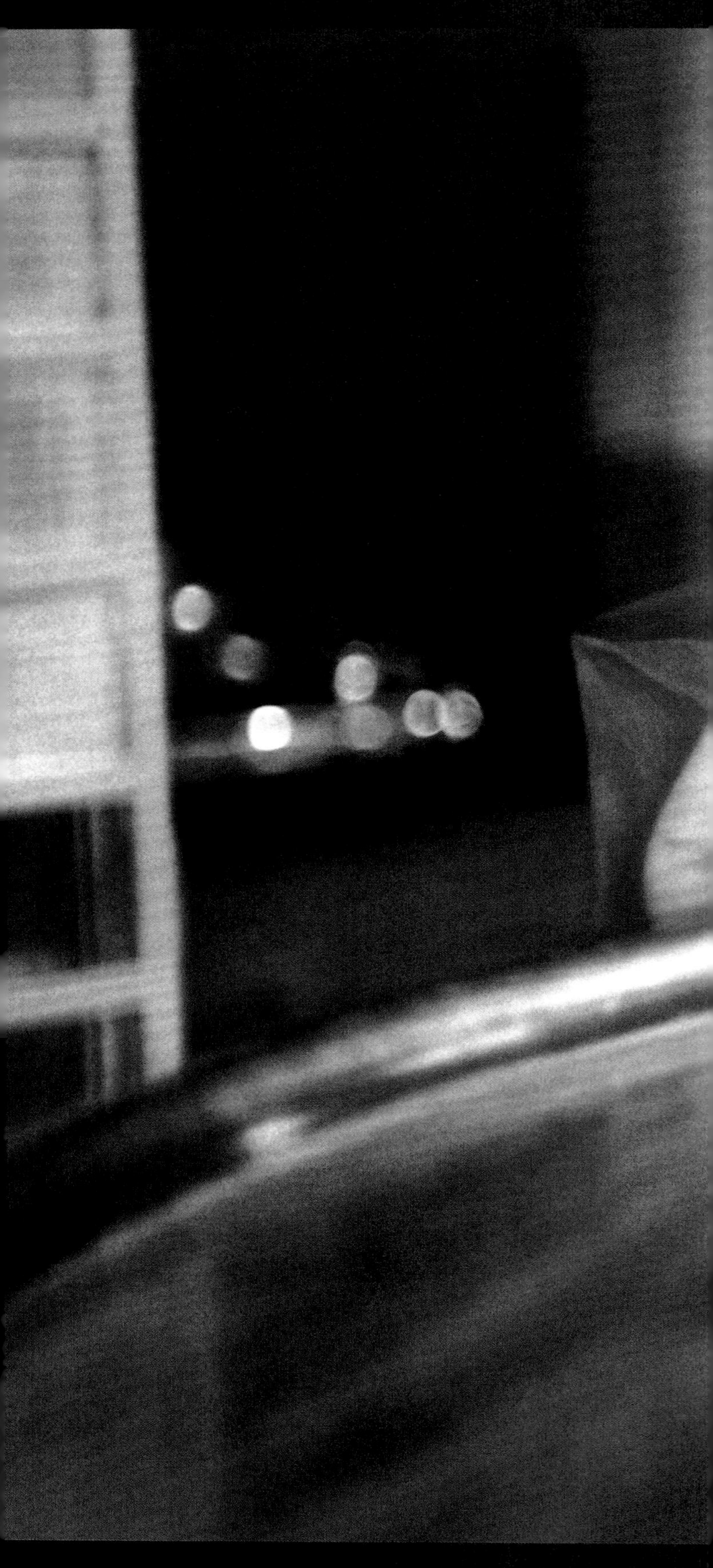

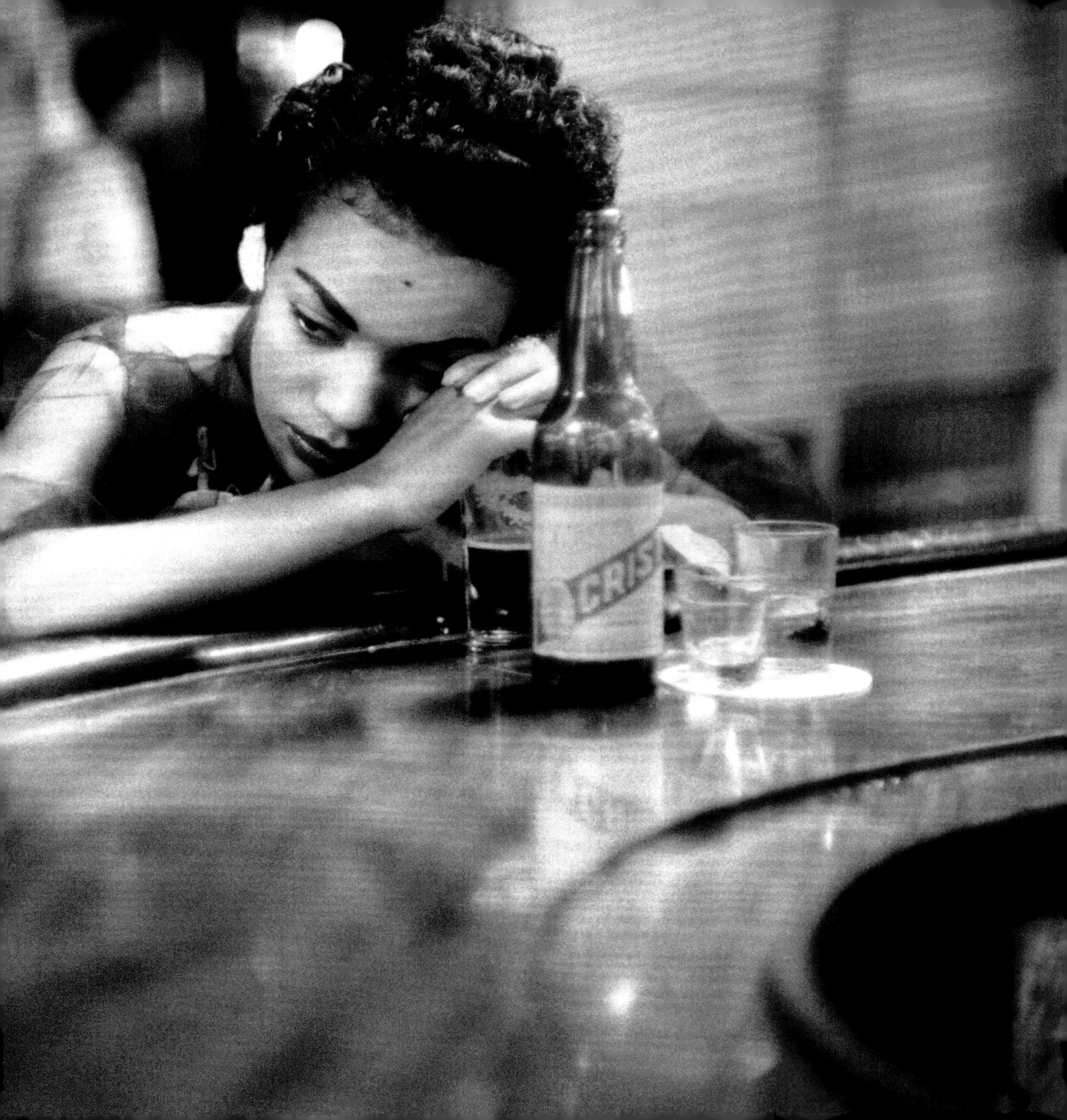

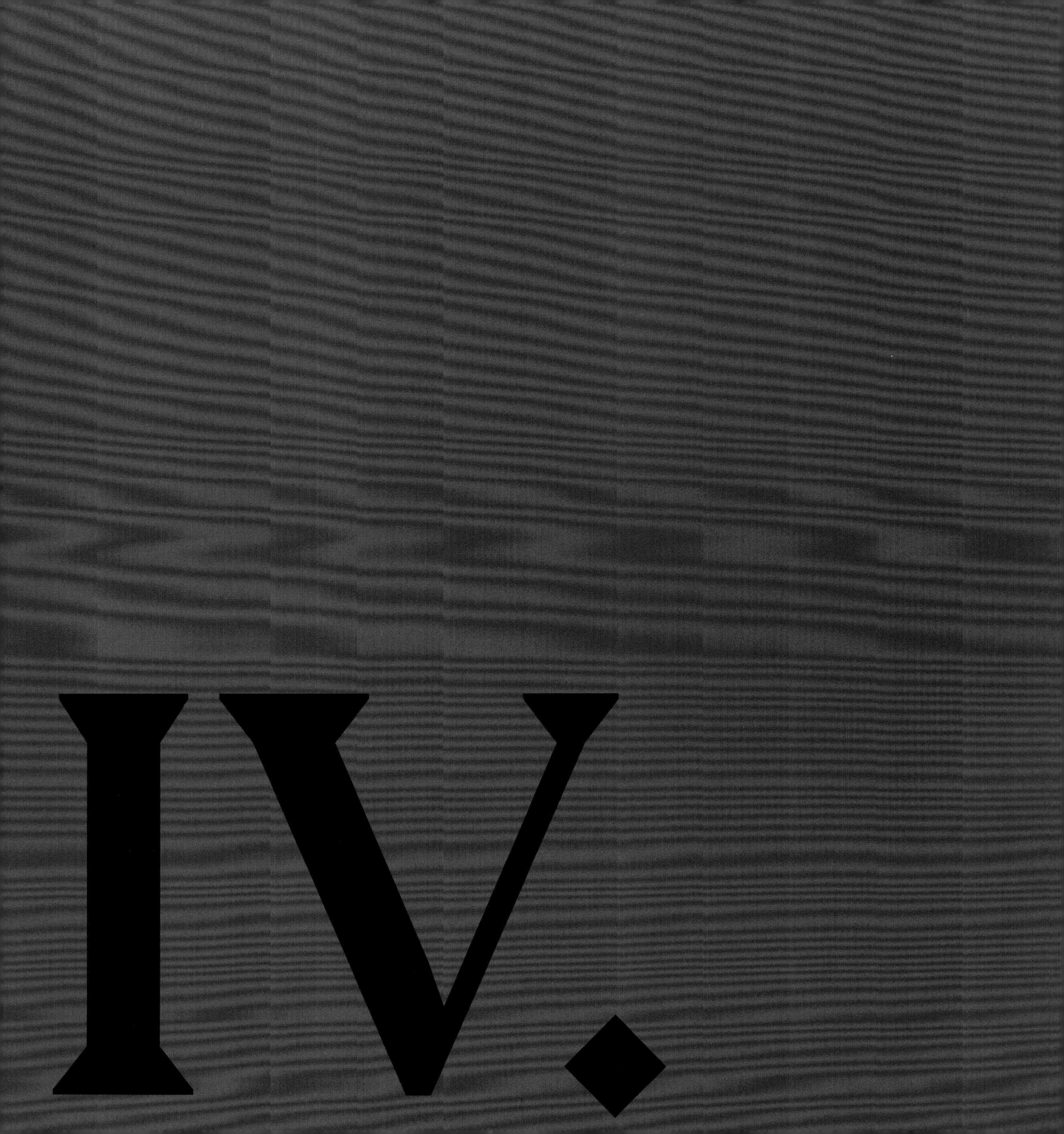
IV.

1960 to 1999

Yves Klein
(French, 1926–1962)

ANTHROPOMETRY OF THE BLUE PERIOD *1960*

On 9 March 1960, Yves Klein staged his painting-performance *Anthropométrie de l'Époque Bleue (Anthropometry of the Blue Period)* at the Galerie Internationale d'Art Contemporain in Paris. Although Klein had been making 'anthropometries' (body paintings) with models in his studio for a couple of years, this was the first live presentation in which an audience was invited to share how they were made.

In a room covered in white paper, three nude women smeared themselves with IKB (International Klein Blue, Klein's patented vivid ultramarine, blue paint) and then pressed themselves against pieces of paper to make an imprint. Klein choreographed the models without touching them or the paint, searching for results that resembled the indentations left on white mats by judo contestants (judo was a lifelong passion of his). The painting-performance was accompanied by an orchestra playing Klein's *Monotone-Silence Symphony* (a single note played for 20 minutes, alternated with 20 minutes of silence), while the audience – dressed in dinner jackets and evening dresses – watched in respectful silence.

While the idea of using naked women as 'living brushes' might raise alarm bells to a contemporary ear and eye, it was not perceived that way at the time, by either the artist or the models. They saw it as a collaborative experience and a way to share with the audience some of the creative process.[38] Later in the year, Klein became one of the founding members of the Nouveaux Réalistes. Many of the group's artworks are the result of 'action-spectacles', in which the performance is part of the creation of the artwork, including Klein's *Anthropometries* and Saint Phalle's shooting paintings (p. 150). Klein's use of the human body as a material for art (instead of just the subject) and the theatricality of the event also makes this an early example of both body art and performance art – types of art-making that would gain momentum throughout the 1960s and beyond.

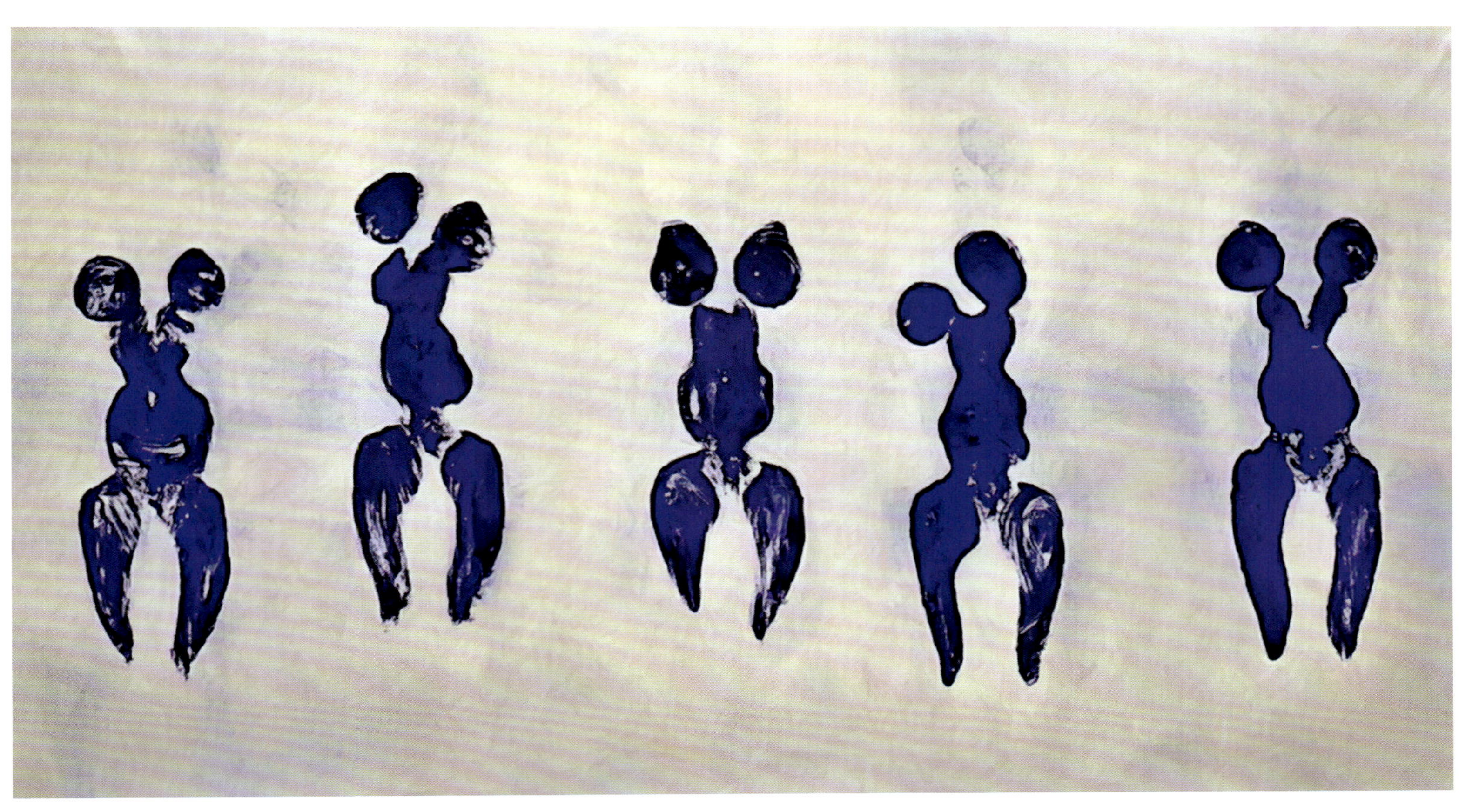

VENUS DE MILO *1962*

In 1961, Niki de Saint Phalle burst onto the international art scene with a literal 'bang', when she produced her first shooting paintings (*Tirs*) in Paris. To create the works, containers of paint were embedded within assemblages and sculptures, which burst when they were shot with a pistol or rifle by Saint Phalle or others. Saint Phalle also became the only female member of the Nouveau Réalistes, a group of young European artists (including Yves Klein – see p. 148) with 'new approaches to the real'.

Venus de Milo was created in New York in 1962. During *The Construction of Boston*, a live theatrical event, Saint Phalle was called on to provide culture for the new American city of Boston.[39] Dressed as a Napoleonic artillery officer, Saint Phalle shot a plaster cast of the Venus de Milo with a rifle. The sculpture bled red, green and brown paint from the face and chest, turning the idealized representation of femininity into a 'murdered', paint-spattered corpse.

The figure of Venus – a symbol of ancient culture and the Louvre, a human figure and a goddess – provides a rich array of associations and possible interpretations for the viewer. Based on a parody of male aggression, the attack on the body of a woman – on the feminine myth of beauty and perfection – could be seen in the context of Saint Phalle's performance as an appropriation of power, as a woman responsible for both creation and destruction, life and death. It may equally be seen as the acceptance of male violence and female helplessness.

—

'Dressed as a Napoleonic artillery officer, Saint Phalle shot a plaster cast of the Venus de Milo with a rifle. The sculpture bled red, green and brown paint from the face and chest'

Saint Phalle has described her shooting assemblages as a symbolic act of protest and liberation against the image of woman imposed by contemporary society. Saint Phalle's own complicity in reinforcing that unattainable ideal, by working as a fashion model in the 1940s and 1950s, further complicates the attack – is she shooting at herself, at her past?

The artist's focus on the female figure and its representation in art presages both the imagery and topics of feminist discussions about art in the 1970s, and Saint Phalle's later three-dimensional works, the *Nanas* (French slang for 'chick' or 'girlfriend'). In these works, she would transform her anger and violence into creating joyful, exuberant, powerful female bodies that grace museums and public spaces around the world.

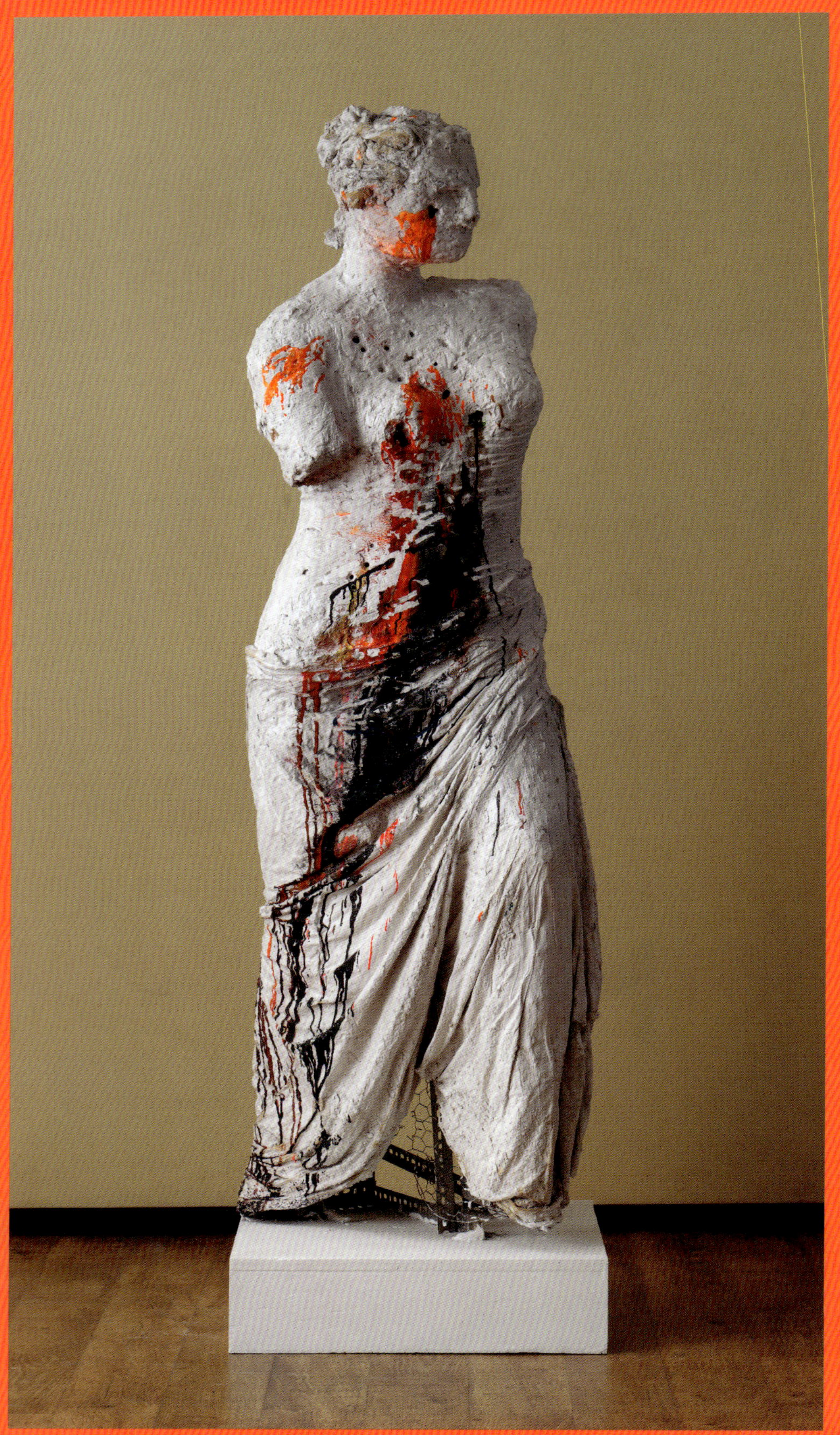

Venus de Milo,
1962

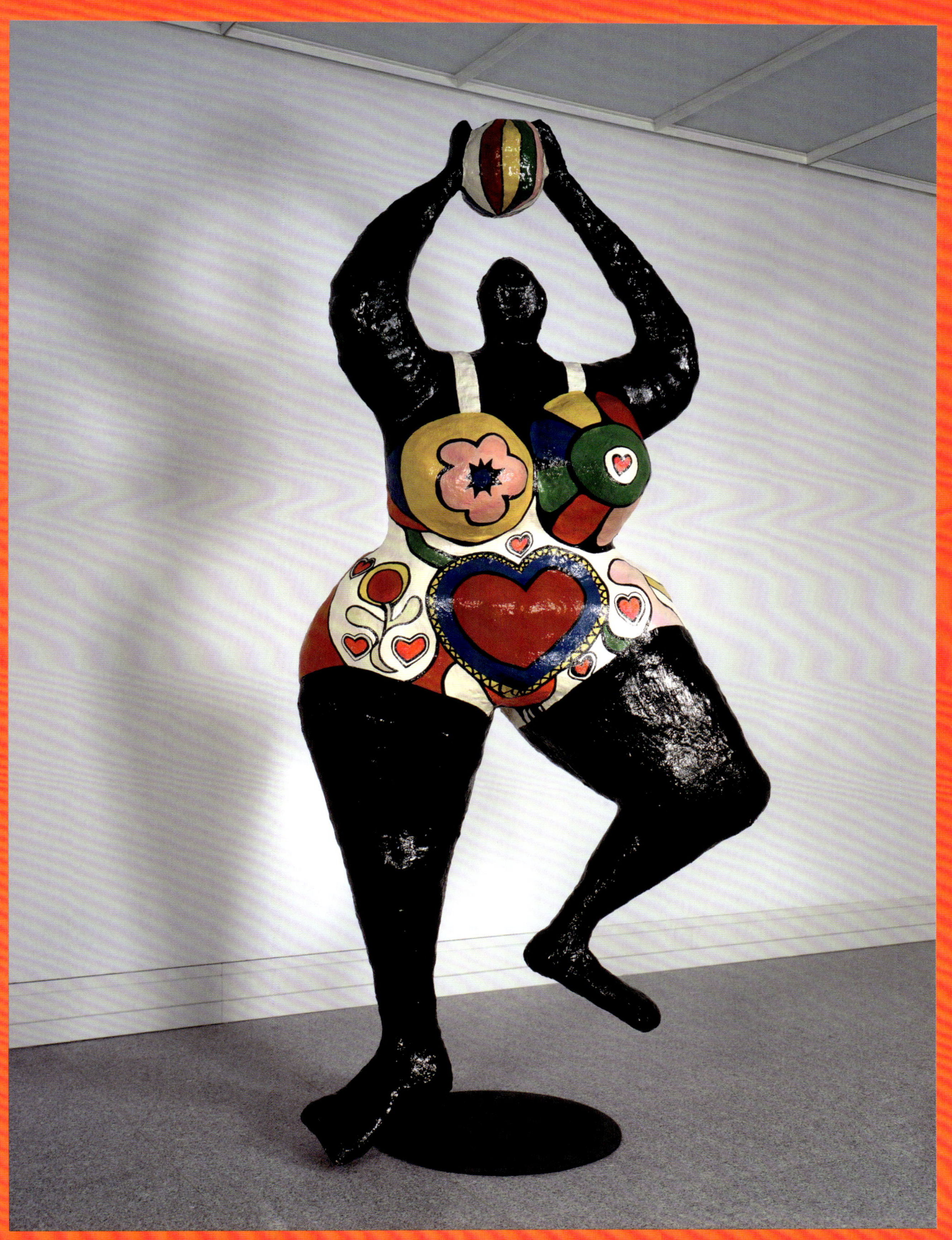

Black Venus,
1965–1967

Andy Warhol
(American, 1928–1987)

SHOT SAGE BLUE MARILYN *1964*

Andy Warhol was fascinated with popular culture and painted an array of iconic women and celebrities, his portraits adding to both the star's glamour and Warhol's fame. None was more famous or intriguing than Hollywood superstar, Marilyn Monroe, whose legendary looks were almost a caricature of historical ideas of feminine beauty. Warhol never met Monroe, but he painted her numerous times after she died of an overdose in 1962. While the world mourned the tragic death of a beloved film star, Warhol paid tribute to her in his own unique way, painting the most famous woman in the world in her most 'sex bomb' mode, all based on the same publicity still from her 1953 film, *Niagara*. These are not portraits of a 'real' person, per se, but a portrait of celebrity; of a familiar image from popular culture.

The title of this particular painting – *Shot Sage Blue Marilyn* –identifies which Marilyn it is in his inventory by the colour of the background (sage blue). Marilyn became one of his stock characters, and the five Marilyns in his 1964 series each have a different single colour background with Marilyn's face on top of it. The 'shot' in the title refers to an incident at Warhol's New York studio, The Factory, when the painting was shot by the performance artist, Dorothy Podber. Warhol had given the artist permission to shoot the paintings, thinking she meant to 'shoot' them with a camera, not a gun.

Warhol took an image from popular culture and transformed it into art. In doing so, he also took on the intrigue and glamour of his celebrity subjects and became an icon of popular culture himself. This is no longer a portrait from a photograph of Marilyn Monroe, but a 'Warhol' or a 'Warhol Marilyn'.

In the 21st century the painting is recognizable as a 'Warhol Marilyn' even by those who don't know who Marilyn Monroe was. For those who do, Warhol's Marilyn has become the defining image of her, long overtaking the original photograph. These two global superstars are now forever entwined, and the duration of her fame is ensured by his, which supersedes (or at least equals) hers. Warhol's phenomenal success made 'his' Marilyn a part of our shared popular culture and enshrined Marilyn's version of idealized feminine beauty in the popular preconscious for the foreseeable future.

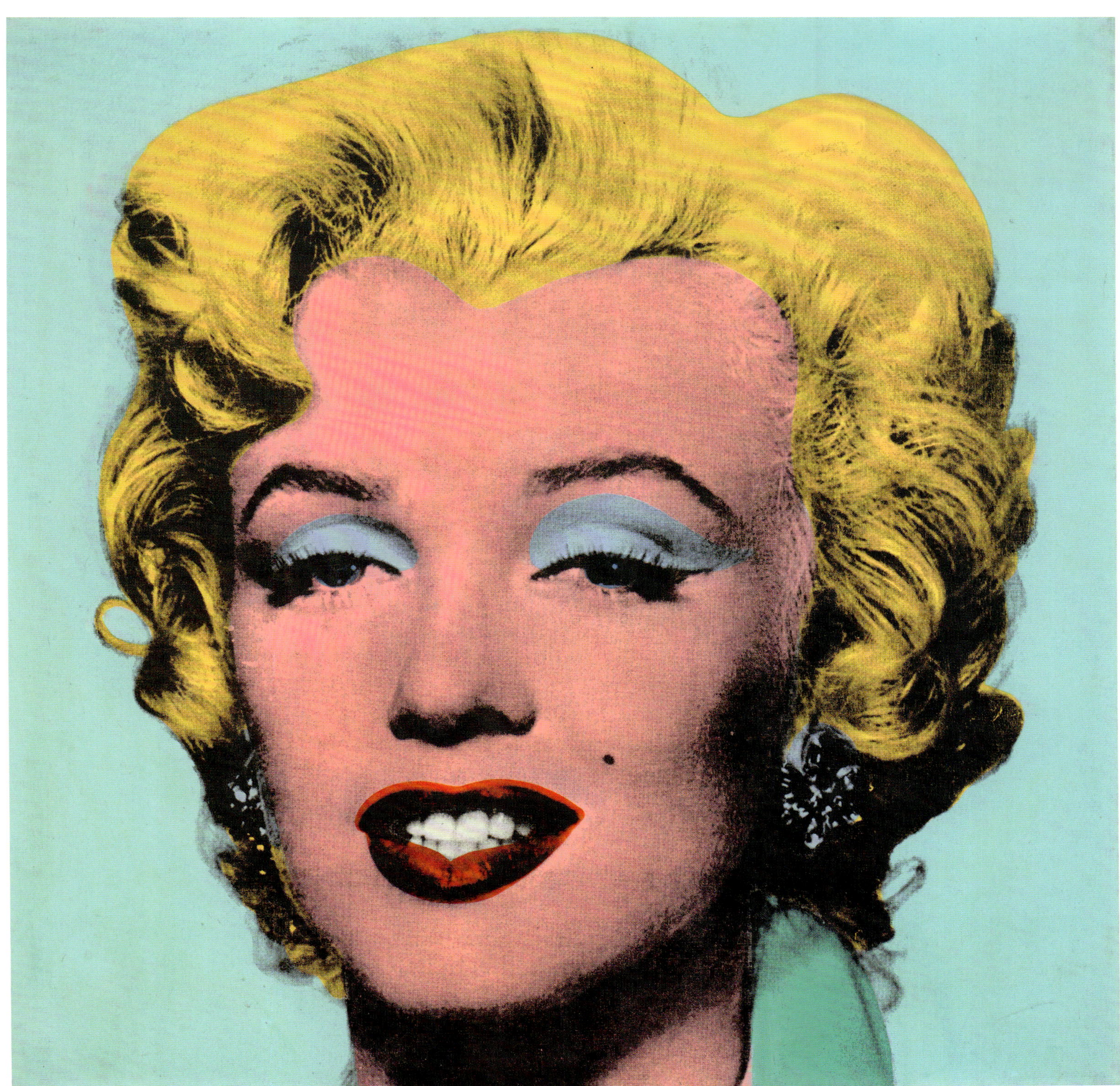

Carolee Schneemann
(American, 1939–2019)

MEAT JOY *1964*

The American painter, performance artist, filmmaker and writer, Carolee Schneemann, used the 'body as a source of knowledge'[40] in her controversial works with social, sexual and art-historical resonances. One of her best-known pieces was *Meat Joy,* in which she brought together touch, smell, taste and sound in a multi-sensory work of art. For the piece, seven participants joined Schneemann in her quest to create a new 'total art' that took the nude off the canvas and used it as one of many materials in the performance. Whereas the performance aspect of Yves Klein's *Anthropometries* (p. 148) or Niki de Saint Phalle's shooting paintings (p. 150) was part of the creation of the artwork, here the performance itself was the art. Although photographs and videos serve as records of it, the actual artwork exists only in the memories of those present.

Meat Joy was first performed at the First Festival of Free Expression at the American Center in Paris, on 29 May 1964. Describing the event in *France-Soir,* Carmen Tessier recalled how 'Half-naked men and women sprawled on a heap of papers and daubed themselves with red, green and yellow paint. Then they threw mackerels and a blood-covered chicken at one another's heads. Meanwhile a rotating jet sprayed the spectators.'[41] The multimedia erotic 'celebration of flesh as material'[42] was performed later in the year in London and New York.

While it was certainly a reflection of some of the prominent socio-political issues of the 1960s – sexual and female liberation – Schneemann's piece can also be read as a challenge to the male-dominated art world; as a progression from (and a subversion of) Klein's performance-painting, *Anthropometries.* In *Meat Joy,* Schneemann claimed the directorial power as a woman, orchestrating the animalistic behaviour of both men and women, and making art that is as messy and complicated as life itself.

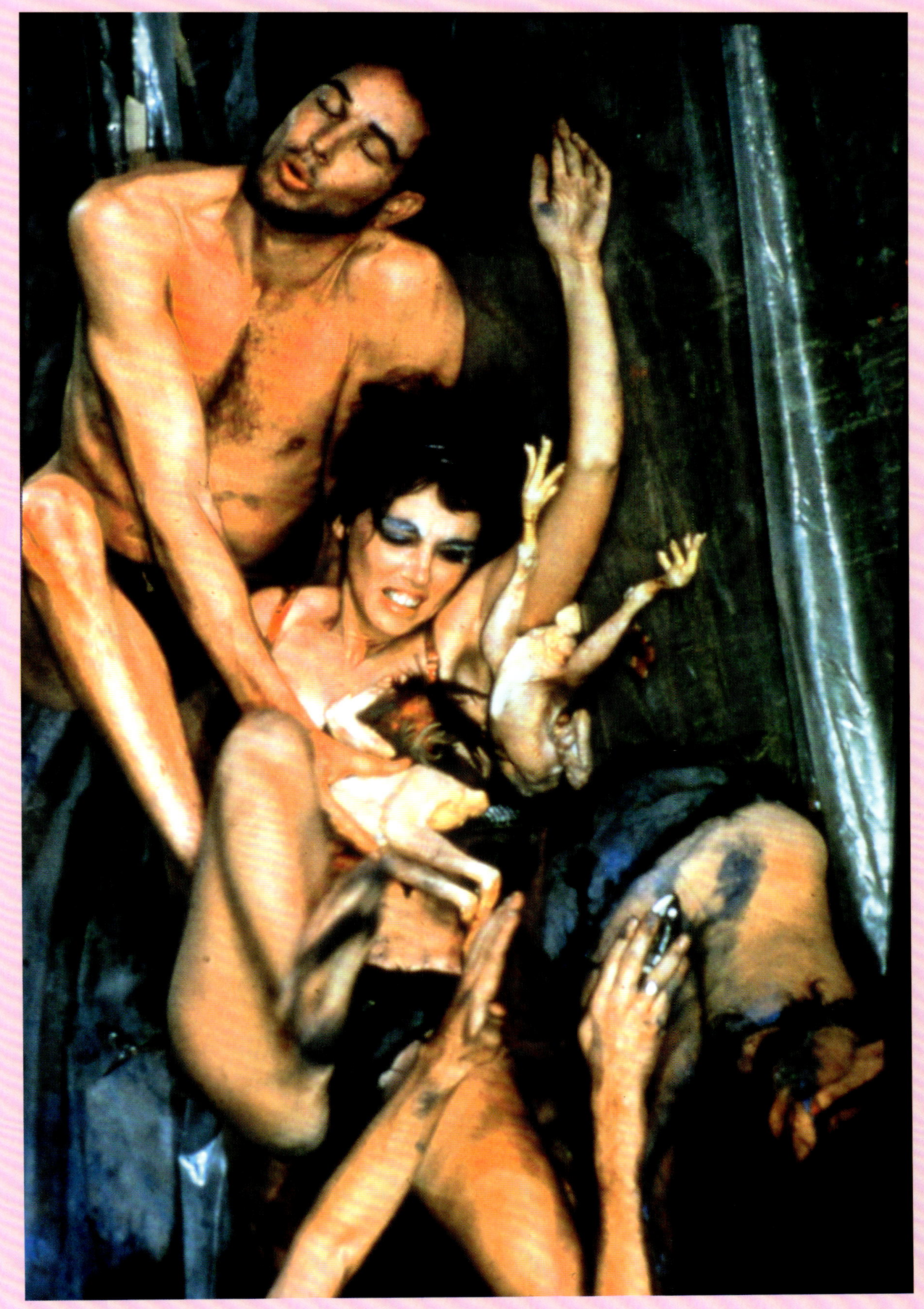

Michelangelo Pistoletto
(Italian, b. 1933)

VENUS OF THE RAGS *1967–2024*

Arte Povera (Impoverished Art) was the name given to a group of Italian artists who came to attention in the 1960s. The group questioned the nature and definition of art itself, as well as its role in society, with its name alluding to the humble (or 'poor') non-art materials they used. Their richly layered artworks were characterized by unexpected juxtapositions of objects or images, the use of contrasting materials, and by the fusion of past and present, nature and culture, art and life.

Perhaps the best-known Arte Povera artwork is Michelangelo Pistoletto's *Venus of the Rags*. The life-sized reproduction of a classical Venus sculpture facing a mound of rags holds a mirror up to Italian society where the surreal juxtapositions of past and present are a part of everyday life. It seems to ask if the idealized, perfect past is preferable to the colour and chaos of the present, and how the two can coexist.

Pistoletto's powerful artwork also resonates with more contemporary concerns, as it could be read as a comment on over-consumption and waste; a clarion call to reuse and recycle, as Venus – the goddess of love and beauty – is being drowned by consumer castoffs and urban debris. To me it brings to mind the horrible images of landfill sites, the problems with fast fashion and the essential need for more sustainable practices.

'Pistoletto's artwork could be read as a clarion call to reuse and recycle, as Venus – the goddess of love and beauty – is being drowned by consumer castoffs and urban debris'

Pistoletto made numerous versions of *Venus of the Rags*, including a monumental outdoor one for the city of Naples, Italy, in 2023. However, just two weeks after it was installed it was destroyed by an arson attack. A crowdfunding campaign was launched to rebuild the installation, but the funds raised were subsequently diverted to local charities when Pistoletto offered to donate a new sculpture to the city; the new *Venus of the Rags* was unveiled on 6 March 2024. The vandalism of the original piece strengthened the sense of ownership within the community and it became a part of its story and DNA, turning the artwork into 'a symbol of resistance, hope and rebirth'. As Pistoletto explained, it 'is supported by the wreck that survived the fire on 12 July … Like a phoenix risen from its ashes.'[43]

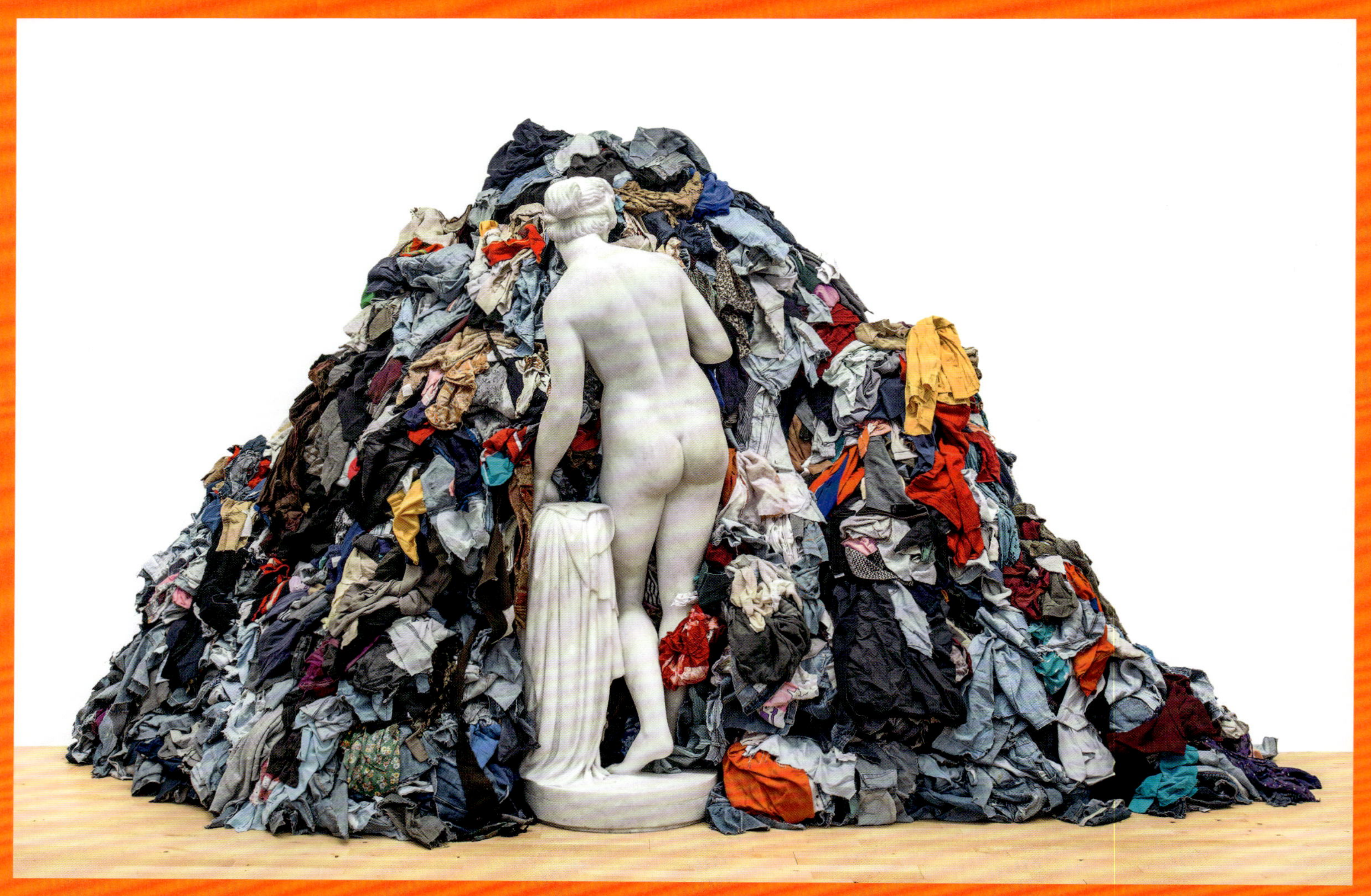

Venus of the Rags,
1967, 1974

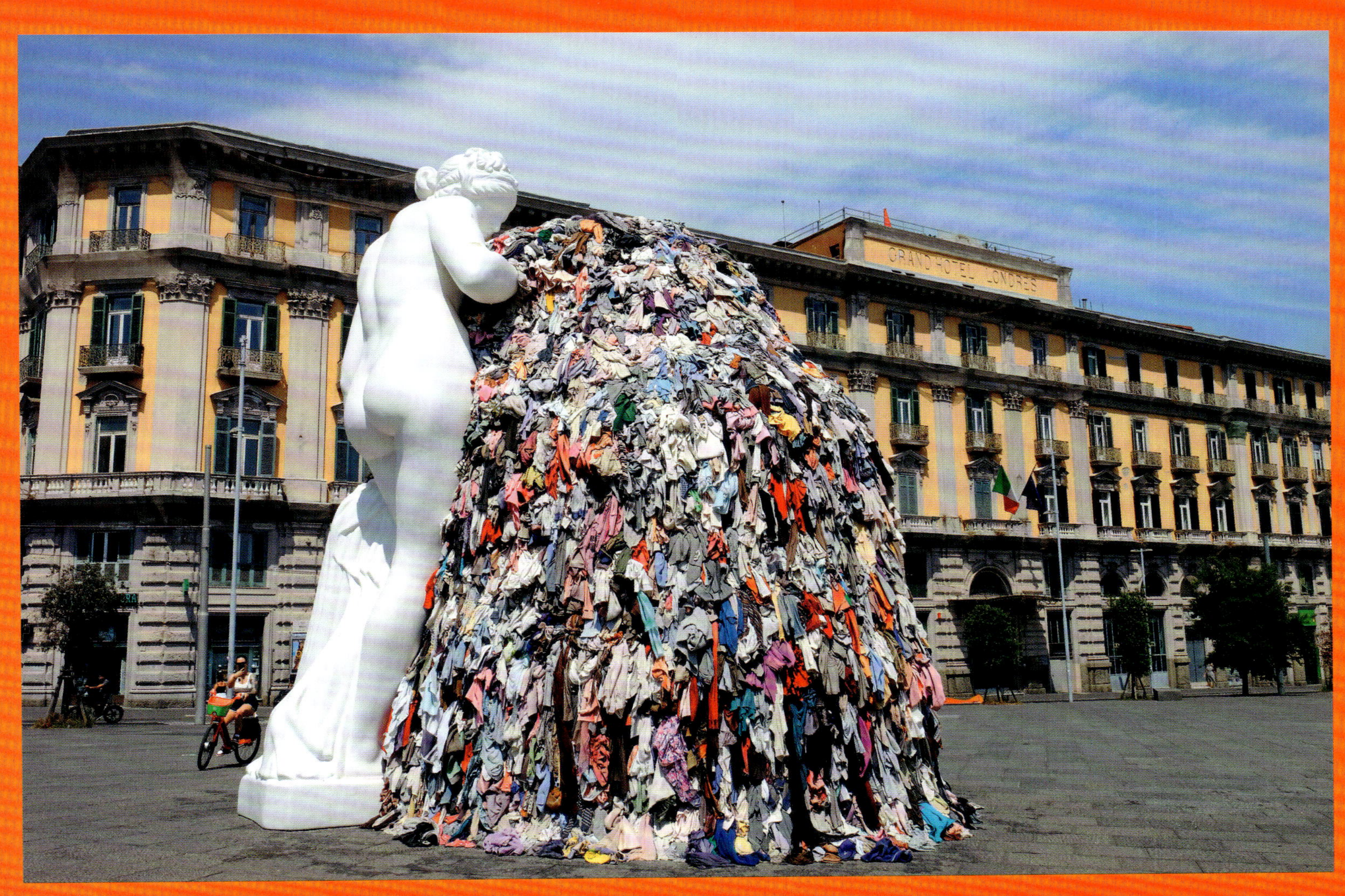

Venus of the Rags,
Naples, Italy
2023–2024

Barkley L. Hendricks
(American, 1945–2017)

LAWDY MAMA *1969*

Barkley L. Hendricks is known primarily for his large-scale portraits of urban Black Americans. His subjects are not aristocrats or celebrities, but ordinary people ennobled in bold, life-sized portraits. Hendricks's sitters served as a point of departure for figurative paintings of people of colour that celebrate their essence, style and the spirit of the times. With his paintings of real people – friends, family and interesting-looking strangers – he enacts a call and response with art history and its traditions, and in so doing he simultaneously points out, and fills in, some of the missing portrayals of Black figures in Western art.

Lawdy Mama – a portrait of one of Hendricks's relatives – is on a canvas with an arched top, like a medieval icon. The arch frames the subject's Afro hair, which looks like a halo. Here is a beautiful young woman standing in front of a glittering gold background that not only brings out the rich, dark golden tones of her skin, but creates the impression that she is emerging from, or floating in front of, the backdrop. The title, which is derived from lyrics in Nina Simone's 1967 song, *Blues for Mama* (Lawdy/Lord, Mama/Madonna) also references Christianity, if rather irreverently.

While the use of gold leaf and the title evoke the divine and the devotional, this is also a portrait of a real young woman. The way she is standing makes it look to me as if she is shy or uncomfortable (perhaps bored?), and slightly daunted by all the attention. Maybe she doesn't want to be a devotional object, an icon or a shiny thing that people want to look at or touch?

Whatever 'Our Madonna'[44] is thinking, Hendricks's lovingly painted portrait radiates such warmth that we are drawn to her. The gold background evokes Byzantine and medieval religious icons, as well as the paintings of Klimt (p. 108), while the three-quarter length portrait, stylish outfit and direct gaze take us on a trip from the Renaissance of Leonardo (p. 18) via the Grand Manner portraiture of Gainsborough (p. 56) and fashionable society portraits of Sargent (p. 88), to late 1960s urban America. With *Lawdy Mama*, Hendricks continues the tradition of beautiful paintings of venerable women as objects to inspire or admire, whether they are the Virgin Mary, a socialite or a family member. However, he gives it his unique twist, creating a portrait that is both of its time and timeless.

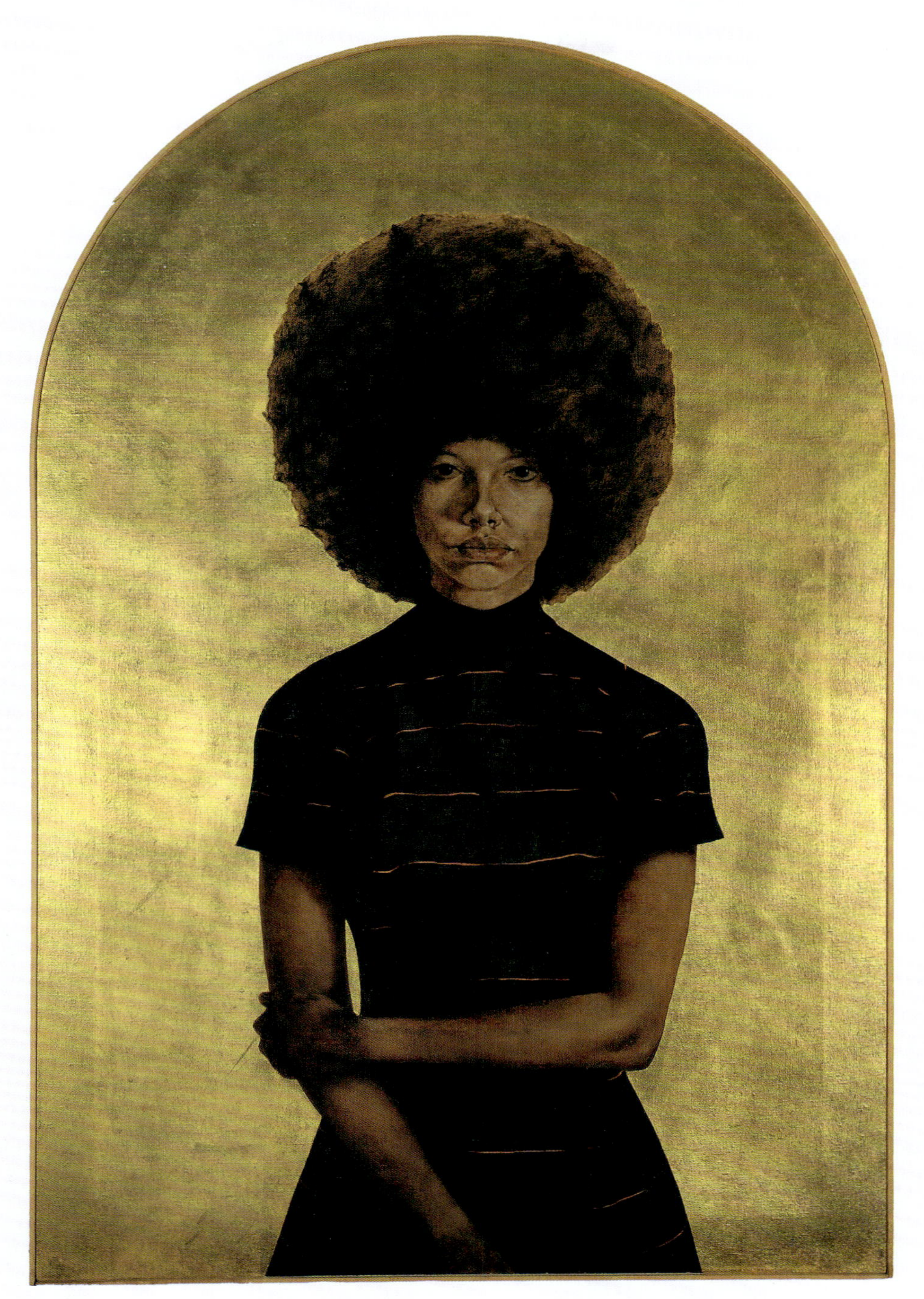

HÔTEL DU PAVOT, CHAMBRE 202

(Poppy Hotel, Room 202) <u>*1970–1973*</u>

Dorothea Tanning grew up in small-town Illinois where she said 'nothing happens but the wallpaper'.[45] To escape the 'eerie, bourgeois calm'[46] she immersed herself in Gothic literature and then Surrealism, which she discovered in 1936 at the 'Fantastic Art, Dada, Surrealism' exhibition at the Museum of Modern Art in New York. She recalled being bowled over and thought 'Gosh! I can go ahead and do what I've always been doing.'[47]

Tanning developed her own type of haunted Surrealism, often centred on the female form, fear and desire. In the late 1960s she began making stuffed soft sculptures, culminating in *Hôtel du Pavot, Chambre 202* (*Poppy Hotel, Room 202*). In what might be her most Surrealist work, the installation took her disturbing dreamlike vision into three dimensions, featuring a full-sized fictional hotel room filled with tortured, twisting bodies emerging from the walls and creepy headless creatures oozing from the chimney and fireplace. In a space that is part horror film, part funhouse, women are becoming furniture, are a part of the wallpaper, buried in the walls and draped over the table. Are they overlooked, sat on, taken for granted? Trapped by domesticity?

Tanning once wrote that she wanted it to look like 'the wallpaper will further tear with screams'.[48] The hallucinatory associations are furthered by the title, as 'Poppy Hotel' suggests an opium den, while 'Room 202' is taken from a song that was popular in Tanning's youth, about a gangster's moll who poisoned herself in room 202 of a Chicago hotel: 'In room two hundred and two / The walls keep talkin' to you ...'[49]

We are definitely not in Kansas any more (or Illinois, as the case may be) as the 'eerie, bourgeois calm' of Tanning's childhood has become something altogether more sinister – a Gothic nightmare where the action is definitely in the wallpaper.

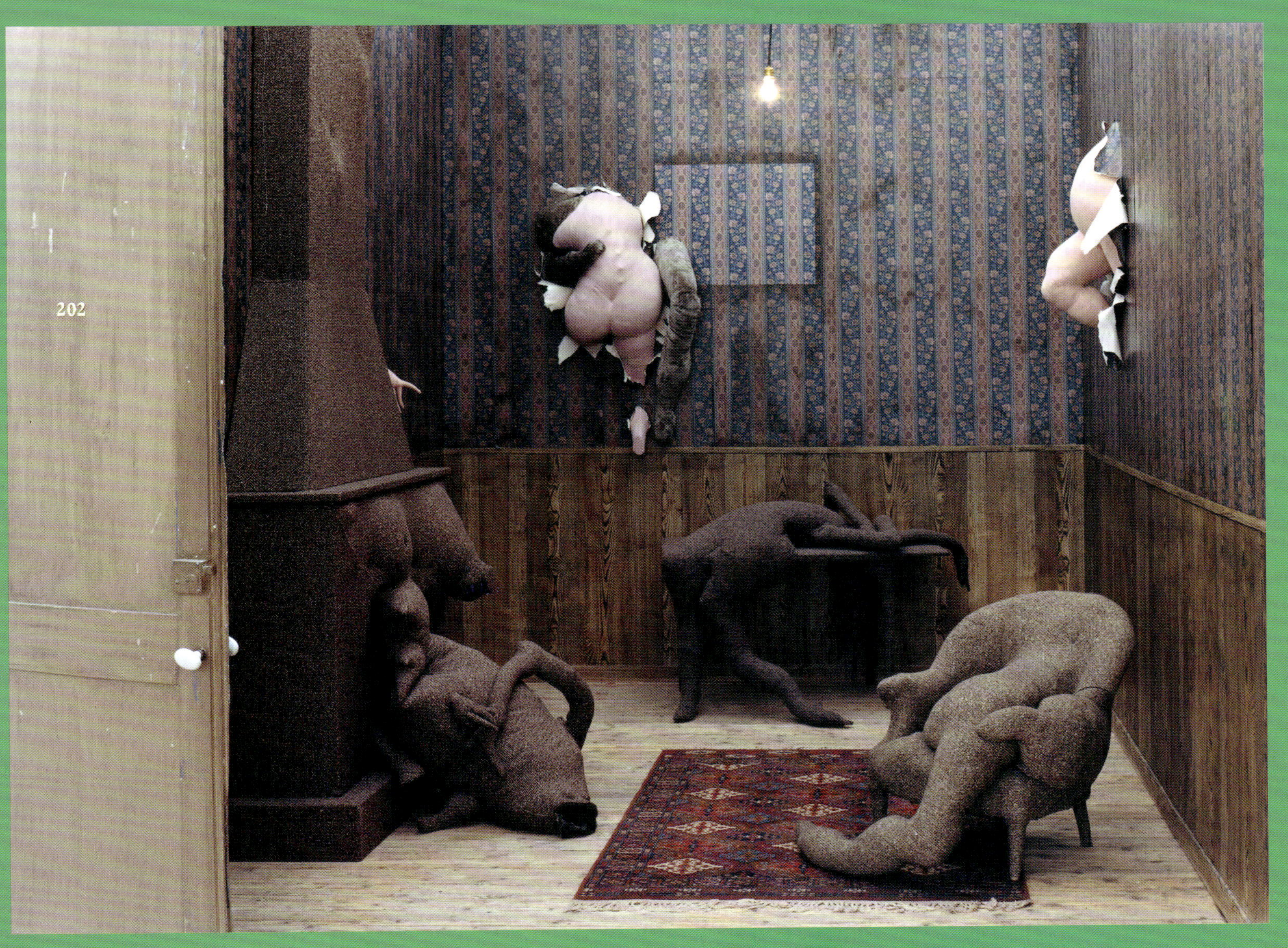

Marina Abramović
(Serbian-American, b. 1946)

ART MUST BE BEAUTIFUL, ARTIST MUST BE BEAUTIFUL *1975*

Marina Abramović is not only a pioneer of performance art, but is also its champion and archivist, and a nurturer of new practitioners. In 1975, she performed *Art Must Be Beautiful, Artist Must Be Beautiful* at a festival in Copenhagen, Denmark, in which she violently brushed her hair and face with a metal comb and brush for almost an hour, while repeating, mantra-like: 'Art must be beautiful, artist must be beautiful.' It had to have been disturbing viewing for the audience as her actions became more intense and harmful.

Although her piece was videoed at the festival, Abramović was displeased with the result and had it deleted. She then re-staged the performance for the camera on her own; this performance-for-video was now under her control. In the video, Abramović framed her head and hands in close-up as she performed to the camera.

As the camera takes on the role of a mirror, it evokes a number of characters associated with their reflection, from Venus and Narcissus to the Evil Queen in the Brothers Grimm's *Snow White* ('Mirror, mirror on the wall, who's the fairest of them all?'). It also calls to mind the 'rule' for thick, shiny hair ('Brush your hair 100 times a day') and punishments meted out in school where the same line has to be written over and over again to drill it into your consciousness.

With her performance, it is as if Abramović is berating herself for forgetting that art and the artist are 'supposed' to be demure and beautiful, rather than difficult and challenging. It makes for uncomfortable but compelling viewing, because the artist is beautiful and the growing intensity gives it a trancelike, ritualistic quality, convincingly conveying Abramović's belief that art shouldn't be easy.

Reflecting on this piece in 1999, Abramović said: 'At that time, I thought that art should be disturbing rather than beautiful. But at my age now, I have started thinking that beauty is not so bad.'[50]

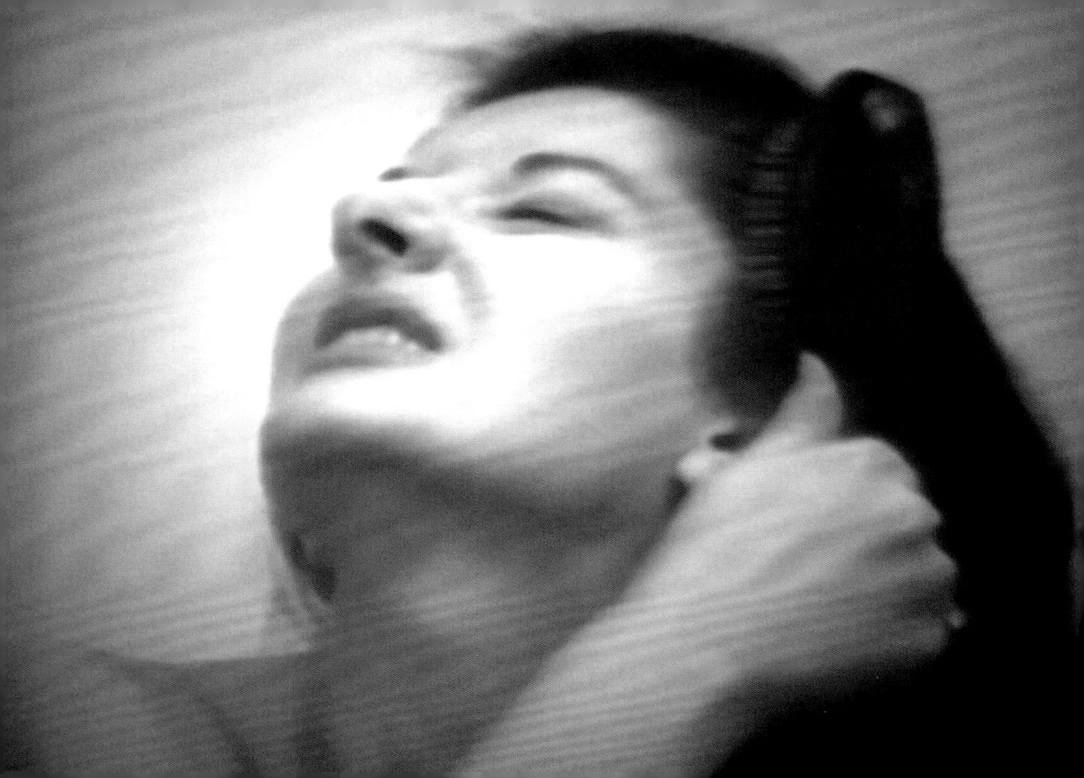

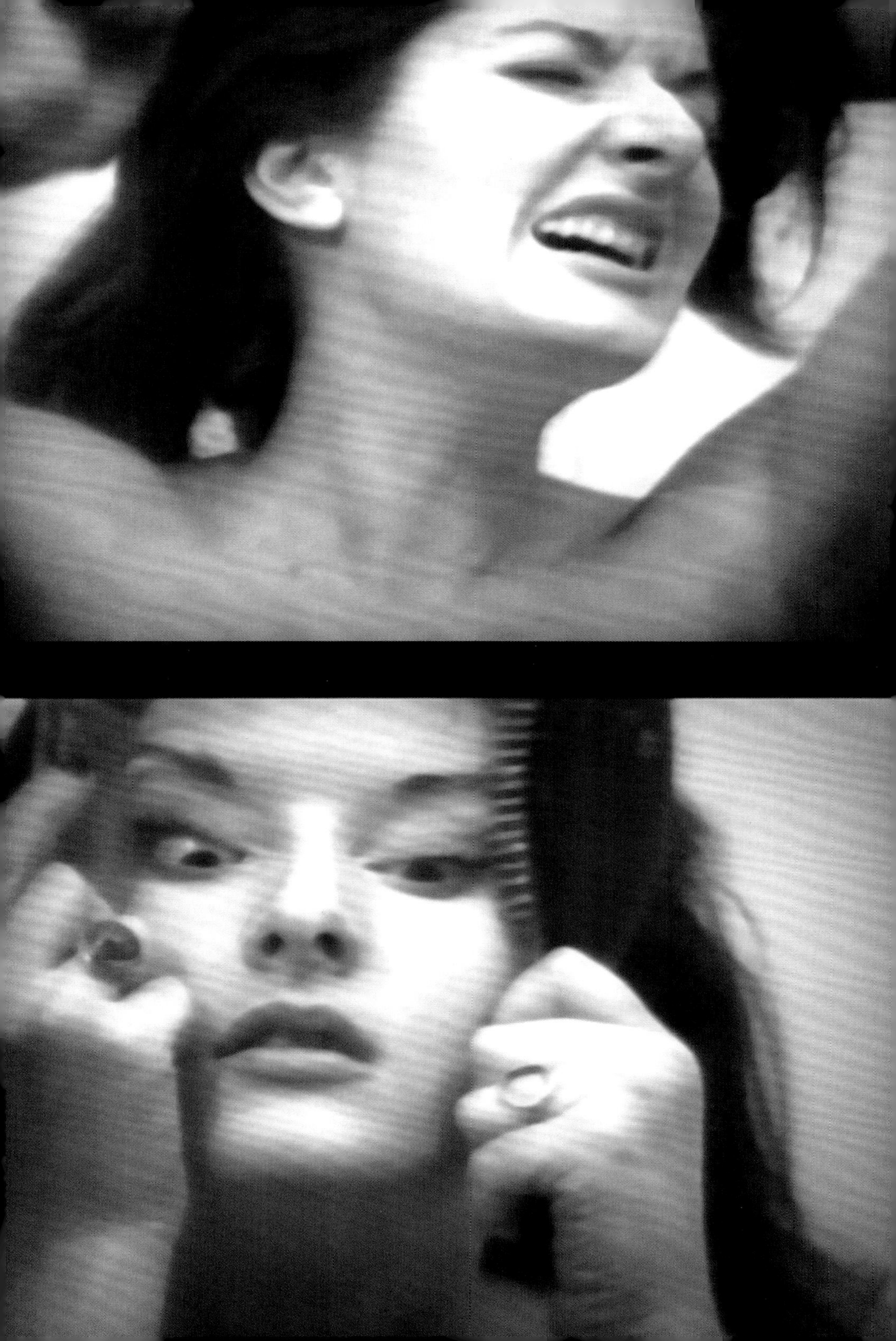

TREE OF LIFE *1976*

Throughout the 1970s, the Cuban-born artist, Ana Mendieta, made more than 200 'earth/body-works' in which she placed her body or its imprint in a relationship with nature to 'become one with the earth'. *Siluetas (Silhouettes)* was a series of performative works made between 1973 and 1980. In them, she used her body and the elements of life – earth, air, fire and water – to make her mark on locations such as Iowa and Mexico, by outlining herself with gunpowder, stones, flowers or fireworks.

In 1981, she explained: 'I have been carrying on a dialogue between the landscape and the female body (based on my own silhouette). I believe this has been a direct result of my having been torn from my homeland (Cuba) during my adolescence. I am overwhelmed by the feeling of having been cast from the womb (nature). My art is the way I re-establish the bonds that unite me to the universe.'[51]

Much of Mendieta's work was ephemeral and photographs are the only traces of the private performances/rituals that remain. *Tree of Life* was created at Old Man's Creek, Iowa, in 1976. For this piece, Mendieta covered herself with greenish mud and grass and stood against an oak tree in a goddess-like pose. The image and action show her connecting with, or surrendering to, the natural world, as she becomes 'an extension of nature and nature becomes an extension of my body.'

Viewed almost 50 years after its making, Mendieta's *Tree of Life* seems to me to be an urgent reminder that we are a part of nature and serves as a call to protect the environment. The way that her body is fused with the tree evokes images of 'tree-huggers' and environmental protesters who chain themselves to trees to save them from destruction.

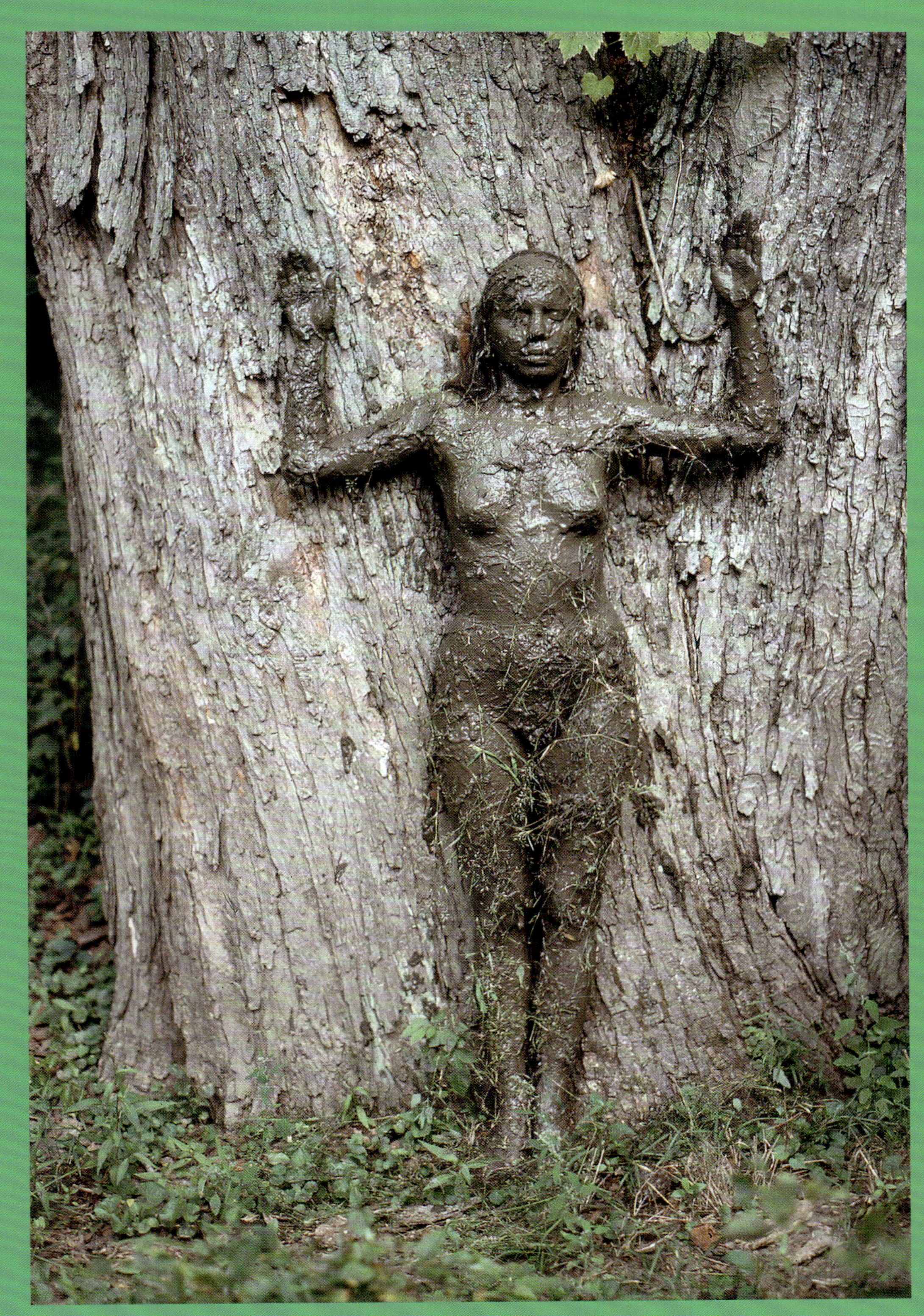

CIRCE *1977*

Romare Bearden was an American artist, writer, songwriter and activist whose body of work positioned African Americans and Black culture as core subjects of modern American art. During the civil rights movement in the 1960s, he became well-known for his mixed-media collages portraying scenes of the everyday life of African Americans in both the rural south and the urban north.

Collage provided him with a way to bring stories from the past into contemporary dialogue and to draw on his wide-ranging influences and interests, which included Greek mythology, European art history, Afro Caribbean culture, jazz and blues. This resulted in richly layered artworks that chronicle the complexities of African American life in a way that is both specific and universal.

In 1977, Bearden produced *A Black Odyssey*, a series of 20 collages based on episodes from Homer's epic tale, *The Odyssey*, reimagined for a contemporary audience. Bearden hoped that making the characters Black would make the ancient Greek myth more interesting and relevant to African American children and that everyone would be able to identify with the hero's tale of trying to get home – of overcoming trials and tribulations to find your place in the world.

Within *The Odyssey* is Circe, a powerful sorceress and goddess of magic who Odysseus encounters on his travels. She could bewitch men with her voice and magic potions and turn them into animals. Bearden took Homer's description of the goddess as possessing beautiful hair and awesome powers, and conflated her with the mythical 'conjure woman' from African American folklore (who also has magical powers that can heal or kill), presenting us with a colourful, edgy image of a strong woman in charge of her fate – and quite possibly yours!

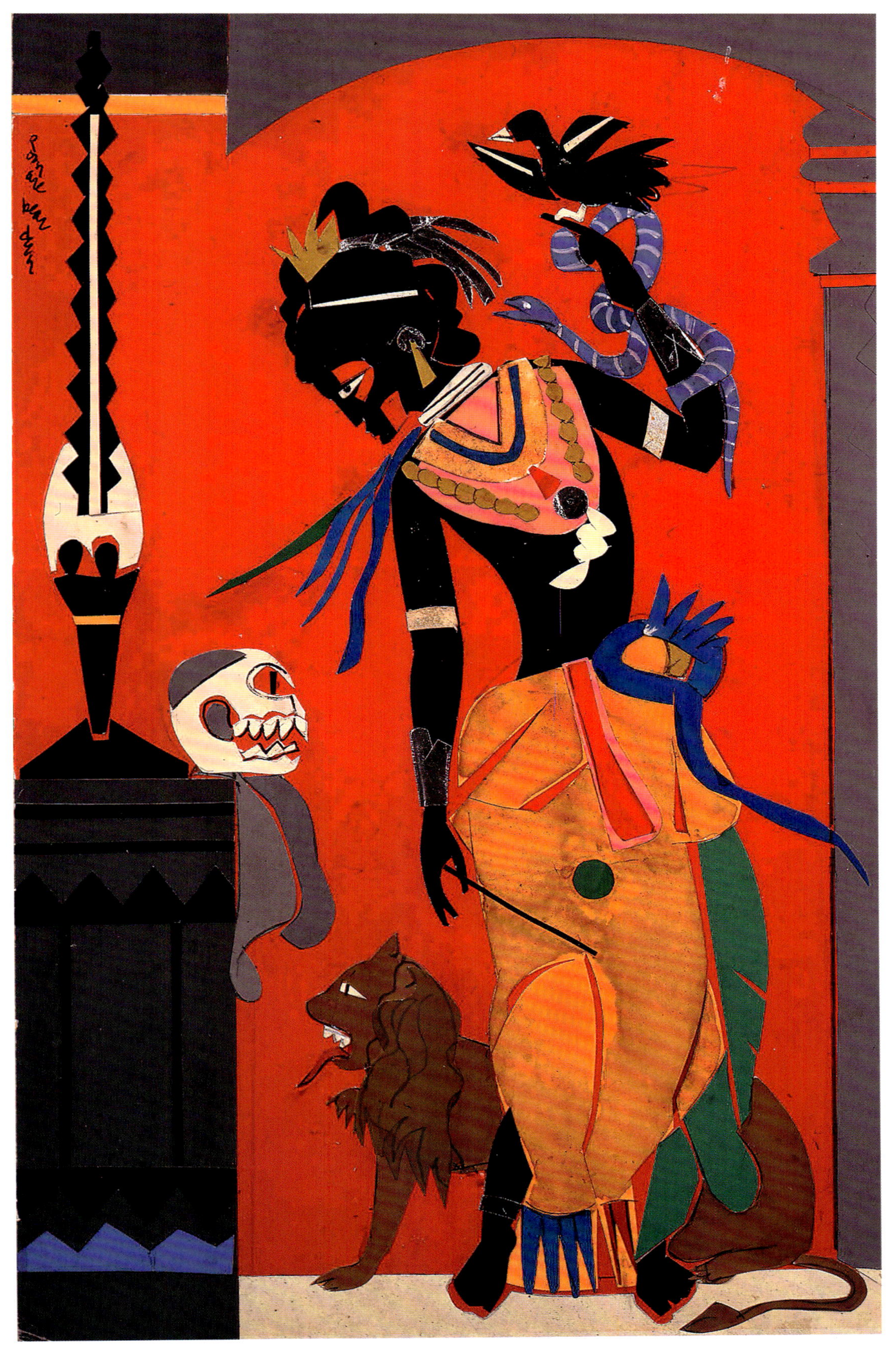

UNTITLED FILM STILLS *1977–1980*

American artist Cindy Sherman burst onto the art scene in the late 1970s with photographs exploring various aspects of female identity. Although Sherman is the sitter in her photographs, they are not self-portraits, as the images are not designed to tell us anything about Cindy Sherman the person. Instead, Sherman poses as a figure in recognizable scenes – from B-movies, girlie magazines, television programmes, advertising, Old Master paintings – effacing her own identity to bring into question the stereotypes she adopts.

Sherman's best-known work is *Untitled Film Stills*, a series of 70 black-and-white photographs presented in the same size and format as if they were stills from actual films. Film stills are the publicity shots that are used to promote a movie and are either staged photographs taken on set or an individual frame isolated from an actual film. However, Sherman's are neither. Each photograph was conceived, constructed, directed and 'starred in' by Sherman to create the illusion of being a film still from a real film.

Within each frame, Sherman appears as a stock female character – ingénue, bombshell, bored housewife, career girl – in scenes that evoke films and television from the 1950s and 1960s. With her impersonations of fictional women who would have been played by actors, Sherman blurs reality and fiction, creating a sort of fusion of *Alfred Hitchcock Presents* and *I Love Lucy* that feels both familiar and entirely original.

The artworks draw our attention to the construction of identities that women 'perform' on a daily basis and serve as a wake-up call for us to think about the images of women that are presented all around us – don't assume that a photograph presents 'truth' or 'reality'. By exposing the fiction of there being a 'real' woman behind these stereotypes of femininity, the work seems to be trying to release us from them and offer encouragement to be whoever we want to be. While Sherman's work tackles serious, thought-provoking issues and observations, there is also no shortage of fun and humour on offer – who wouldn't want to dress up every day and try on a new persona? It is unsurprising that her serio-comic theatrical photographs have captured imaginations since the 1980s and remain both enormously popular and influential.

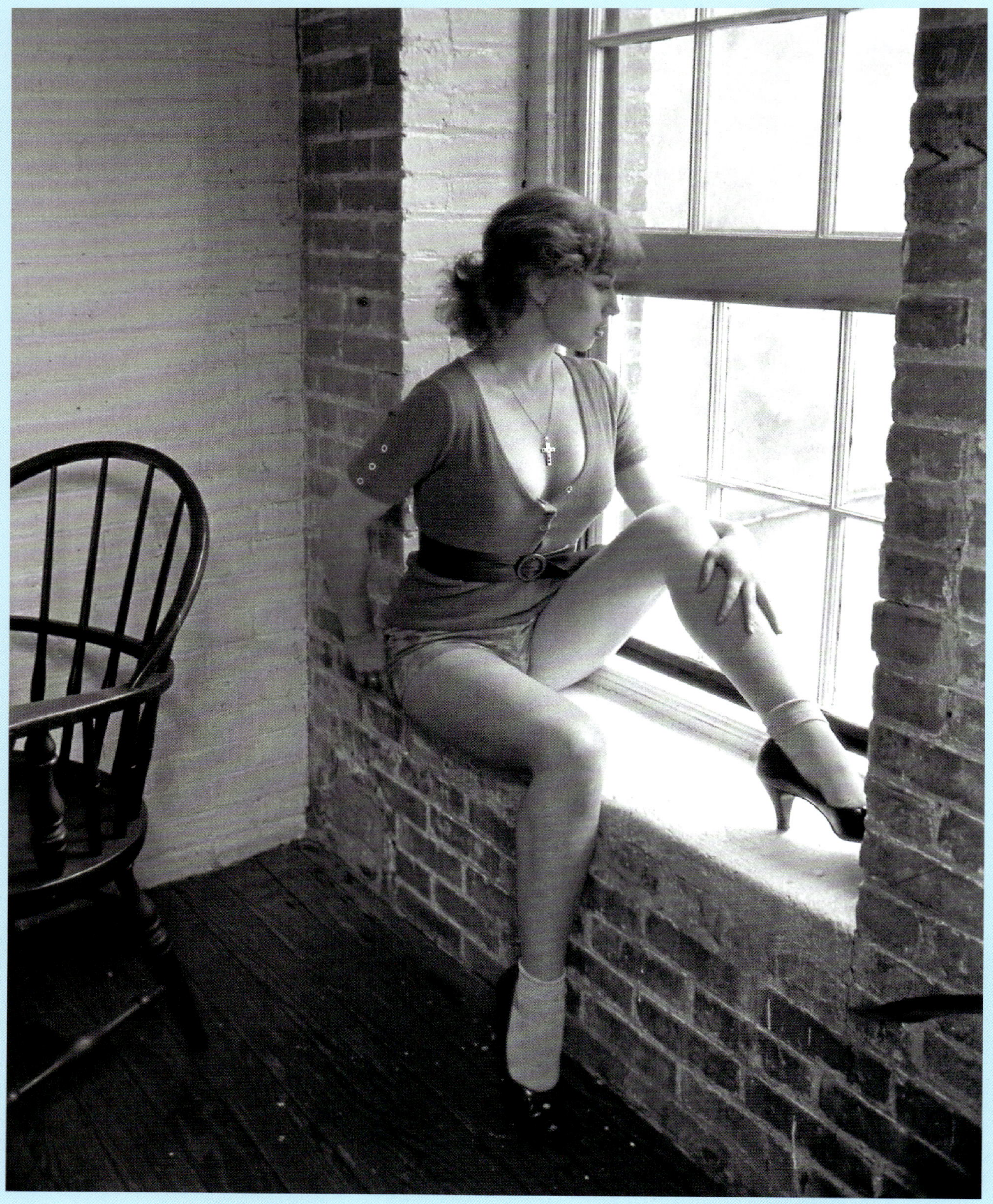

Untitled Film Still #15,
1978

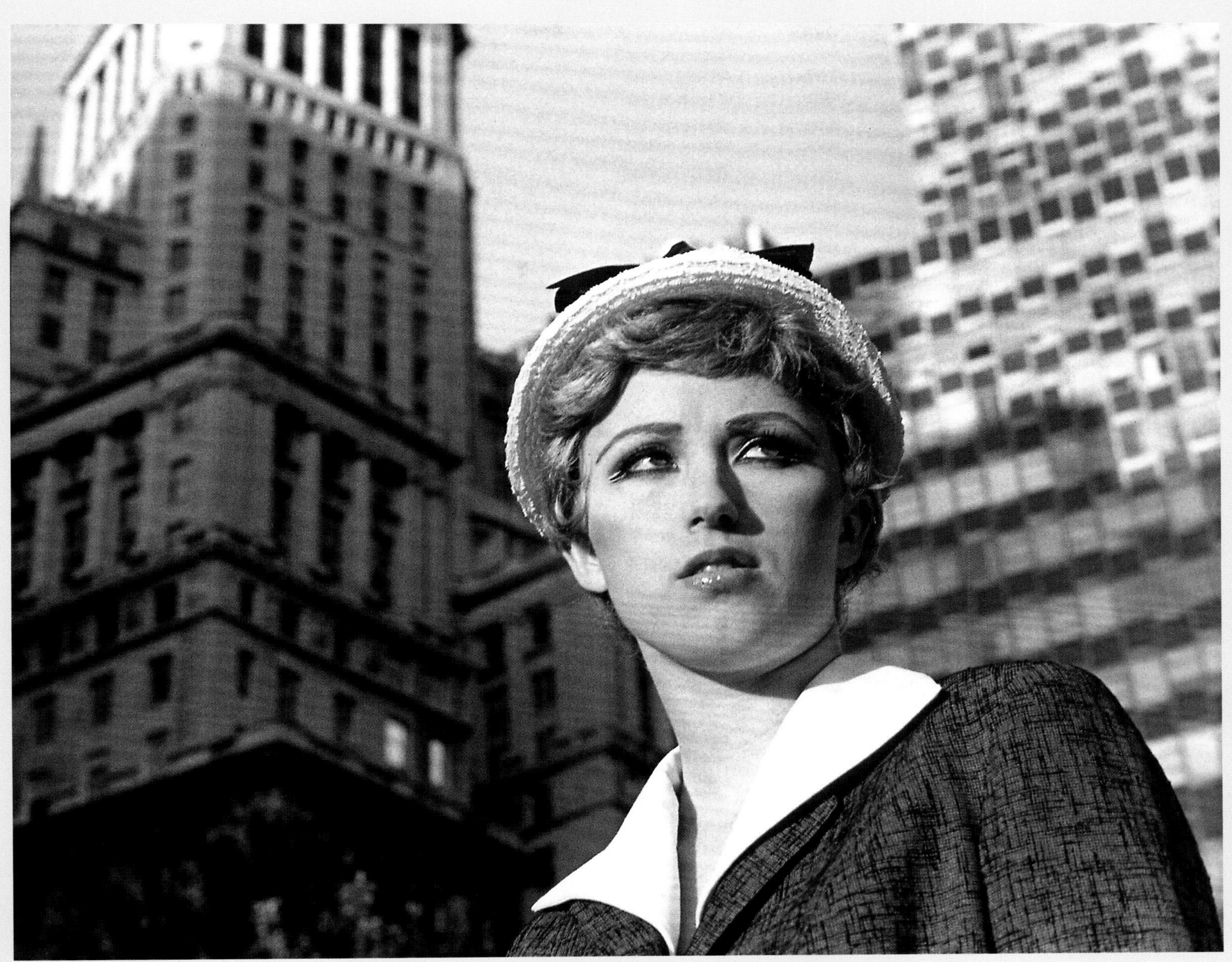

Untitled Film Still #21,
1978

NUESTRA SEÑORA DE LAS IGUANAS

(Our Lady of the Iguanas) <u>1979</u>

One of Latin America's most influential contemporary photographers, Graciela Iturbide, has been documenting the lives of Indigenous people in rural communities in her native Mexico since the 1970s. Working primarily in black and white, her powerful, sympathetic photographs have been exhibited widely in Europe and North America, bringing international exposure and fame to her and the communities that she has photographed.

In 1979, she was invited to photograph the Zapotec people in the Indigenous town of Juchitán in the Mexican state of Oaxaca. Over the following seven years, Iturbide immersed herself in the community in a series of visits, growing to know the people so she could photograph them and their way of life on their terms. The Zapotec are descendants of an ancient matriarchal society and women are still at the forefront of their society, organizing finances, businesses and religious festivals, while men work as farmers or fishermen. She found these socially and economically independent women inspiring and featured them in her break-through series, *Juchitán de Las Mujeres 1979–1989* (*Juchitán, A Town of Women 1979–1989*).

Our Lady of the Iguanas is the most famous image from the series. Iturbide was delighted when she saw Zobeida Dias carrying the iguanas on her head on the way to market to sell them. She recalled that 'only one photo from the 12 I took of her was good, because it was the only one where the iguanas raised their heads as if they were posing.'[52] The iguanas create a fabulously surreal crown and add to Zobeida's 'ethereal sense of self-possession'. Iturbide believes that 'the photographer's job is to synthesize, to make strong and poetic work from daily life.' She certainly achieved that with this photograph, which the community has claimed and dubbed 'The Juchitán Medusa'.

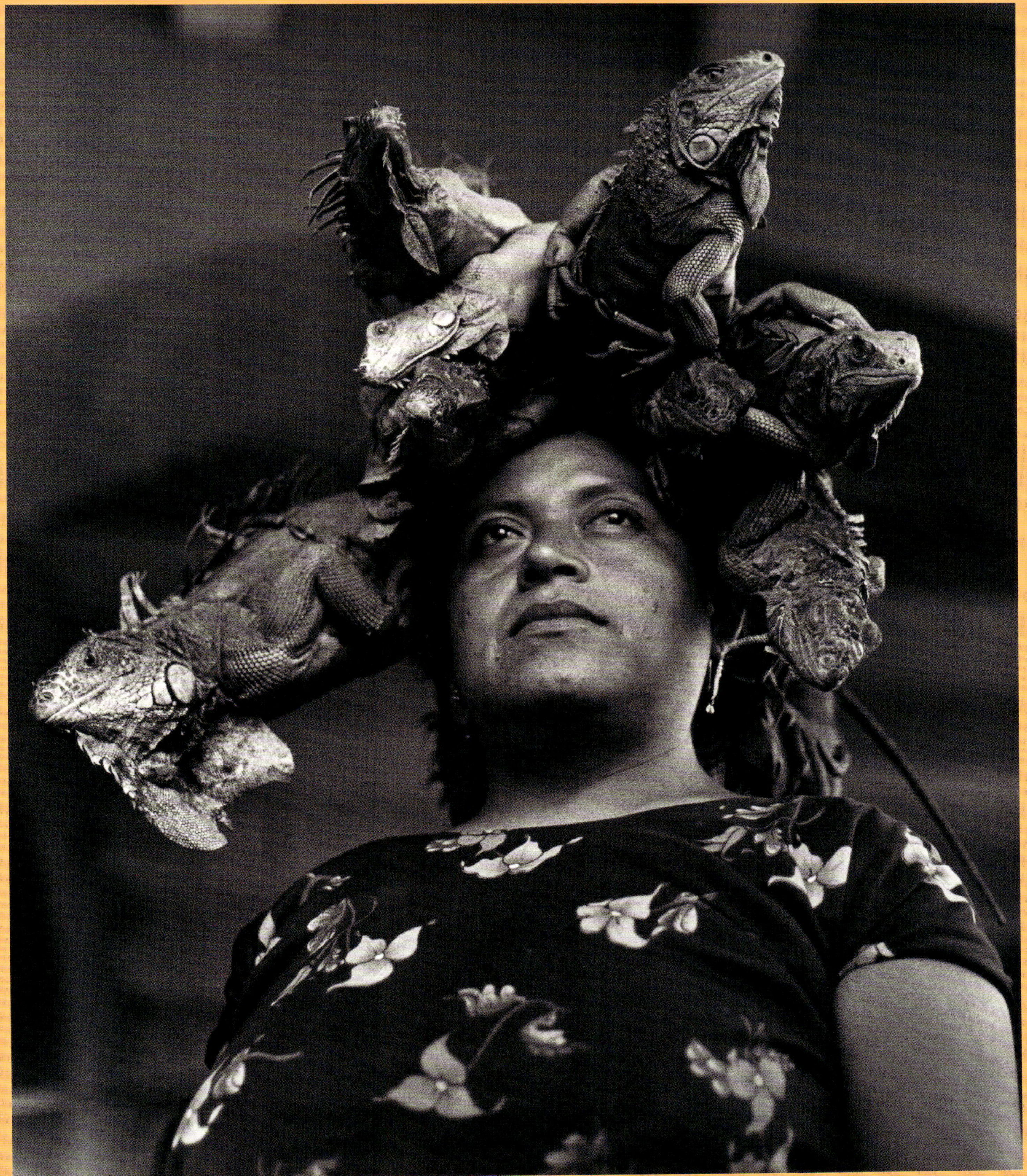

DO WOMEN HAVE TO BE NAKED TO GET INTO THE MET MUSEUM? *1989*

The Guerrilla Girls is a collective of anonymous female artist activists, which formed in New York in 1985 with the motto: 'We intend to be the conscience of the art world.' Outraged that the International Survey of Recent Painting and Sculpture exhibition at the Museum of Modern Art (MoMA) in 1984 featured just 13 women out of a total of 169 artists, they took to the streets to protest about the inequalities rampant in the art world, not to mention society as a whole.

The collective uses humour and fact-based texts to unmask and critique individuals and institutions that exclude or under-represent women and minorities, presenting their work via fly posters, stickers, comics, billboards and actions. Members maintain their anonymity by wearing large rubber gorilla masks and using the names of dead women artists, such as Hannah Höch (p. 114) and Frida Kahlo (p. 132), as pseudonyms, which also helps to raise the profiles of those kindred spirits.

In 1989, their most famous poster posed the provocative question: *Do Women Have to be Naked to Get into the Met Museum?* The Guerrilla Girls co-opted Ingres's *La Grande Odalisque* (p. 66), gave her a gorilla mask and put her to work to help draw attention to the fact that while women's bodies had long been a core subject for artworks, very few artworks by women artists had been collected or displayed. The poster first appeared on the side of New York City buses before travelling around the world questioning the representation of women at other cultural sites.

The Guerrilla Girls continue to be the conscience of the art world, striving to right gender imbalance so that our cultural institutions present more truthful, complete reflections of the cultures they serve.

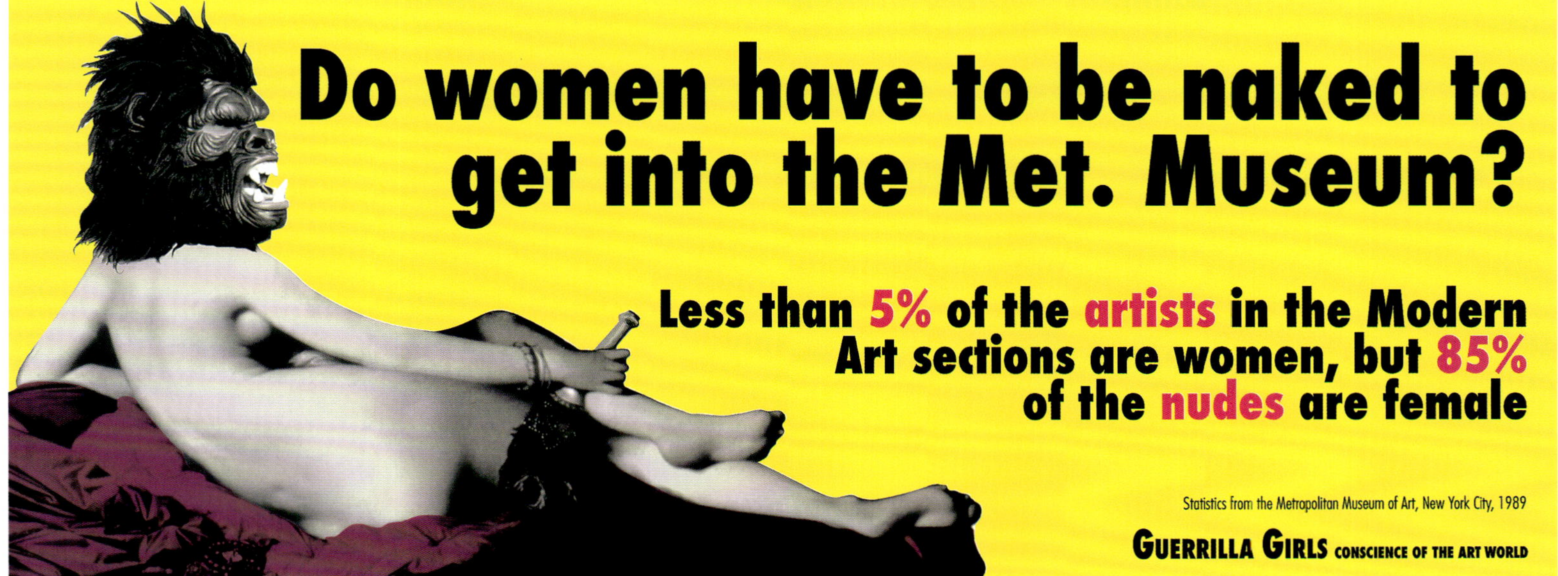

Do women have to be naked to get into the Met. Museum?

Less than 5% of the artists in the Modern Art sections are women, but 85% of the nudes are female

Statistics from the Metropolitan Museum of Art, New York City, 1989

GUERRILLA GIRLS CONSCIENCE OF THE ART WORLD

UNTITLED (YOUR BODY IS A BATTLEGROUND)

1989/2019

In the late 1970s, Barbara Kruger, a former chief graphic designer at *Mademoiselle*, started producing photomontages that stylishly combined images with unsettling captions. This included works such as *Untitled (Your Gaze Hits the Side of My Face)* (1981), in which conventionally unexamined aspects of social behaviour (men looking at women) were exposed to scrutiny. Kruger uses posters and billboards, as well as immersive installations, to put forth messages that challenge and deconstruct prevailing attitudes. Her large-scale image-text works combine pithy statements and sharp wit with strong graphic images and social commentary, and by employing language and techniques familiar from advertising and politics, she speaks clearly and directly to the viewer – she does not allow them to accept the status quo easily or without thinking.

One of her most famous pieces, *Untitled (Your Body is a Battleground)*, was made in 1989 in response to the March for Women's Lives in Washington DC, in support of women's reproductive freedom. A tightly cropped woman's face is split down the middle by positive and negative exposure, graphically presenting the divisive nature of the issue with the woman as a battleground, while the bold type and red frame scream the urgency of the situation. The use of 'Your' in the title involves the viewer directly, whatever gender, because as Kruger puts it: 'Pronouns really cut through the grease.' For Kruger, this is about more than one issue, as she sees it as 'a very free-floating statement about bodies too. It can allude to men, women, non-binary people … I believe in the possibility of the multiplicity of bodies and all bodies are vulnerable.'

'Kruger's large-scale image-text works combine pithy statements and sharp wit with strong graphic images and social commentary. She speaks clearly and directly to the viewer and does not allow them to accept the status quo'

Kruger's poster has been used as a rallying cry for numerous protests around the world and has become more relevant again, as women's reproductive rights have come under attack, particularly in the United States. In 2019, Kruger revisited the work and made a new version – a 'replay' – using new modes of communication and technologies in the form of short videos displayed on LEDs. The moving images animate the now-iconic poster and show it being put back together like a jigsaw puzzle, as if it has been pulled off the shelf and called back into action again. As Kruger herself has stated: 'It would be great if my work became archaic, if the issues that they try to present, the commentary I'm trying to suggest, were no longer pertinent. But unfortunately, that's not the case at this point.'[53]

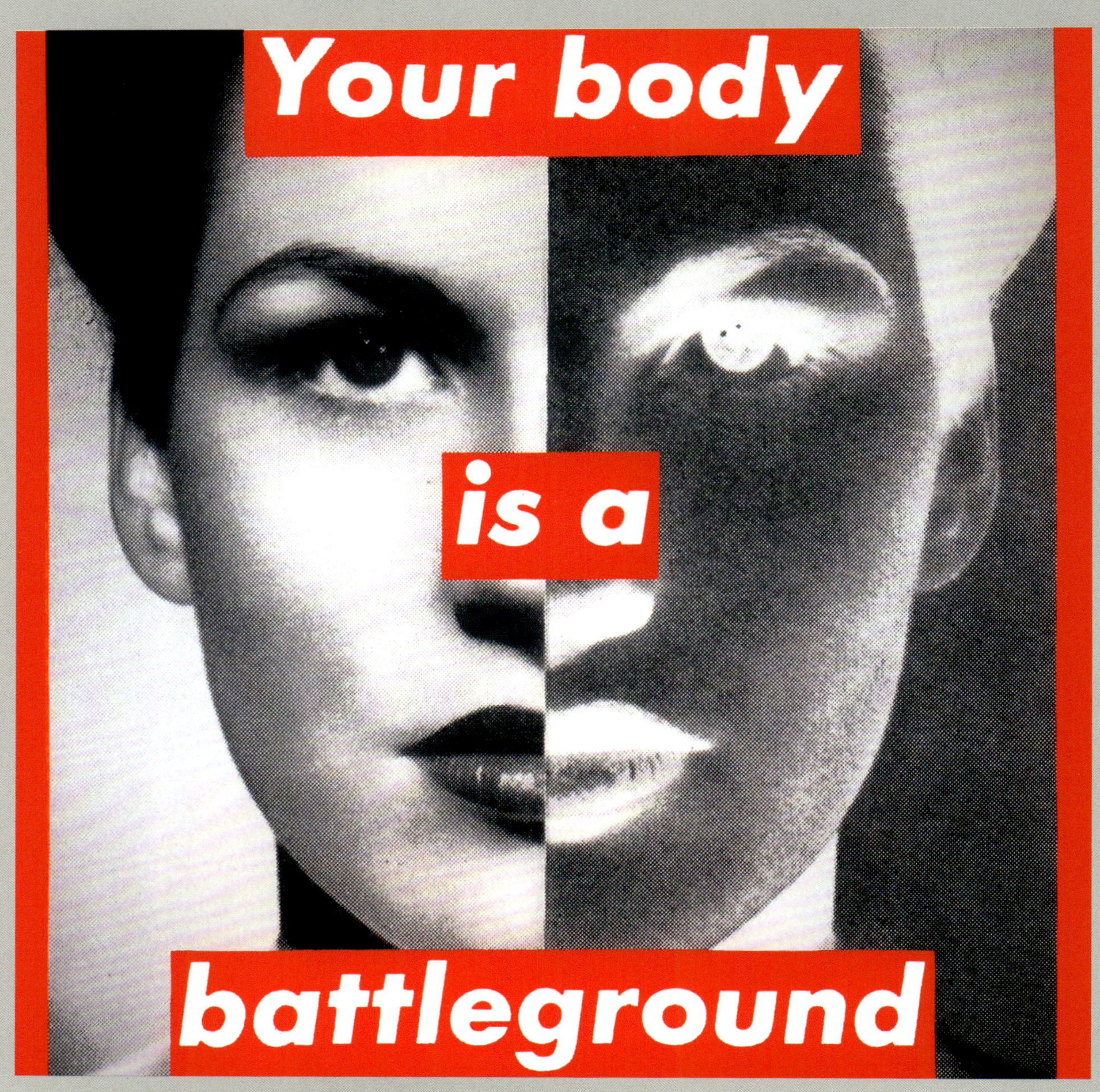

*Untitled (Your Body
is a Battleground),*
1989

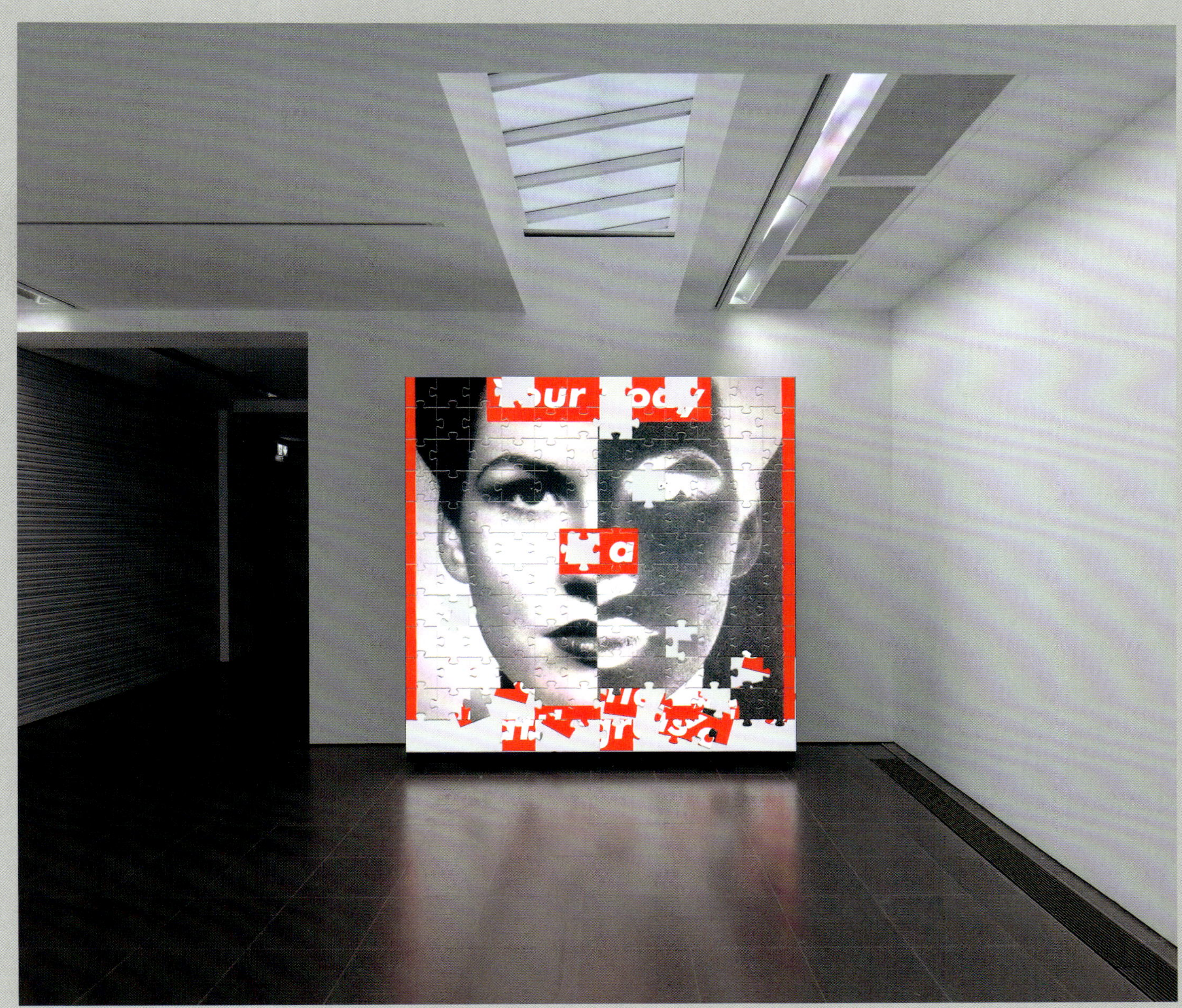

*Untitled (Your Body
is a Battleground),
1989/2019*

PROPPED *1992*

In the 1990s, British artist Jenny Saville reinvented the portrayal of the female nude with her huge canvases that seemed to barely contain substantial female bodies. Seen from below, and often decorated with contour lines or writing, the works are confrontational and compelling representations of femininity and the body. Her beautifully rendered Rubenesque bodies in awkward, uncomfortable positions, with the marks, textures and blemishes of the skin painted with relish, question standards of beauty and notions of 'good taste'.

In her nude self-portrait of 1992, *Propped*, Saville shows a woman perched precariously on top of a small stool, her breasts squeezed together by crossed arms, hands gripping and kneading her fleshy thighs. She looks quizzically at herself in a cloudy mirror inscribed with a quote from 'When Our Lips Speak Together', an essay by the French feminist, Luce Irigaray, theorizing that women function as mirrors for male narcissism.

Plan (1993) is a 2.75 metre (9 foot) high painting showing a naked woman with a plastic surgeon's preparatory marks on her body, which look like contour lines marking out elevation on a topographical map. The immense size of the paintings intimidate and overwhelm the viewer. As Saville explained: 'I'm interested in the physical power a large female body has – [someone] who occupies a lot of space, but who's also acutely aware that contemporary culture encourages her to disguise her bulk and look as small as possible.'[54]

In an era that saw an increase in eating disorders, harmful dieting, cosmetic surgery and body shaming, Saville's paintings stand as unconventional and defiant celebrations of the human body, complete with bulges and blemishes on show, forcing a rethink of what the idealized nude should look like.

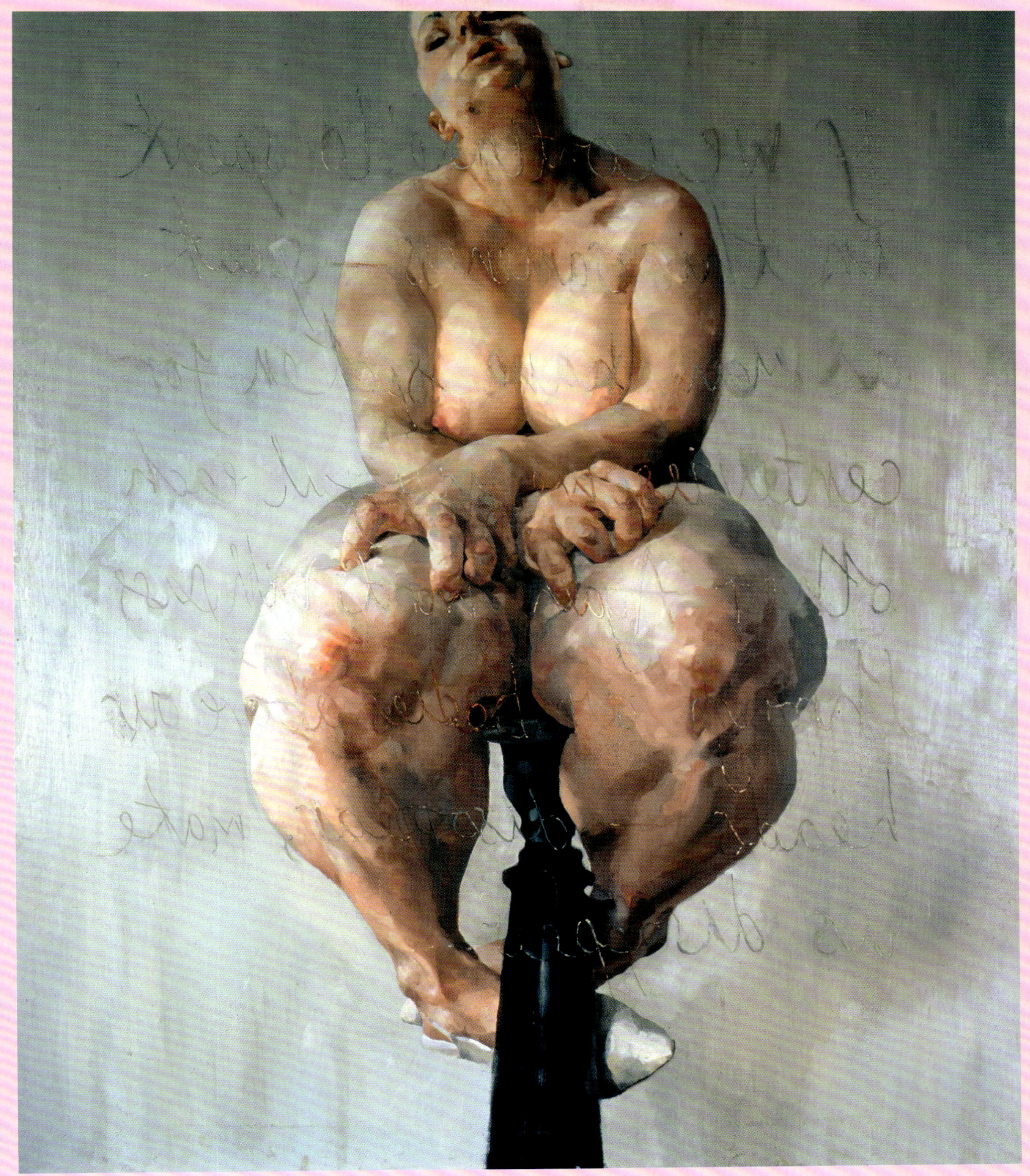

I AM ITS SECRET *1993*

Shirin Neshat was born and raised in Iran before moving to the US in 1975 to study. The Islamic Revolution (1978–1979) and the Iran–Iraq war (1980–1988) prevented her from returning to Iran to visit until 1990. In a body of work that is both tender and critical, personal and political, she examines stereotypical portrayals of Muslim women from the perspective of an artist who is Iranian, but living in exile, separated from family and country, looking in from the outside; from the West. Her work also reflects her experiences as an immigrant living in the USA.

Women of Allah (1993–1997) was her first major body of work as an artist. It was informed by her reactions to the dramatic political, social and religious changes that her native country had undergone in her absence, and how the lives of Iranian women – both those who stayed and those who had been displaced – had been affected. She worked through her complex emotions in a series of black-and-white photographs of veiled women (often herself), which were overlaid with texts from controversial Iranian women writers. In doing so, Neshat explored notions of femininity, violence and resistance in powerful staged photographs that encourage multiple readings.

I Am Its Secret is one such image: a portrait of Neshat wearing a chador, her face covered with swirling black and red Farsi script. The lines are from *I Will Greet the Sun Again*, a poem by the pre-revolutionary poet, Forugh Farrokhzad, which speaks of hope, resilience, perseverance and love. Her hair and mouth might be covered, but her thoughts cannot be controlled and the red ink on the otherwise black-and-white image seems to assert that women will always find modes of self-expression and resistance. While a meditation on the lives of women living in the Islamic Republic, the evocative image also seems to be Neshat pondering what it means for those like herself who are part of the Iranian diaspora.

Neshat's arresting images have made Muslim women and their lives visible to the international art world. These are women who hold our gaze and do not let us look away – or forget them. Her powerful images give cause for thought about the lives of Muslim women in the Middle East and Western countries, as well as the stereotypes surrounding them.

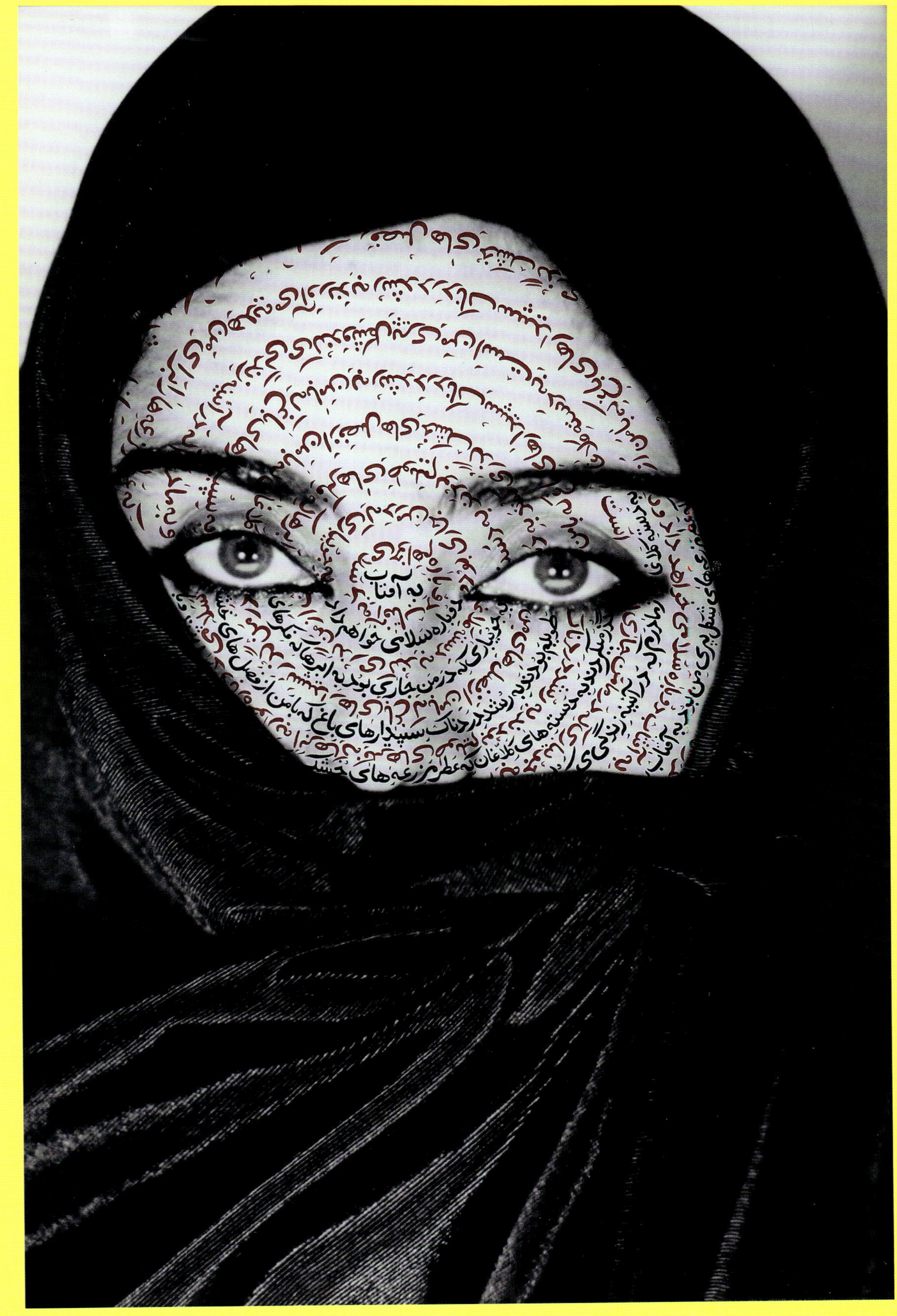

ABORTION SERIES TRIPTYCH *1998*

Paula Rego is known for hard-hitting figurative paintings that tackle difficult subjects, such as depression, fear and mental illness, and for creating art with the aim to effect social and political change, especially in regard to women's rights and their place in the world.

Her unsettling *Abortion Series* was created in response to the failed 1998 referendum in Portugal to decriminalize abortion. She poured her fury and frustration with the outcome into the creation of 10 large pastels in the space of six months. Each image focuses on an individual woman and her experience, the unflinching portrayals showing in no uncertain terms the physical, emotional and psychological pain endured. Drawn in by the beautiful colours and compositions, the viewer is taken behind closed doors to witness the reality of the back-street options.

Having spoken openly about her own abortions and seen the dangers that face those who cannot access or afford safe legal procedures, she explained that the series 'highlights the fear and pain and danger of an illegal abortion, which is what desperate women have always resorted to. It's very wrong to criminalize women on top of everything else.'

'Each image focuses on an individual woman and her experience, the unflinching portrayals showing the physical, emotional and psychological pain endured'

Etchings of the series were published in several Portuguese newspapers in the run-up to a second referendum in 2007, where they served as a stark reminder that criminalizing abortion does not stop women from having abortions – it only endangers more lives. The president of Portugal credited Rego's powerful images for raising awareness and helping to sway public opinion, resulting in legalized abortion in Portugal.

As access to safe and legal abortions continues to be restricted around the world, Rego's *Abortion Series* continues to pack a punch with its continued relevance. Interviewed in 2019, in reference to state laws restricting abortions in the USA, she said: 'It seems unbelievable that these battles have to be fought all over again. It's grotesque.' Shortly after Rego's death in 2022, the US Supreme Court overturned Roe vs. Wade, ending almost 50 years of abortion rights in America. The fight goes on.[55]

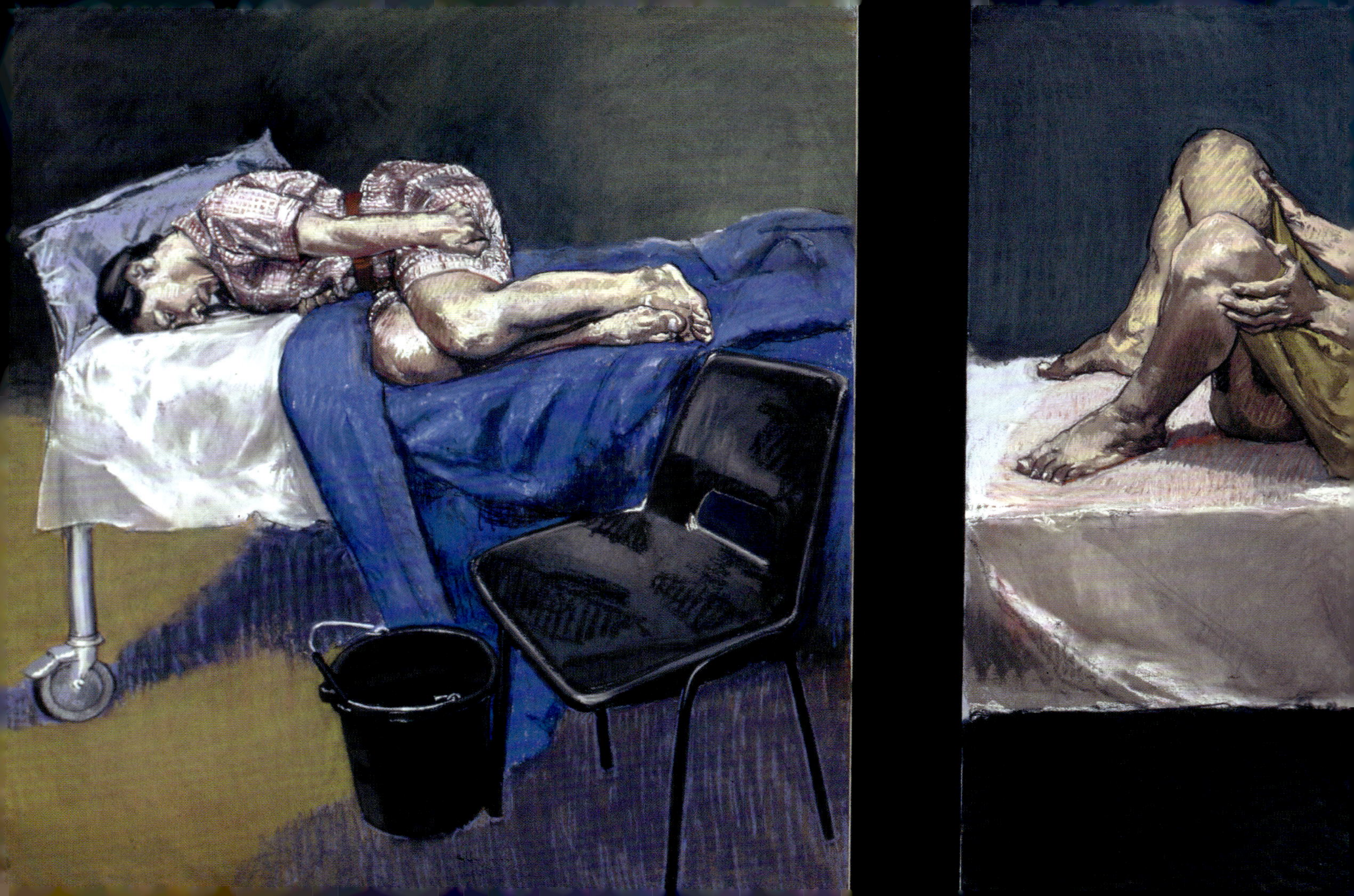

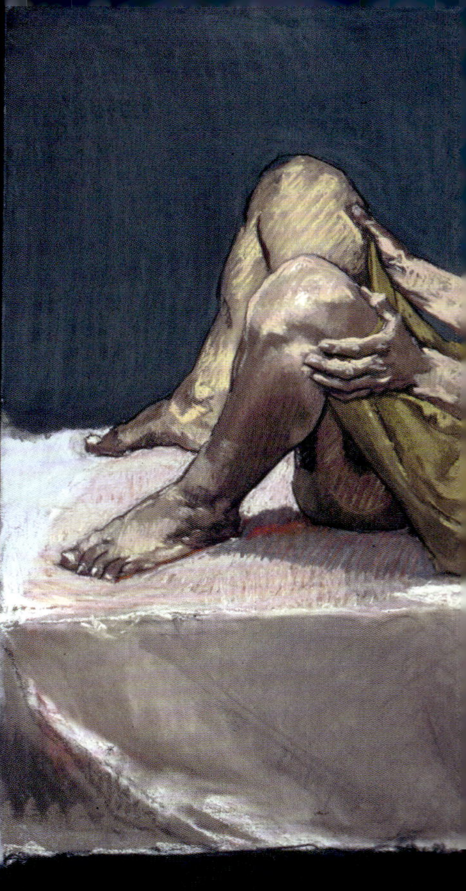

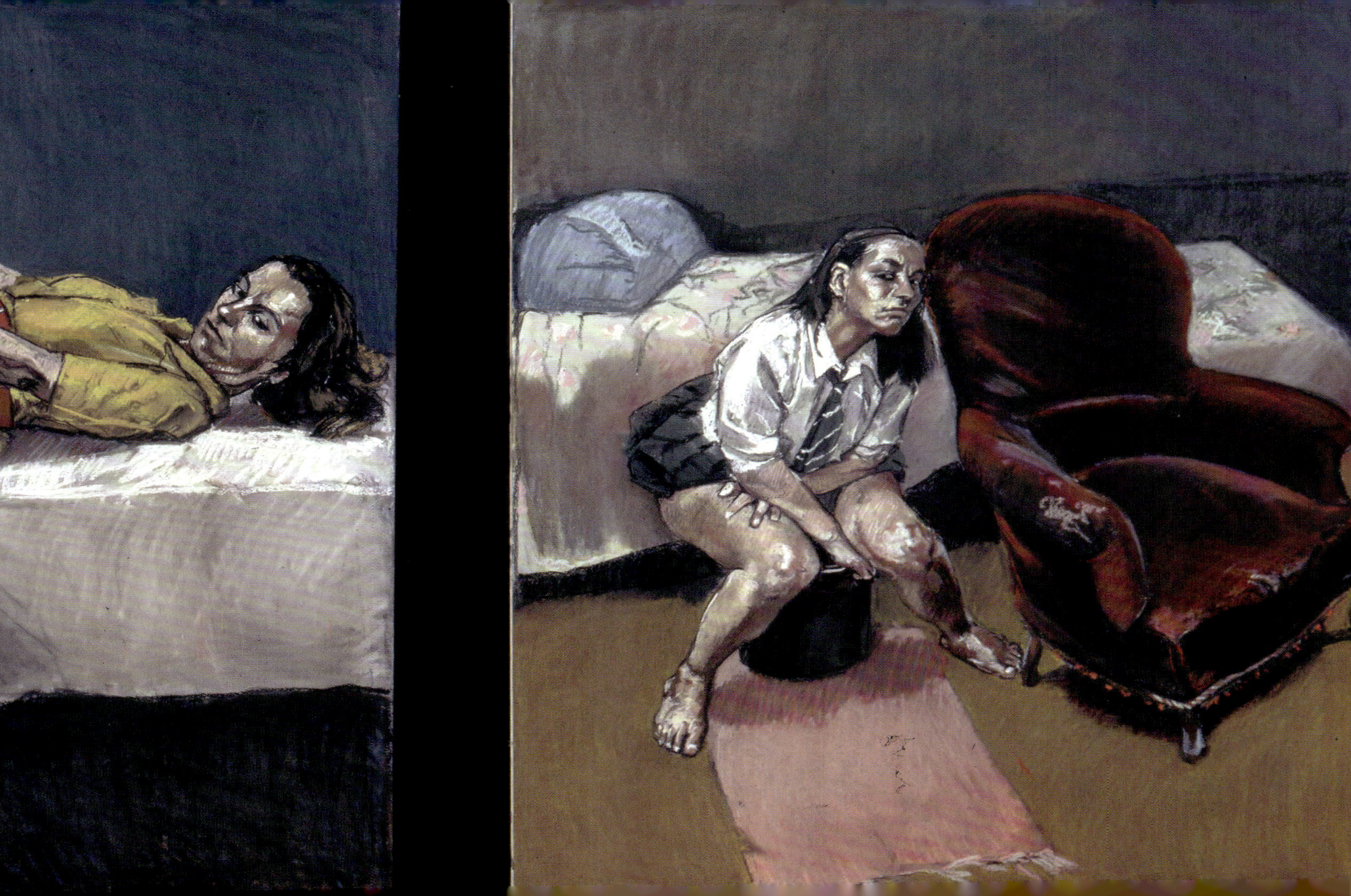

DO NOT ABANDON ME *1999*

Motherhood and abandonment are recurring themes in the vast body of work by Louise Bourgeois, in which she explored the physical, psychological and intellectual expressions of a range of human emotions: fear, loneliness, anxiety, love, abandonment, jealousy, rage, loss and guilt. Her search for self-discovery led to raw, honest, autobiographical art about the body, sexuality and relationships – as daughters, mothers, partners and friends – expressed in images of the body or stand-ins for the body (such as spiders) in varying media, forms and sizes. She explained that 'my subject is the rawness of the emotions, the devastating effect of the emotions you go through. The materials are my medium.'[56]

Do Not Abandon Me, which was made in 1999 when Bourgeois was in her late 80s, speaks to the intense emotions involved in giving birth and becoming a mother, as well as those of being a child. This work seems to mine Bourgeois's relationship with her mother, as well as reflect on her own role as a mother. Many of the artist's late sewn sculptures are a tribute to the act of restoration and reparation; her mother, a tapestry restorer, was often ill and died when Bourgeois was 20.

Do Not Abandon Me freezes the moment when a woman abandons the self that she has been for the past nine months – from 'being pregnant' to 'being a mother' – with all the conflicting emotions of joy and fear that accompany that transition. The soft, simple figures are reminiscent of rag dolls, but their still, stiff bodies also evoke the mummified bodies of Pompeii and the petrifying fear that comes with the overwhelming responsibility of raising another human being. The child is still connected by the umbilical cord, but the cord is attached to the mother on the outside, so that we can see it. To me, the sculpture is a potent image of 'separation anxiety' and the complexities of the parent-child relationship – who ultimately abandons whom? Please don't leave me …

Bourgeois's brave, bold visceral art has had a huge influence on others searching to express their authenticity, such as Tracey Emin (p. 210), with whom she collaborated on a series of prints just before she died. These were also entitled *Do Not Abandon Me* (2009–2010).

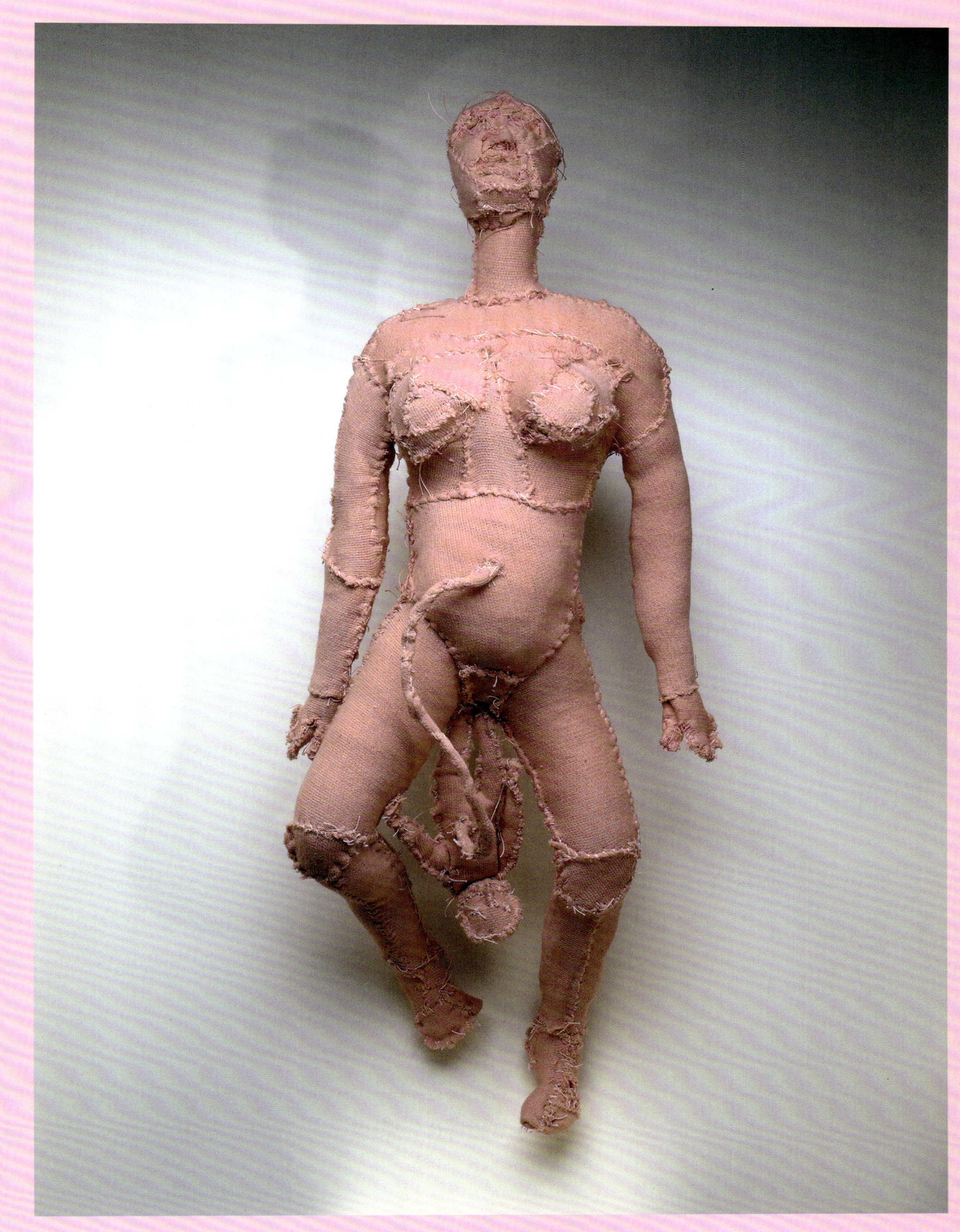

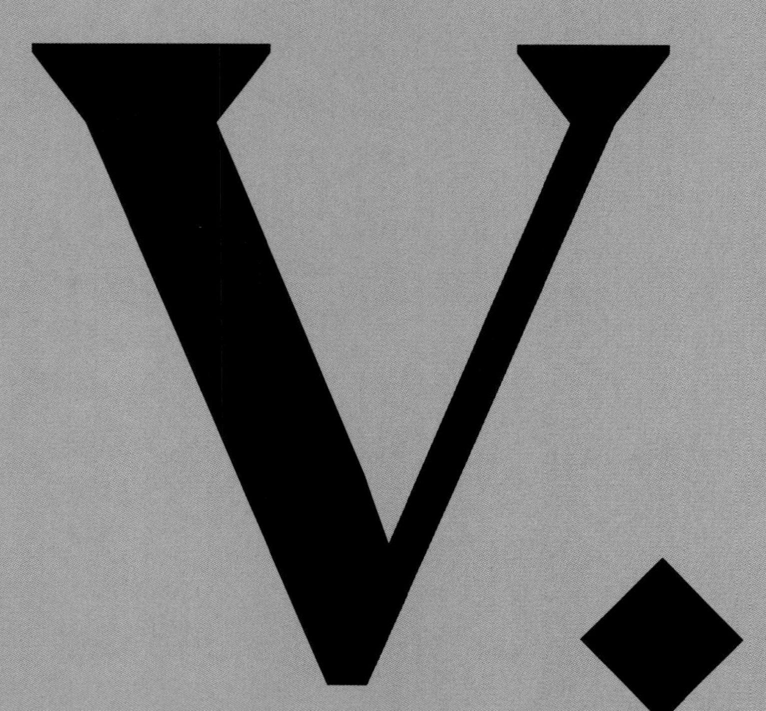

V.

2000 ONWARDS

Mickalene Thomas
(American, b. 1971)

AFRO GODDESS LOOKING FORWARD *2015*

When Mickalene Thomas was studying art and art history, she couldn't find images of strong Black women like those who raised her and inspired her in real life, so she set about filling the void. Her portraits of Black women in decorative 1970s themed domestic interiors often adopt the reclining poses of a Titian (p. 24), Manet (p. 82) or Ingres (p. 66), assertively claiming the spaces they inhabit.

Afro Goddess Looking Forward is a self-portrait, and its title and image capture the essence of Thomas's work. The composition references art of the past and places the Black female body in position to take the tradition forward. With a black-and-white photograph of her eyes, Thomas looks out from the riot of patterns that make up her outfit and background. She is collaged into her background – a domestic setting that envelopes her like a loving caress. Her flatly painted skin and patterns are brought to life by the light and texture of the shimmering rhinestones that outline her body and appear in her hair.

Thomas elevates the presence of Black women in her large paintings, photographs, collages and installations, which place her subjects firmly in the spotlight. Often using the real women of her life – her mother, friends and lovers – the results are big, bold, positive statements that counter the often-negative, mass-media stereotypes of Black women.

As a queer woman, Thomas's work also celebrates the female gaze as she shares with the viewer her love and respect for the important women in her life and their sensuality and strength. Harnessing the power of grand portraiture, she bestows on her friends and family the gravitas, grandeur, glamour and visibility that were enjoyed in the past by white nobility and socialites.

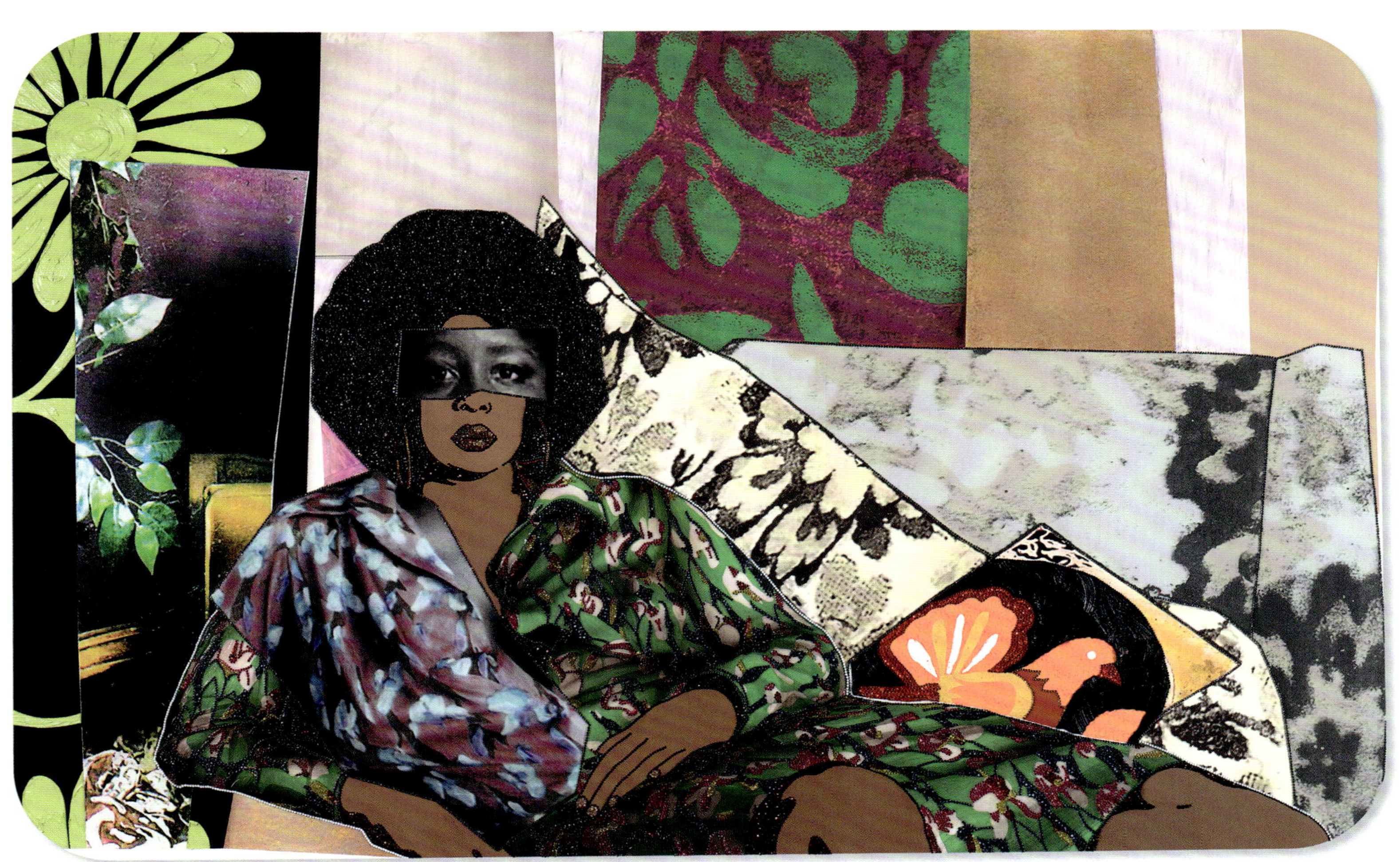

Mari Katayama
(Japanese, b. 1987)

BYSTANDER #014 *2016*

Mari Katayama is a Japanese multimedia artist, model and singer who creates hand-sewn objects, photographs and installations using her body as the raw material. Katayama was born with congenital tibial hemimelia, which led to the amputation of her lower legs at the age of nine to enable her to walk with prosthetics. The focus of her work is living within her own body as well as thinking about ideas around artificial beauty, or as she puts it: 'How much of this is you, and how much is not you?'[57]

For her *bystander* series (2016), Katayama photographed the hands of puppeteers from an all-female puppet theatre company, which she translated into hand-sewn soft sculptures. In *bystander #014* Katayama is lying on a beach wearing one of these soft sculptures of stuffed textile arms. She appears to have been washed ashore, like a stranded mermaid, jellyfish or crab – or perhaps a new version of Botticelli's Venus (p. 14). The soft sculptures blend with her own body such that you can't tell where one stops and another begins, a reference to the fact that our identities are all constructed of a variety of elements.

This was the first time that Katayama used other people's bodies in her artwork, which is perhaps an acknowledgement that we can all use a helping hand at times? That no man – or woman – is an island, and that we are all a part of each other and our environment.

That the series was created on the Japanese island of Naoshima, which is filled with contemporary art installations, adds another contextual element, signalling Katayama's position in the international contemporary art scene. The richly layered artworks also beautifully illustrate her belief that 'all human bodies – including ones like mine that have been altered by human hands – are perfect.'[58]

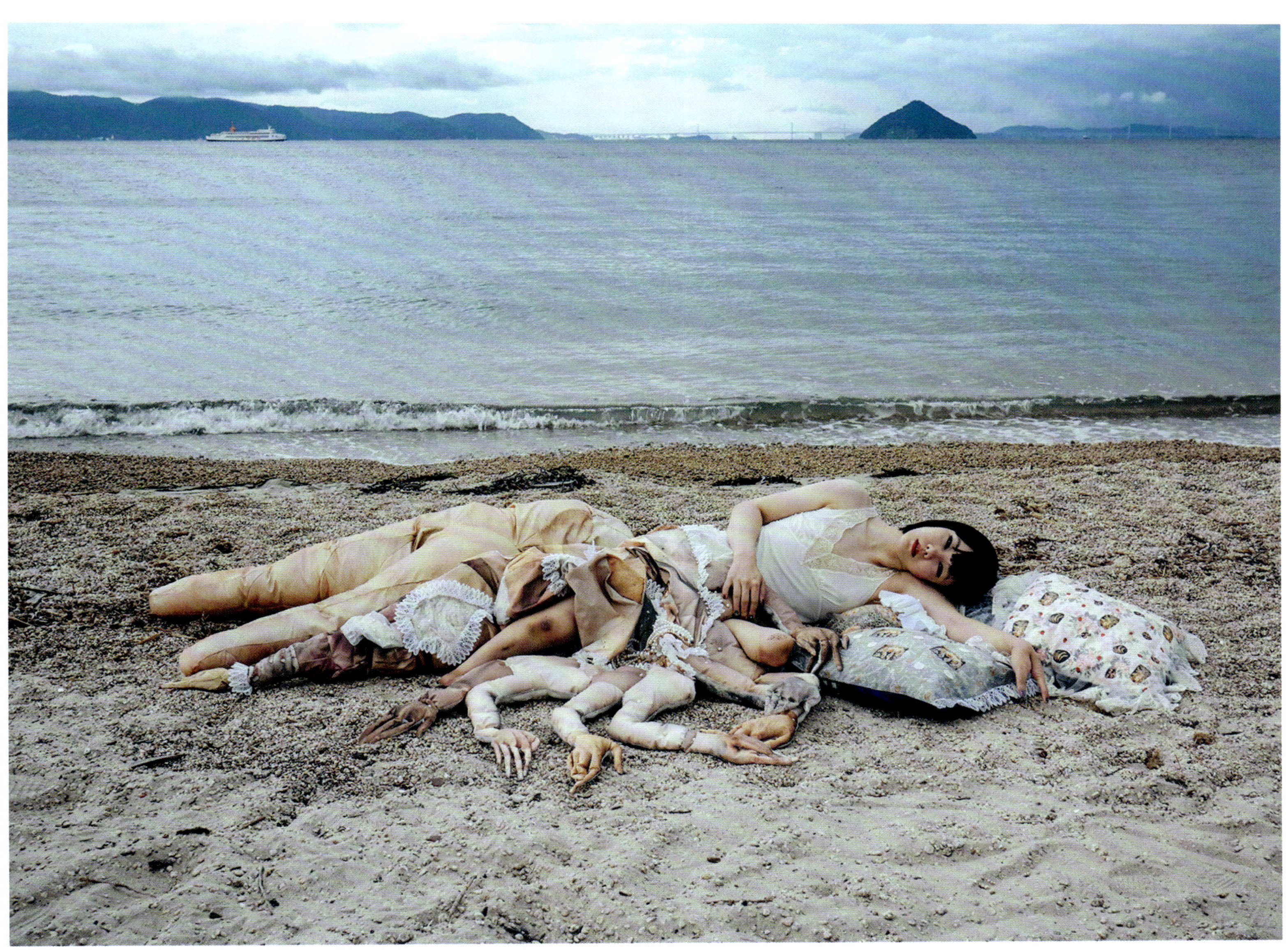

Zanele Muholi
(South African, b. 1972)

SEBENZILE, PARKTOWN _2016_

South African artist Zanele Muholi (pronouns: they/them/theirs) began their visual activist practice by raising awareness of the hate crimes suffered by Black lesbians in South Africa. They then began documenting and celebrating South Africa's Black lesbian, gay, trans, queer and intersex communities. Through photography, and more recently, sculpture, they tell the stories of the prejudice and gender-based violence suffered by members of their communities, as well as capturing more joyful, positive moments and advocating for change.

Faces and Phases (2006–) is a collective visual archive, featuring more than 600 portraits of Black lesbians, transgender and gender non-conforming people in different stages of their lives, while *Brave Beauties* (2014–) is a series of portraits of trans women, gender non-conforming and non-binary people in the guise of cover shoots for fashion magazines. As well as capturing the lives of others, in 2012 Muholi began an ongoing series of self-portraits taken in different cities around the world, *Somnyama Ngonyama (Hail the Dark Lioness). Sebenzile, Parktown,* is one of these, which was made into wallpaper for the 22nd Biennale of Sydney (2020). The striking, beautiful, powerful images of Muholi in various costumes and characters, reference traditions of art, moments of political history and conventions of self-portraiture and fashion photography. They draw you in to have a closer look at, and think about, moments of pain, resistance, defiance and transformation.

As Muholi explains, 'It is important to mark, map and preserve our mo(ve)ments through visual histories for reference and posterity so that future generations will note that we were here.'[61] Muholi's extraordinary body of work does just that.

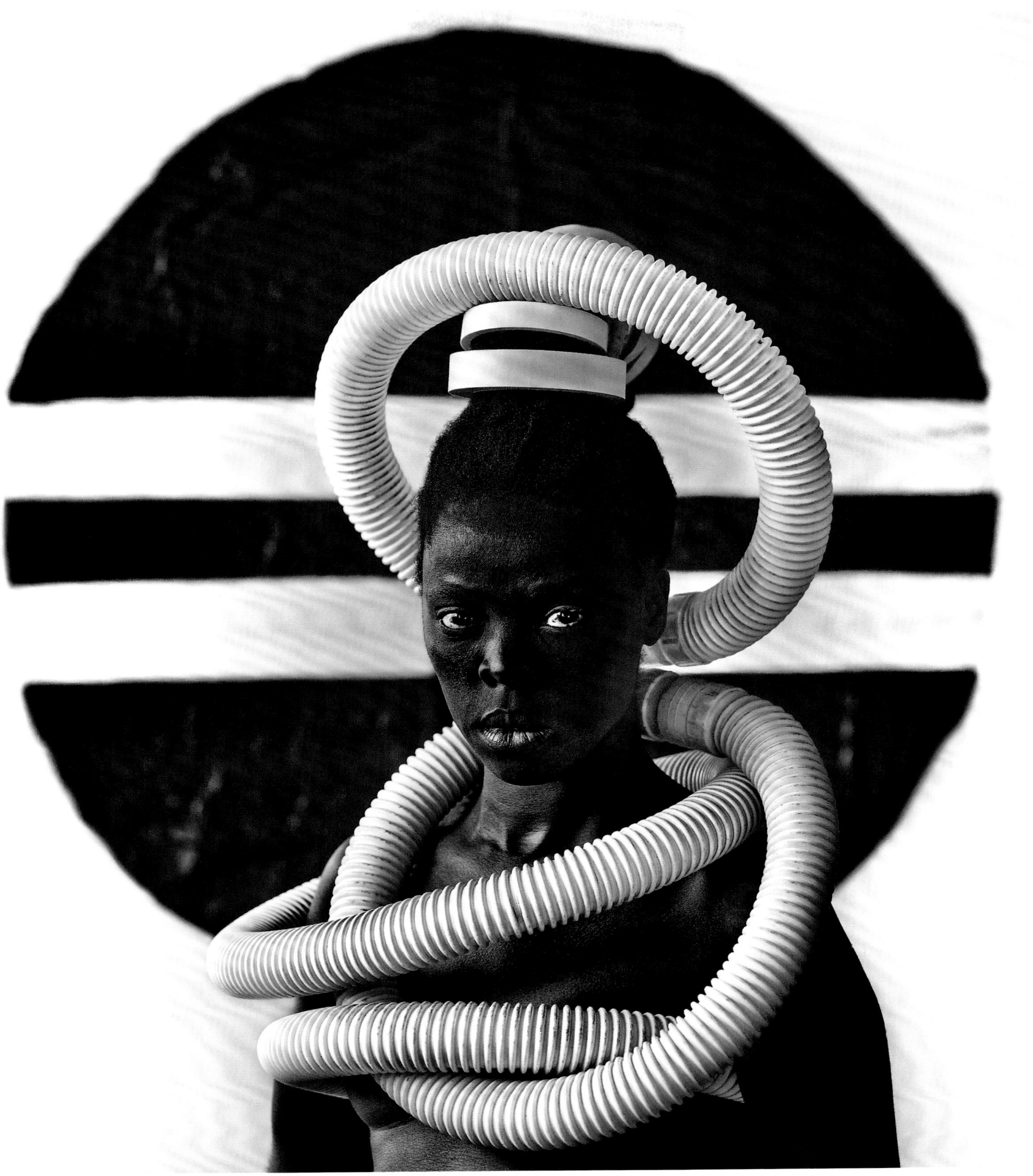

THE ADVENTURESS CLUB, EST. 1922 _2016_

Toyin Ojih Odutola is known for her multi-layered compositions, in which she explores many of the big issues of the 21st century: race, identity, migration, class, queer history and colonialism. Her visual storytelling of the lives of imagined people is set in scenes and narratives that seem familiar and plausible enough to invite closer examination. They posit whole new worlds and encourage the viewer to consider these alternatives; to wonder 'what if' and 'if only'. The scenes are rendered in her distinctive textured marks, in a sumptuous style influenced by Japanese prints (p. 60), comics and the fashionable portraiture of artists such as John Singer Sargent (p. 88) and Barkley L. Hendricks (p. 162).

Ojih Odutola's representation of women throughout is overwhelmingly positive – and matter of fact. *The Adventuress Club, est. 1922* presents us with four striking, well-dressed women, not cowed or weighed down by life, but in charge of it. They appear confident, stylish and at ease with themselves and the world. Travel for them is not displacement, but adventure and excitement, as it should be.

The portrait is part of an epic body of work 'documenting' the imagined lives of two fictional aristocratic Nigerian families united by the same-sex marriage of their sons. 'Adventuress' was a euphemism for 'lesbian' in the early 20th century in America and the UK. Ojih Odutola used it for the title as a nod to the way that 'unmarried/unattached, childless women are suspiciously viewed in societies, not solely in Nigeria, but globally as well.'[59] Ojih Odutola's imaginary Nigeria is one where colonialism and the transatlantic slave trade are not aspects of its past, and the Same Sex Marriage (Prohibition) Act 2013 is not a part of its present. Misogyny and patriarchy are also refreshingly absent.[60]

Ojih Odutola provides us with an image of the kind of women we can all hope to be when we grow up – or at least hang out with: strong, intelligent, adventurous, interesting, attractive, wealthy, beautifully dressed and in charge of their own destiny. What if? If only? And especially – why not?

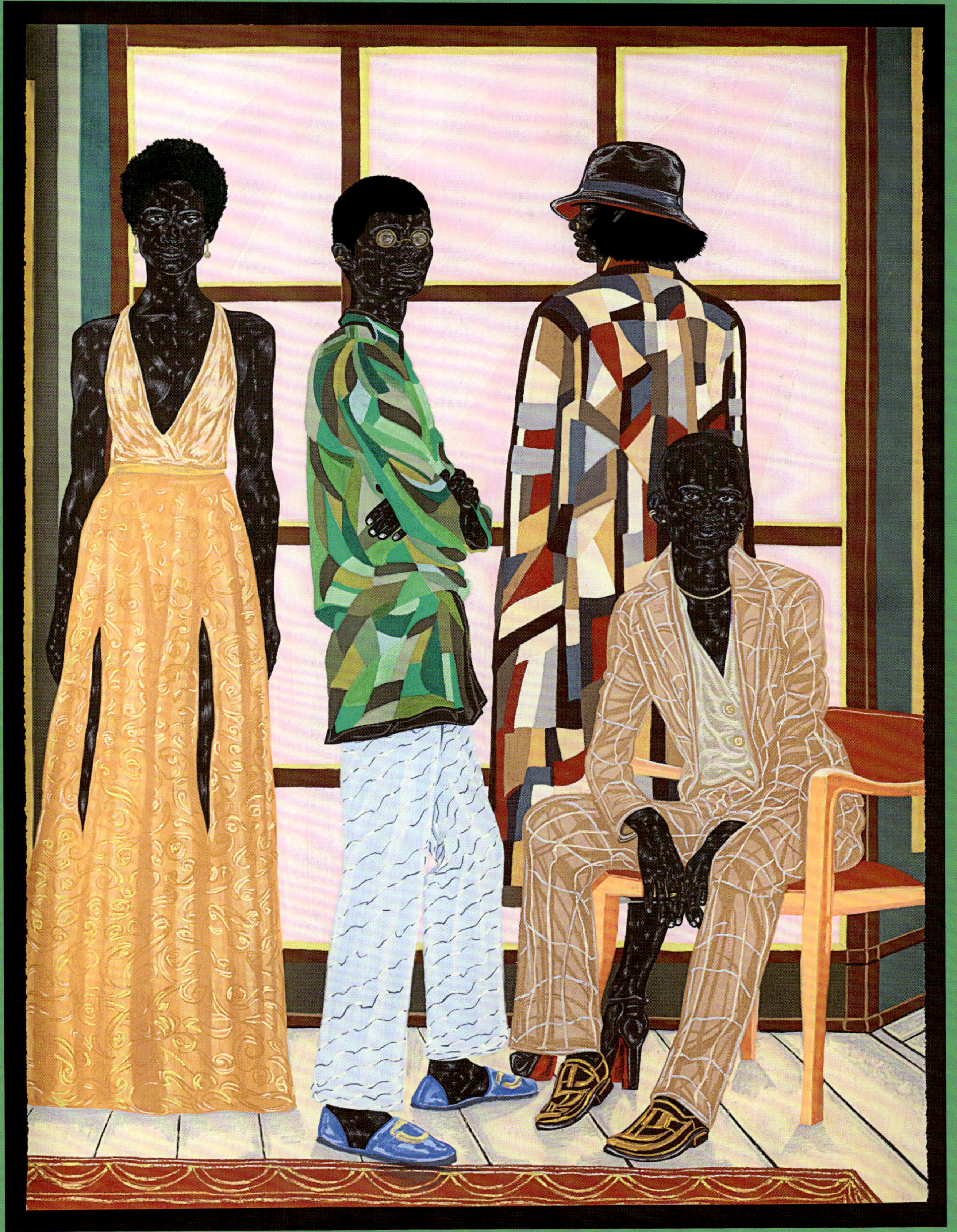

Yuki Kihara
(Sāmoan/Aotearoa New Zealand, b. 1975)

NAFEA E TE FA'AIPOIPO? WHEN WILL YOU MARRY?
(After Gauguin) <u>2020</u>

Yuki Kihara is an interdisciplinary artist who lives and works in Sāmoa. Her body of work addresses aspects of Pacific colonial history, gender identity and gender and racial stereotypes. In Sāmoa, gender classification is based on gender identity and spirituality rather than biological sex. There are four recognized cultural genders: female, male, fa'afafine ('in the manner of a woman') and fa'afatama ('in the manner of a man').

In *Paradise Camp*, Kihara (herself a fa'afafine) cast fa'afafine and fa'afatama as the main subjects in 12 photographs, shot on location at Upolu Island, Sāmoa. Many of the images engage directly with paintings by Paul Gauguin, recasting his exoticized fantasy vision with real people from the Pacific Islands as in this reimagining of the French artist's painting, *Nafea faa ipoipo? (When Will you Marry?)* (p. 94). Using familiar images from Gauguin's paintings as a starting point helps to draw the viewer in to have a closer look and see real Pasifika people. It also furthers conversations about whether or not Gauguin was actually painting Indigenous third-gender people at the time.

Paradise Camp was shown at the 59th Venice Biennale in 2022, and Kihara was the first Pasifika, first Asian and first fa'afafine to represent New Zealand. Presenting the fa'afafine vision of paradise on this international stage allowed her to challenge stereotypes and make her community visible, so they become part of our shared visual vocabulary. *Paradise Camp* imagines a world outside the binary gender system of most Western societies, a paradise that is inclusive and diverse, where one can be oneself without fear or discrimination. As Kihara explains, the aim of her work is to 'interrogate the Western representation of people in the Pacific, and specifically Sāmoa, and I'm hoping that it also gives licence for people to be their own self and to live a meaningful life that is authentic to them.'[62]

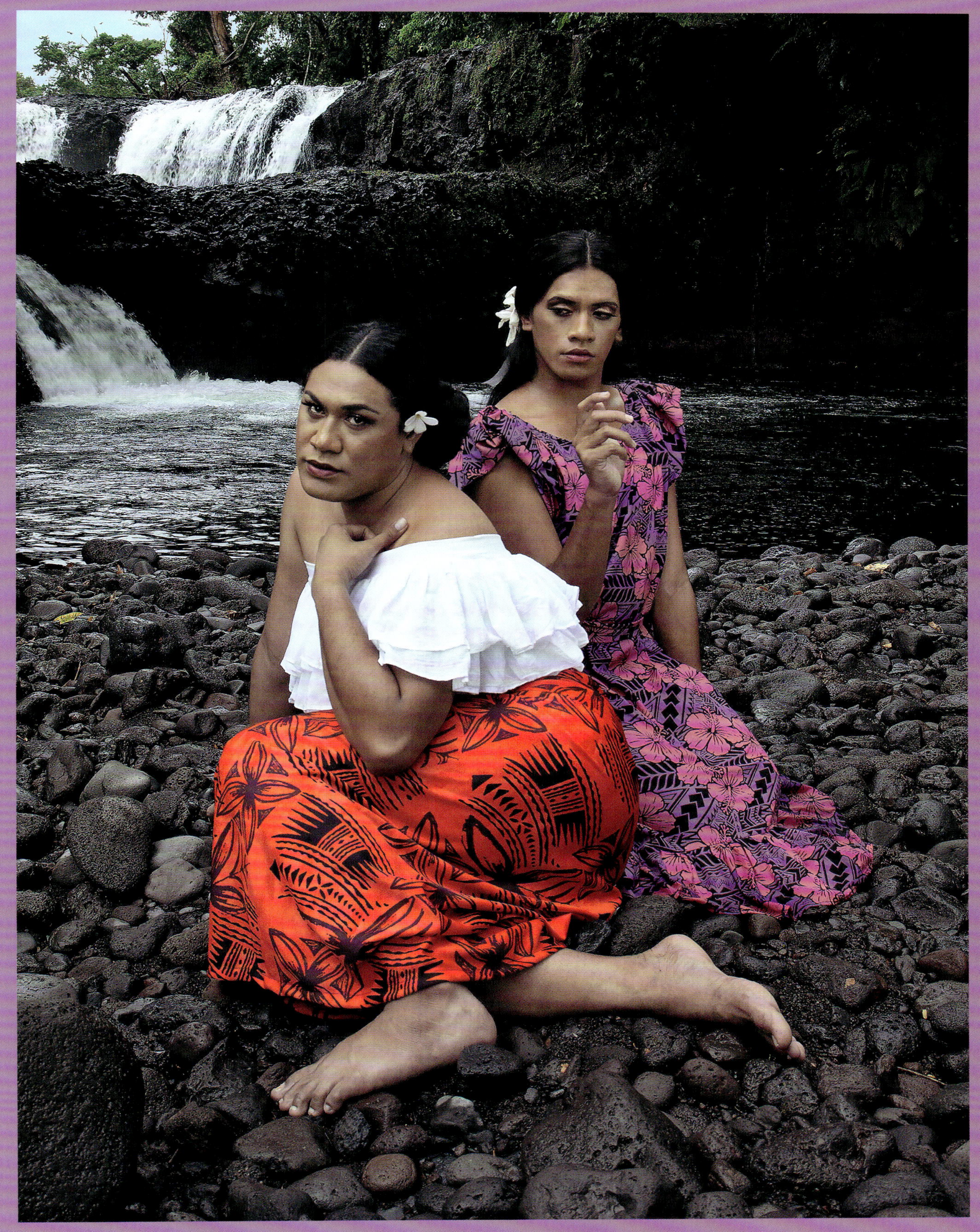

Hayv Kahraman
(Iraqi-Swedish, b. 1981)

SNAKES *2021*

The female bodies that Hayv Kahraman depicts in her highly stylized, seductive, decorative paintings are those of refugee and diasporic women. Her semi-autobiographical work is informed by her Iraqi/Kurdish heritage and experiences as a refugee in Sweden, where she lived as a teenager, and then as an immigrant in the USA where she settled as an adult.

The genesis of the bodies that populate her work is her own. She started from photographs of herself to bring forth a troupe of fierce, strong, athletic women taking on racial and gender stereotypes and investigating the effects of displacement and dislocation from forced migration. Weaving together aspects of Middle Eastern aesthetics and Western traditions of art with her own personal experiences and research, she creates challenging, often violent, disturbing images of naked and semi-naked women that both attract and horrify.

While an erotic reading of a pyramid of exotic, bikini-clad, athletic women cavorting with snakes in front of a ziggurat[63] made of Kurdish textiles needs no decoding, other possible associations and readings suggest themselves as well. Instead of (or in addition to) seeing the snakes as symbols of evil, temptation, lust and so on, we could see them as a reference to the goddess Medusa, symbolizing matriarchy and female power, protection and wisdom.[64]

Alternatively, we might look to other cultures and times when snakes have been used to represent fertility and regeneration (shedding their skins to reveal new ones) and admired or worshipped for their ability to survive on earth and in the water. The strength to reinvent yourself and adapt to new surroundings is something you would certainly wish for as a refugee or migrant.

Even if you don't know Kahraman's backstory or intentions, you can still see her 'army of fierce women' as cheerleaders for 'girl power'. Her women are not scared of the snakes, but in control of them – the swirling tower of bodies and snakes a celebration of the powerful female body and sisterhood.

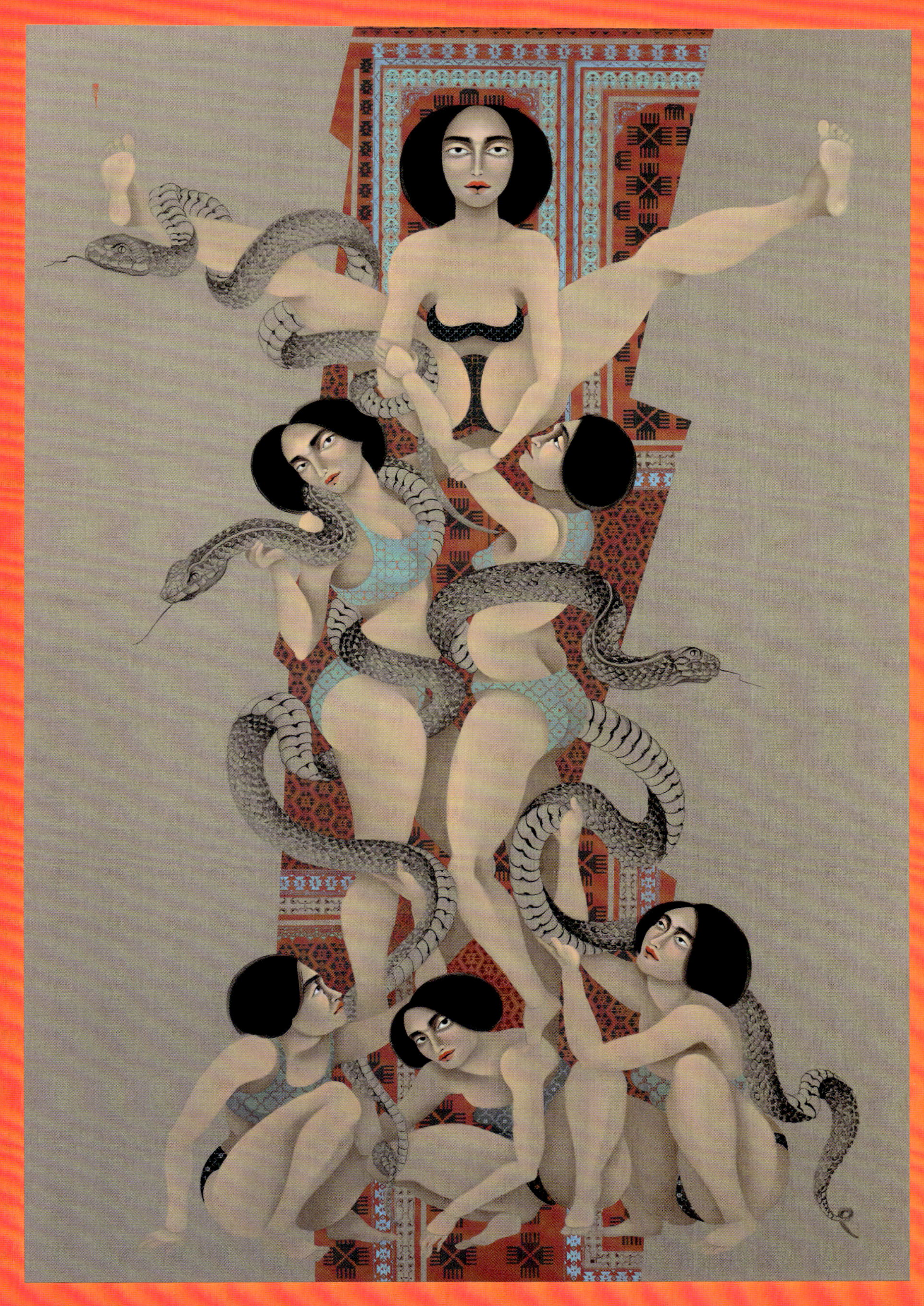

Tracey Emin
(British, b. 1963)

THE MOTHER <u>*2022*</u>

The Mother, by British artist Tracey Emin, is a nine metre (29 1/2 foot) high bronze sculpture of an ageing naked woman kneeling in a field of wildflowers. It is displayed in Oslo, Norway. Norwegian Expressionist artist Edvard Munch (p. 100) is Emin's favourite artist, so she was particularly thrilled to win the international competition to create a public artwork to sit next to the new MUNCH museum. Emin explained her idea: 'Munch's mother died when he was very young. So I want to give him a mother.'[65]

Like Munch, Emin is known for her raw, moving, emotional art made from the stuff of real life, usually her own. This piece is no exception, as the sculpture is a loving depiction of her own mother in old age: 'It's not a beautiful young woman, it's my mum. It's a figure of a woman of about 80. But it doesn't matter about the age, it's a metaphor for the universal mother that looks after us all, wherever she is. Haven't you ever loved someone who is old?'[66]

While public monuments have traditionally commemorated political and military events, *The Mother* is simultaneously heroic and intimate, a tender ode to motherhood and to the ageing female body. It has not been polished smooth but instead retains the feel of the handmade clay model, conveying the sense of a body actually lived in, rather than an idealized representation of one. Despite its monumental size, this loving homage to Emin's mother and favourite artist is imbued with the feel of the artist's touch. With this, the artist has made both the portrayal of the female nude and the tradition of heroic colossal sculptures as symbols of places her own.

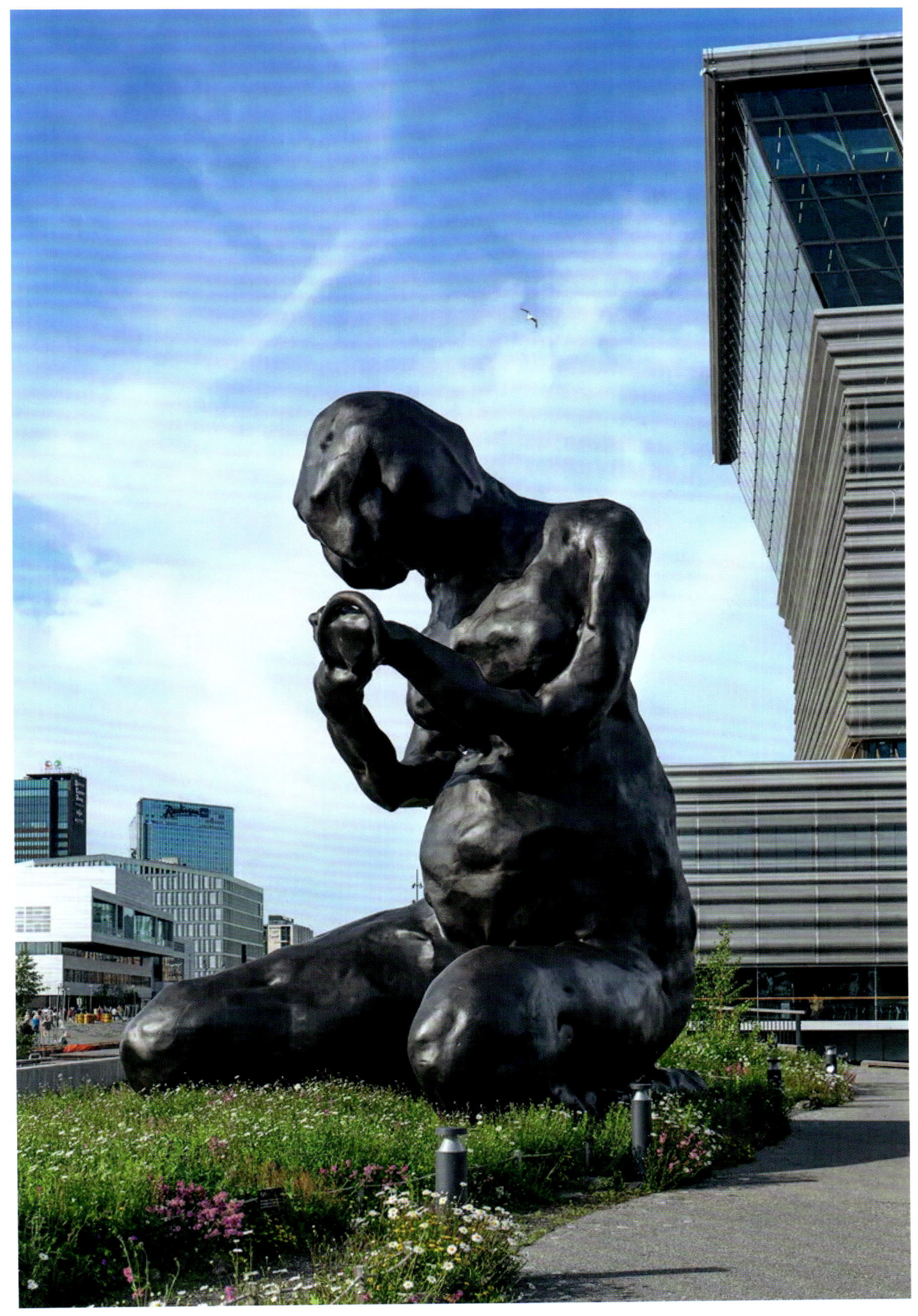

Rose B. Simpson
(American, Santa Clara Pueblo, b. 1983)

COUNTERCULTURE

2022

Rose B. Simpson is a woman on a mission: to help us love ourselves, treat each other with compassion, respect and kindness, and to appreciate and cherish the natural world. The art that she creates – sculptures, ceramics, installations, performances – are manifestations of her engagement with various aspects of the human condition, be it personal growth and development, the challenges and responsibilities of parenthood, or how to be – and be better – in this post-colonial, post-apocalyptic world.[67]

Her work is informed by her personal experiences as a Native American woman and the traumas that haunt her community, such as the legacy of the Indian Boarding School era of 1860–1978 and the ongoing crisis of MMIW (Missing and Murdered Indigenous Women). However, it is also able to speak of the trials and tribulations that we all face, and the artist uses the human form – female or androgynous – so that anyone can identify with the struggles or emotions that her figures are expressing. As she wants to create an empathic response in every viewer, her figures are necessarily abstract enough to be open and inclusive, yet at the same time realistic enough to allow for identification.

Counterculture is a site-specific installation of 12 female humanoid characters, each about 3 metres (10 feet) tall. It was installed in Williamstown, Massachusetts, on the ancestral homelands of the Stockbridge-Munsee Band of Mohicans, who were forcibly relocated to Wisconsin. This band of warrior women of different hues (all earth tones, derived from Mother Earth) looks out over the land – a land that is beautiful, but scarred by the past.

The figures, which Simpson calls 'spirits', are adorned with necklaces of clay beads, which are signs of empowerment and femininity, strength and beauty. The mask-like faces have holes for eyes that allow the light to shine through, giving them an otherworldly appearance

'This band of warrior women of different hues looks out over the land – a land that is beautiful, but scarred by the past'

and making them seem alive; the spirits are definitely watching, witnessing man's inhumanity to man over the years, as well as man's destruction of the planet's natural resources. From this awareness, this testimony, the stern women of _Counterculture_ embody a call for serious conversations to be had about bringing change.

After the initial installation in Massachusetts, figures from _Counterculture_ travelled around the USA, surveying other landscapes wrested from Indigenous Peoples. In 2024, a number of the figures took up residence at the Freedom Monument Sculpture Park in Montgomery, Alabama. There, these 'empowered vessels', these female bodies, honour the Indigenous Peoples forcibly removed from the land, those forcibly enslaved and brought to it, and the amazing resilience of the human spirit. These watchful guardians are there to make sure that we acknowledge historical traumas and figure out how to help everyone heal, enabling humankind not just to survive but to thrive.

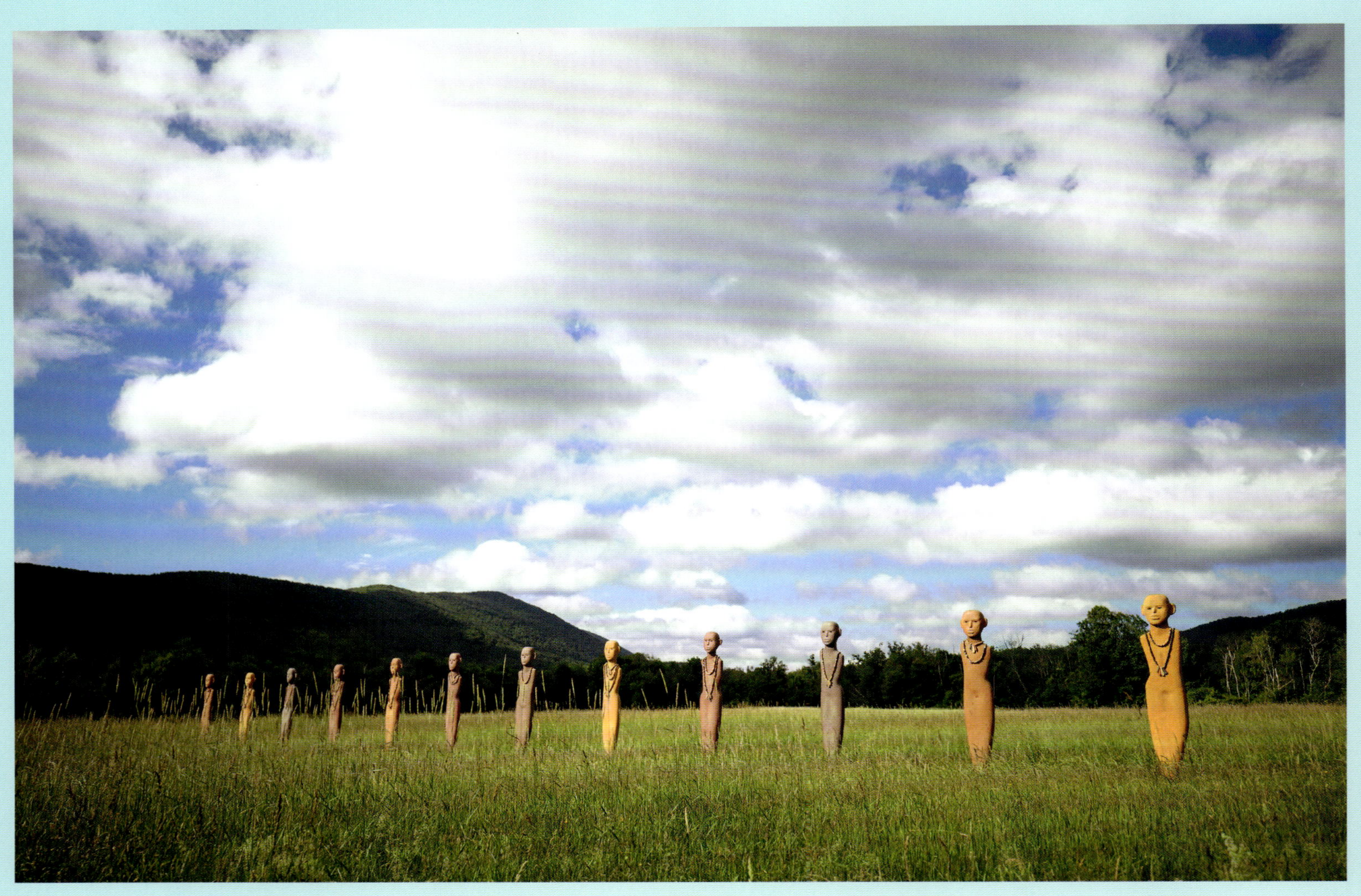

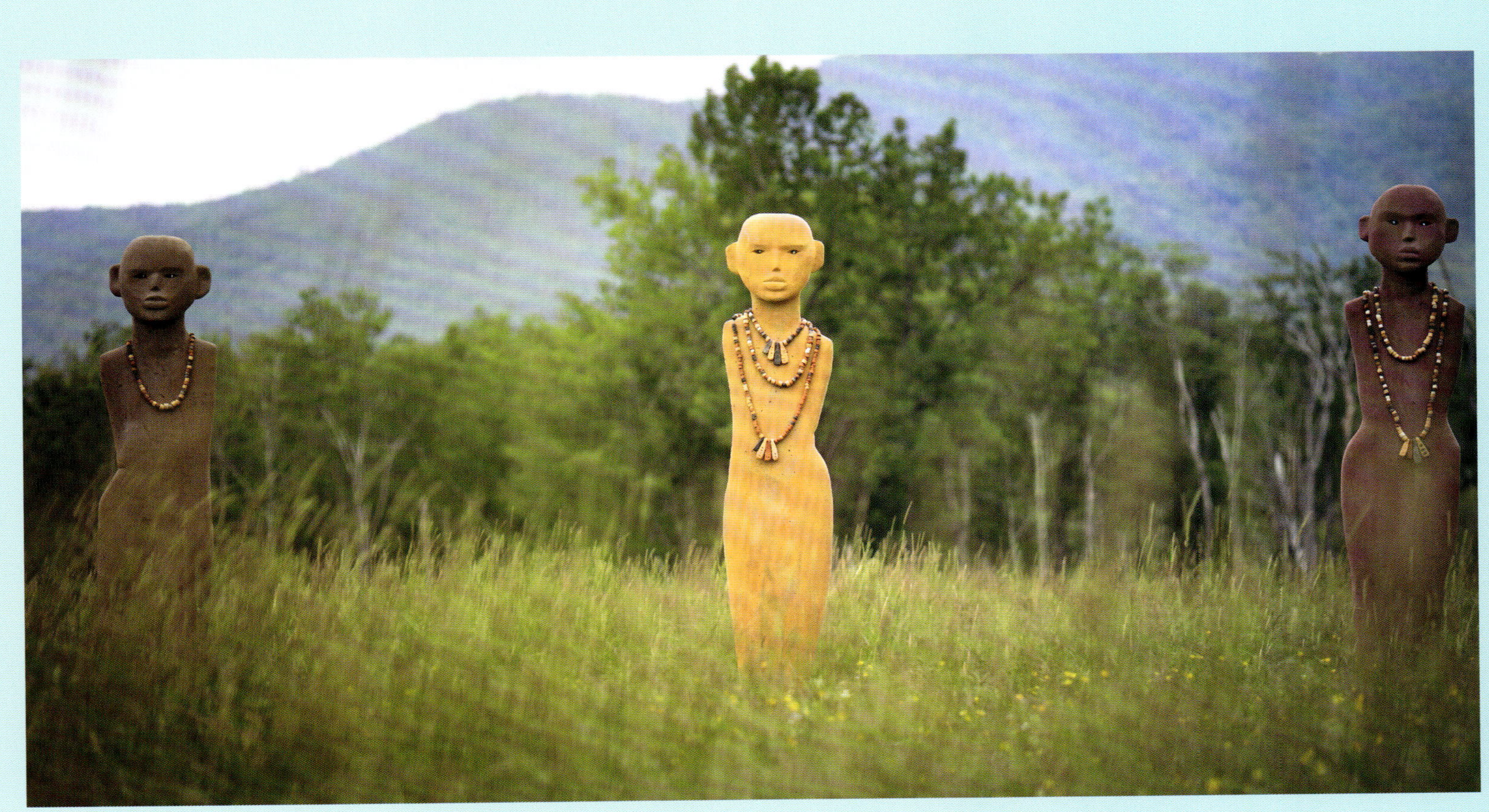

THE THREE GRACES *2023*

Kehinde Wiley is famous for his 2018 commissioned portrait of former US President Barack Obama and his large-scale portraits of contemporary urban people of colour in the guise of Old Master paintings. His 21st-century models are found on the streets of the city, in a process he calls 'street casting', and are depicted wearing their own clothes. The young Black and Brown men and women are rendered in a photorealistic mode and adopt the exaggerated poses of the historical white subjects they are mimicking from art history.

Instead of the trappings of wealth and power used in grand society portraiture, Wiley places his subjects against highly decorative backgrounds in a style that has become unmistakably his own. Through a careful study of art history, Wiley uses the tools of painting to elevate and celebrate ordinary people who would not necessarily find themselves gracing the walls of a museum. Wiley wants the viewer to recognize – or at least have a feel for – the paintings he is referencing, in order to take on their aura and claim it for his young people of colour.

In this instance, Wiley gave us his *The Three Graces*, which echoes the pose and setting of the goddesses in Rubens's famous Baroque painting (p. 38). However, the sassy, beautiful Black women in Wiley's painting are most definitely real women of the 21st century and not mythological figures from the artist's imagination. As in the Rubens, the three women appear to be dancing and are integrated with their lush floral background. But where the goddesses in the Rubens are looking at each other, these young women look directly out at us and hold our gaze, as if we have interrupted them. The figures are slightly larger than life and have a commanding presence. The subjects of the painting – Coumba, Mariama and Rokhaya – are clothed and defiant in this welcome update on feminine beauty, which celebrates strong Black women and places them in a conversation with the idealized female bodies of art history.

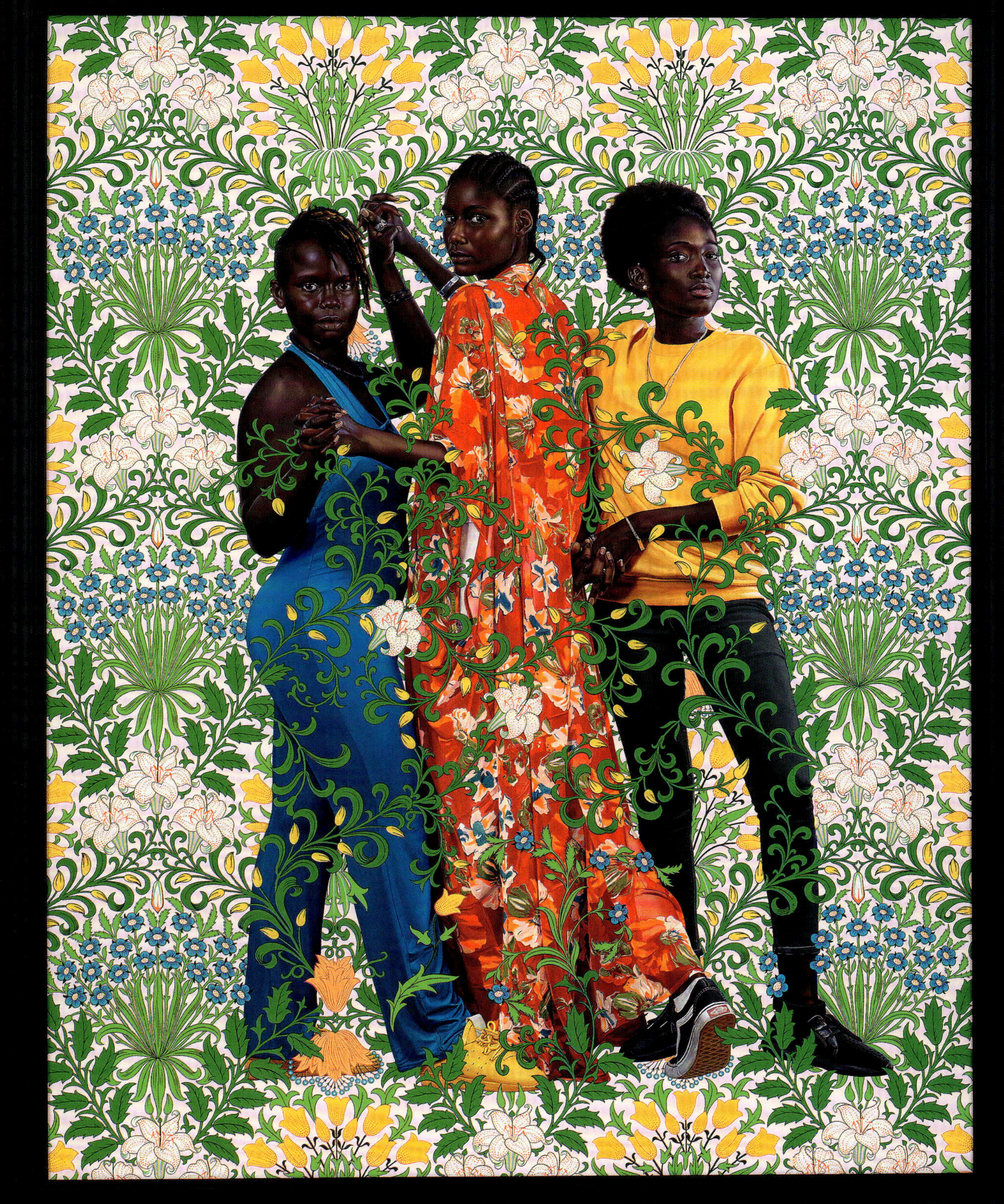

Lorna Simpson
(American, b. 1960)

BLUE TULIP *2023*

Lorna Simpson came to prominence in the early 1990s with her pioneering conceptual photographic works that raise questions about the nature of representation and the way notions of gender, identity and race are constructed. Since then, her practice has expanded to use whatever means necessary – photography, collage, video, installation, sculpture or painting – to investigate how images function in the production of meaning and to examine the ways that gender and culture shape our lives, our identities and desires.

In multi-layered, thought-provoking, eloquent works, she uses the figure – often women – to consider life in America, past and present. Much of her investigation focuses on the historical implications of the iconography of Black culture in the USA and considers how the repetition of images in our everyday lives creates and reinforces stereotypes. She often uses cuttings of glamorous Black women from old *Ebony* and *Jet* magazines as source material and as a catalyst to think about issues of visibility and representation.[68]

In *Blue Tulip*, from Simpson's *Special Characters* series (2019–), a woman has been 'found' in – and constructed from – fashion and wig advertisements from vintage *Ebony* magazines. The black frame gives the 'portrait' the feel of a publicity headshot, film still or negative, and the gorgeous blue-black ink wash lends it a hazy feel, like looking back through the mists of time.

This composite portrait questions the traditions of portraiture and the formation of 'types' of characters – stock types and stereotypes – that arise through the repetition of certain images in our everyday lives. *Blue Tulip* not only adds to our visual image bank of beautiful young American women of the 1950s and 1960s, but the large format of the *Special Characters* series (prints are 170 x 127 cm/67 x 50 in) tells us that Simpson is not going to allow these Black women to be erased from American history.

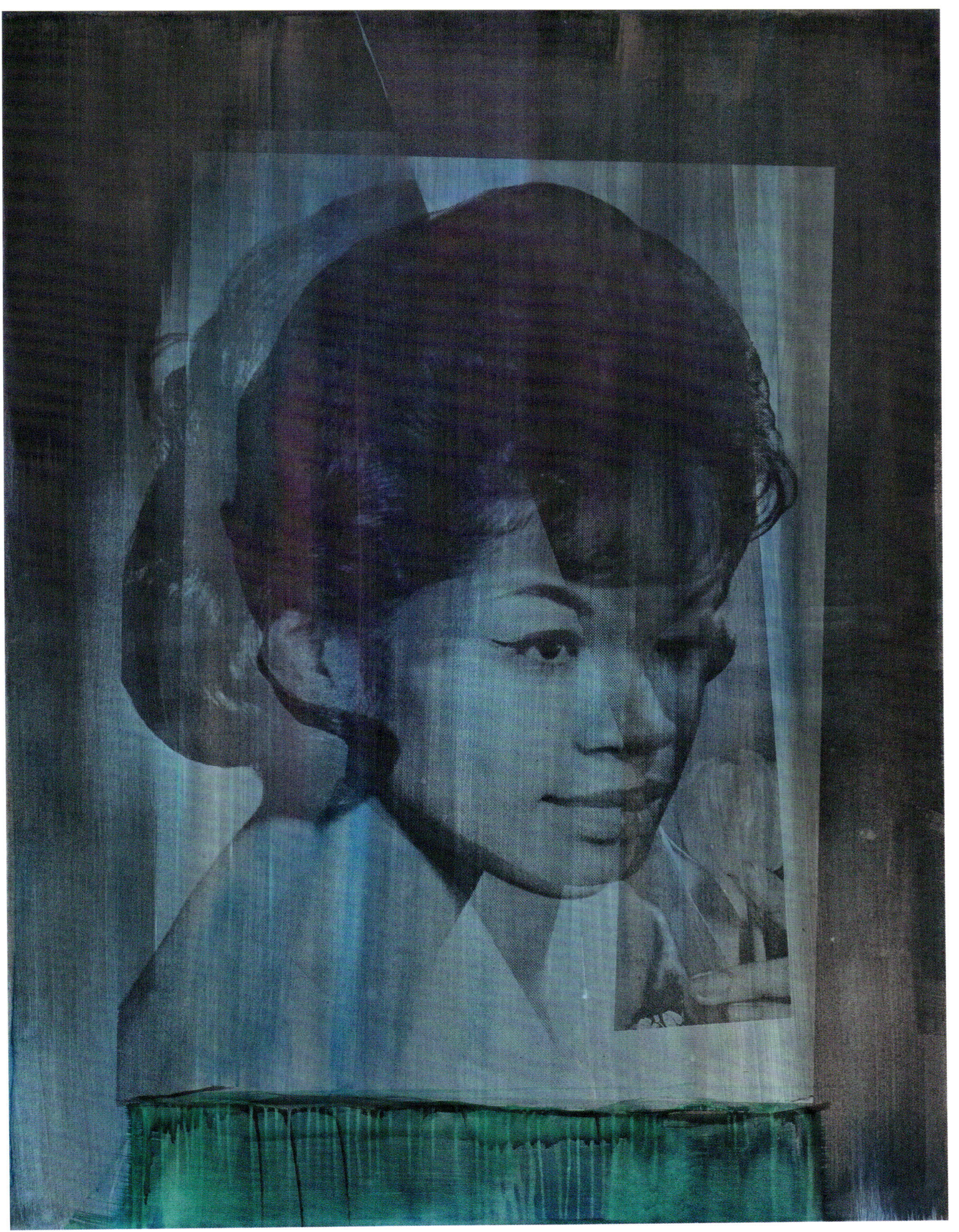

SOMOS
(Standing On My Own Shoulders) <u>2024</u>

Julie Rrap has been addressing the female body and its representation in art and culture since the 1970s through body art, performance, photography, video, painting, installation and sculpture. She often uses her own body as the vehicle to explore the representation of women, using humour and subterfuge to undermine stereotypes and confront the constraints and omissions of history.

Now, after 40 years of feminist art practice, she has turned her attention to the hunt for images of older women's bodies in Western art history. 'Where are the sculptures, where are the paintings? Of course, you can find a few poor old wretches, crones, or witches, but that's about it! I'm definitely interested in pushing against a clichéd view of women's bodies within art.'[69]

In contrast to the abundance of young female bodies in art and culture, there is a distinct lack of images of older women. Rrap's answer to this is *SOMOS (Standing On My Own Shoulders)*, two life-size casts of her own body at the age of 73, one supporting the other. The work is in bronze, defiantly declaring the ageing female body as a worthy subject for heroic monumental sculpture.

The title of the work reflects the doubling of her body in the sculpture and her role as a leading feminist artist in Australia. 'I was thinking about the usual problem of women artists and their lack of historical visibility and about standing on the shoulders of giants, and then I wondered, "Whose shoulders do I stand on?" In a kind of jokey way, I realized I have to stand on my own shoulders.'[70]

Along with Tracey Emin's monumental sculpture on the other side of the world (p. 210), Rrap's sculpture begins to fill the void. As she has pointed out: 'The human body has been used in art since the beginning of time. My intervention is to play around and challenge fixed ideas and conventions about imaging the body, and to renegotiate how we might look at the female body, particularly the older female body.'[71]

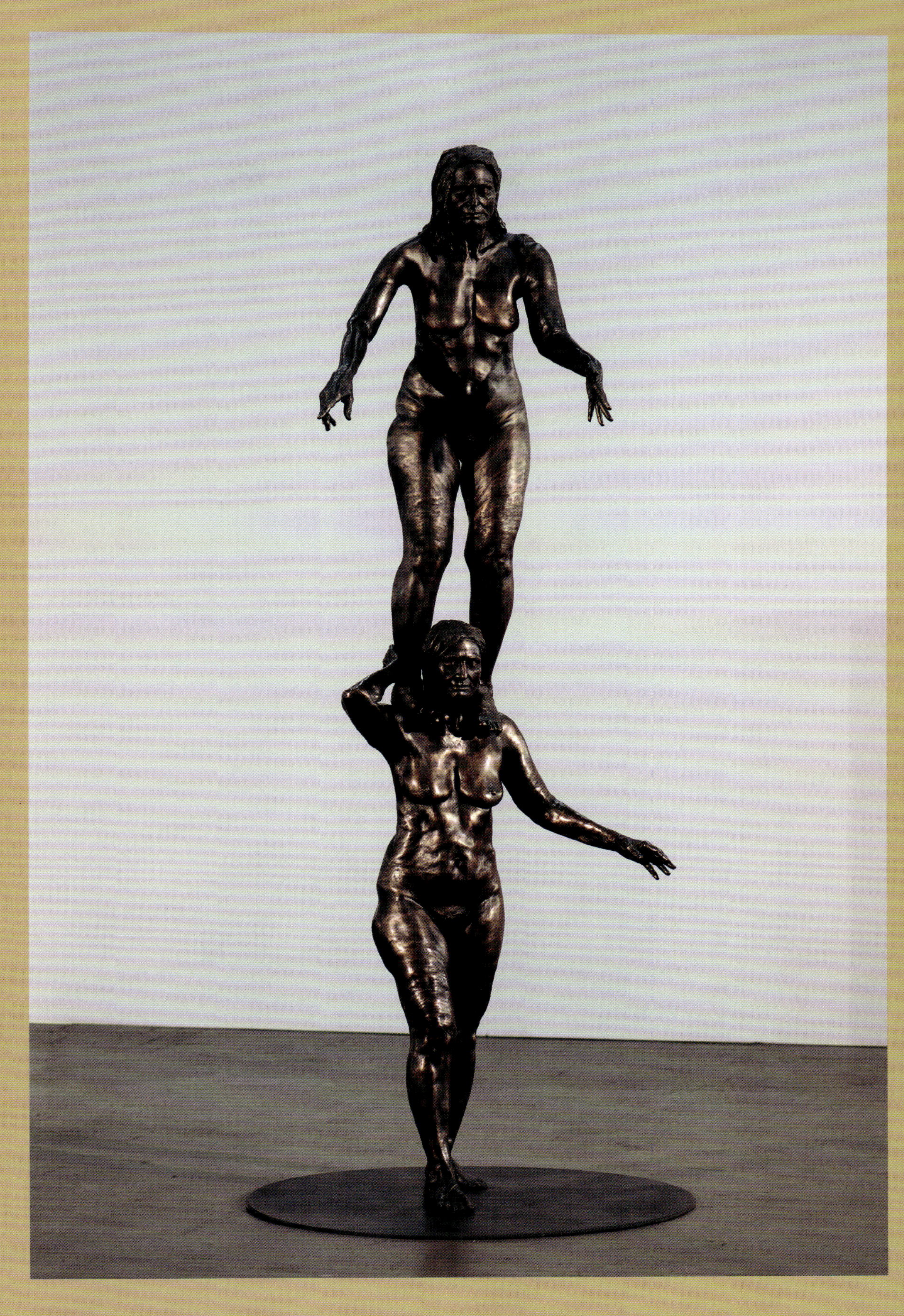

NOTES

1 Giorgio Vasari, *Lives of the Artists* (second edition, 1568), translated by George Bull (1965), pp. 266–67.

-

2 See Jill Burke, *How to be a Renaissance Woman* (2023), pp.131–43 and Catherine McCormack, *Women in the Picture* (2021), pp. 208–13 for discussions about the *Malleus Maleficarum*. Also, H. Diane Russell, *Eva/Ave: Woman in Renaissance and Baroque Prints* (1990), for more about the portrayals of women during the period.

-

3 See Jill Burke, *How to be a Renaissance Woman: The Untold History of Beauty & Female Creativity*, 2023, for more about Marinello's book. See pp. 139–40 for Marinello on body hair and pp. 186–87 for Marinello on head hair.

-

4 Burke discusses *A pleasant new work which teaches how to make various perfumed compositions to make every woman beautiful… titled Venustà* (1526) on pp. 6–8 of *How to be a Renaissance Woman: The Untold History of Beauty & Female Creativity*, 2023.

-

5 Giorgio Vasari, *The Lives of the Most Excellent Painters, Sculptors, and Architects*, second edition, 1568.

-

6 Renaissance female beauty standards were described in detail by Giovanni Marinello in *The Ornaments of Ladies*, 1562. See Jill Burke, *How to be a Renaissance Woman: The Untold History of Beauty & Female Creativity*, 2023, for more on Marinello's book.

7 For an in-depth analysis of the sitter's dress and accessories, see Kenne Libes, '1583/5 – *Annibale Carracci, Portrait of a Woman Holding a Clock*', *Fashion History Timeline*, 26 June 2020. https://fashionhistory.fitnyc.edu/1583-5-carracci-african-woman-clock/

Another interesting discussion about the portrait is by Jonathan M. Square, 'A portrait that survives the test of time', Nicholas Hall Art, 25 June 2021. https://www.nicholashall.art/journal/a-portrait-that-survives-the-test-of-time/

See also *Revealing the African Presence in Renaissance Europe*, edited by Joaneath Spicer, The Walters Art Museum, 2012. https://thewalters.org/wp-content/uploads/revealing-the-african-presence-in-renaissance-europe.pdf

-

8 In his book *Baroque*, 1977, John Rupert Martin notes that the first observation of the derivation of the pose of Velázquez's Venus from the Borghese Hermaphrodite was by C. Justi in *Diego Velázquez und sein Jahrhundert*, 1888, p. 368. (In Martin, note 219, p. 356.)

-

9 Caroline Vout, Professor of Classics, University of Cambridge in the exhibition and accompanying pamphlet, 'The Cult of Beauty', Wellcome Collection, London, 26 October 2023–28 April 2024.

-

10 The Cabinet Reynst was an extensive private collection of art and antiquities, which was set up as a 'museum' in Amsterdam, Netherlands, and opened to visitors. An album was made containing engravings of some of its highlights, which included Falck's engraving of Strozzi's painting.

11 See Rosenau's book reprinted in Griselda Pollock, *Woman in Art: Helen Rosenau's 'Little Book'* of 1944, 2023, p. 146. The painting can be seen in its original home, as the alms house is now the Frans Hals Museum in Haarlem, Netherlands.

12 In folklore, the horse and the goblin represent evil spirits who torture sleepers and may even have sex with sleeping women. See Dr Noelle Paulson, 'Henry Fuseli, The Nightmare', Smarthistory, 9 August, 2015. https://smarthistory.org/henry-fuseli-the-nightmare/

13 Georgiana's best friend moved in with her and her husband and they ended up having intense relationships with each other.

14 For more see:
James Smalls, 'Slavery is a Woman: "Race", Gender, and Visuality in Marie Benoist's *Portrait d'une négresse* (1800)', *Nineteenth-Century Art Worldwide* volume 3, issue 1, Spring 2004. www.19thc-artworldwide.org/spring04/slavery-is-a-woman-race-gender-and-visuality-in-marie-benoists-portrait-dune-negresse-1800
Dr Susan Waller, 'Marie-Guillemine Benoist, Portrait of Madeleine,' Smarthistory, 26 September, 2018. https://smarthistory.org/benoist-portrait/

15 For more see: Martina Droth and Michael Hatt, '*The Greek Slave* by Hiram Powers: A Transatlantic Object', *Nineteenth-Century Art Worldwide* 15, no. 2 (Summer 2016). www.19thc-artworldwide.org/summer16/droth-hatt-intro-to-the-greek-slave-by-hiram-powers-a-transatlantic-object

16 For more see: Martina Droth and Michael Hatt, '*The Greek Slave* by Hiram Powers: A Transatlantic Object', *Nineteenth-Century Art Worldwide* 15, no. 2 (Summer 2016). www.19thc-artworldwide.org/summer16/droth-hatt-intro-to-the-greek-slave-by-hiram-powers-a-transatlantic-object

17 T. J. Clark, *The Painting of Modern Life: Paris in the Art of Manet and His Followers*, 1984, p. 86 and pp. 284–5, no. 23.

18 J.S. Ingram, *The Centennial Exposition, Described And Illustrated: Being a Concise And Graphic Description of This Grand Enterprise, Commemorative of the First Centennary [!] of American Independence ...* Philadelphia: Hubbard Bros, 1876.

19 The Gibson Girl was the feminine ideal of the late 19th and early 20th century as personified in the illustrations of American artist Charles Dana Gibson in various periodicals of the day. She was young, smart, athletic, upper-middle or upper class, liberated and progressive. Physically, she was beautiful, tall and slender, with an hourglass figure. She often had a haughty expression and a messy updo.

20 John Singer Sargent's letter to Edward 'Ned' Robinson, then Director of the Metropolitan Museum of Art, dated January 8, 1916. Image and transcript of letter available at: 'From the Archives: How Madame X Came to the Met', by Stephanie L. Herdrich, 8 January, 2016. https://www.metmuseum.org/articles/how-madame-x-came-to-the-met

21 See Diane Kelder, *The Great Book of French Impressionism*, 1980, p. 287.

22 Quoted in George Heard Hamilton, *Painting and Sculpture in Europe 1880–1940*, 1989, pp. 23–24.

23 The liberty cap – a soft, conical hat with the top curled forward – became a symbol of liberty and freedom from oppression during the American and French Revolutions of the 18th century, used to show allegiance to the republican cause. Derived from the hats worn by emancipated slaves in ancient Rome, it was also revived as a symbol of freedom from slavery during the abolitionist movements of the 18th and 19th centuries.

24 Quoted in Amy Dempsey, *Styles, Schools & Movements: The Essential Encyclopaedic Guide to Modern Art*, second edition, London: Thames & Hudson, 2010, p. 72.

25 Women in Germany were granted the right to vote in 1919 under the new democratic Weimar Republic (1918–1933), established after Germany's defeat in World War I. The stereotype of the liberated, progressive, urban 'New Woman' of the Weimar Republic was a young woman with an athletic build, wearing masculine-tailored clothing or short skirts, sporting a short bob and smoking, free to pursue a career and remain unmarried and childless, if she so desired.

26 For more see: Maude Lavin, *Cut with the Kitchen Knife: the Weimar Photomontages of Hannah Höch*, New Haven & London: Yale University Press, 1993.

27 Kiki de Montparnasse was the nickname of French artist, singer, artist's model and celebrity, Alice Prin (1901–1953). The embodiment of bohemian Paris, Kiki was Man Ray's lover and muse from 1921–1929.

28 Quoted on website: https://www.delempicka. org/tamaras-life/

29 Quoted in Katy Hessel, *The Story of Art Without Men*, 2022, p. 153.

30 Quoted in Katy Hessel, *The Story of Art Without Men*, 2022, p. 138.

31 Quoted in J.N. Sinha, 'Amrita's Village', *Frontline*, February 20, 2013. https://frontline. thehindu.com/arts-and-culture/amritas-village/ article4431504.ece

32 Dorothea Lange, 'The Assignment I'll Never Forget: Migrant Mother', *Popular Photography*, February 1960.

33 André Breton, *Surrealism and Painting*, translated from the French by Simon Watson Taylor, MacDonald & Co, 1972, p. 210.

34 Quoted in Desmond Morris, *The Lives of the Surrealists*, 2018, pp. 121–22.

35 Quoted in *Germaine Richier*, exhibition catalogue, Louisiana Museum of Modern Art, Humlebaek, Denmark, 1988, p. 28.

36 Quoted in Peter Selz, *New Images of Man*, exhibition catalogue, Museum of Modern Art, New York, 1959, p. 130.

37 Eve Arnold, introduction to *The Unretouched Woman*, Alfred A. Knopf, USA, 1976.

-

38 On the website of Archives Yves Klein (www.yvesklein.com) there are fantastic photographs from the performance, as well as a short film of it. There are also interviews with Elena Palumbo-Mosca, one of the models who took part in the performance-creation, and with Klein's widow, Rotraut Klein-Moquay, who took part in some of the anthropometries in Klein's studio. Both talk about how special it was to be involved.

-

39 4 May 1962: *The Construction of Boston* by Kenneth Koch, directed by Merce Cunningham at the Maidman Playhouse, 42nd Street, New York. With Robert Rauschenberg, Jean Tinguely, Niki de Saint Phalle, Frank Stella, Henry Geldzahler, Maxine Groffsky, Billy Klüver, Oyvind Fahlström, Viola Farber, Steve Paxton, and the Stewed Prunes (McIntyre Dixon and Richard Libertini). Produced by John Wulp. For more on the event see Amy J. Dempsey, *The Friendship of America and France: A New Internationalism*, 1961–1965, PhD thesis, Courtauld Institute of Art, University of London, 1999.

-

40 Odili Donald Odita, 'Conversation with Carolee Schneemann, Part II', 1997. https://plexus.org/connect/texts/interviews/texts/2.html

-

41 Carmen Tessier, 'Sachez tout sur le happening "art total" qui vient d'être découvert à Paris', *France-Soir*, 3 June 1964, quoted in Laurence Bertrand Dorleac, 'Tomorrow you'll all be artists: The art scene in France, 1960–73', *The Sixties: Britain and France, 1962–1973: The Utopian Years*, 1997, p. 43.

-

42 https://www.schneemannfoundation.org/artworks/meat-joy

-

43 Quoted in Jack Guy and Sharon Braithwaite, 'Naples gets new "Venus of the Rags" artwork after original destroyed by fire', CNN, 6 March 2024

-

44 Thelma Golden, Director of the Studio Museum in Harlem, mentions that Hendricks called the painting 'Our Madonna' in 'The Lives and Legacies of Barkley L. Hendricks', 5 December 2023. https://www.frick.org/interact/hendricks_lives_legacies

-

45 Dorothea Tanning, 'Dorothea Her Lights and Shadows (a scenario)', published in the exhibition catalogue, *Dorothea Tanning: 10 Recent Paintings and a Biography*, New York: Gimpel-Weitzenhoffer Gallery, 1979. https://www.dorotheatanning.org/images/Dorothea%20Tanning%20Her%20Lights%20 and%20Shadows.pdf

-

46 Christopher Masters in 'Dorothea Tanning obituary', *The Guardian*, 2 February, 2012: 'Her upbringing in a milieu of eerie, bourgeois calm clearly fed into her art.' https://www.theguardian.com/artanddesign/2012/feb/02/dorothea-tanning-obituary

-

47 Dorothea Tanning interviewed by Gaby Wood, 'Arts Interview: "I've Always Been Perverse"', *The Guardian*, 15 August, 2004, p. 7. https://www.theguardian.com/artanddesign/2004/aug/15/art.fiction

48 Dorothea Tanning, Journal 16 (unpublished), c. 1993, n.p., in the artist's archive, The Dorothea Tanning Foundation/The Destina Foundation, New York, quoted in the exhibition catalogue Dorothea Tanning, Tate Modern, London, 2019, p. 56.
-

49 From 'In Room 202' by Edgar Leslie, Bert Kalmar and Dave Harris (1919).
-

50 Janet A. Kaplan, "Deeper and Deeper: Interview with Marina Abramovic." *Art Journal*, vol. 58, no. 2, 1999, p. 7.
-

51 All quotes from 'Ana Mendieta, 1981, Unpublished statement', in John Perreault, 'Earth and Fire: Mendieta's Body of Work', in *Ana Mendieta: A Retrospective*, ed. Petra Barreras del Rio and Perreault (New York: New Museum of Contemporary Art, 1987), p. 10. The exhibition catalogue can be accessed here: https://d2b8urneelikat.cloudfront.net/media/collectiveaccess/images/9/5/8928_ca_object_representations_media_9558_original.pdf
-

52 All quotes from Beverly Hall Smith, 'Looking at the Masters: Graciela Iturbide', *The Talbot Spy*, 3 March 2022 https://talbotspy.org/looking-at-the-masters-graciela-iturbide/
-

53 All quotes from *Barbara Kruger in conversation with Hans Ulrich Obrist*, 2024. Printed in the exhibition guide accompanying 'Barbara Kruger: Thinking of ~~You~~. I Mean ~~Me~~. I Mean You' exhibition at Serpentine South Gallery, London, 1 February – 17 March 2024.
-

54 Jenny Saville quoted in Karen Hearn, *Portraying Pregnancy: from Holbein to Social Media*, 2020, p. 124.

55 All quotes from Lanre Bakare, 'Paula Rego calls US anti-abortion drive "grotesque"', *The Guardian*, 31 May 2019.
-

56 'Louise Bourgeois in Conversation with Christiane Meyer-Thoss', in Meyer-Thoss, *Louise Bourgeois: Designing for Free-Fall* (Zurich: Ammann Verlag, 1992), p. 123.
-

57 'Mari Katayama', *Tate Etc*, 8 September 2023, https://www.tate.org.uk/tate-etc/issue-59-autumn-2023/mari-katayama See also artist's statement, *bystander, 2016*: http://marikatayama.com
-

58 Katayama interviewed by Chris Campion, 'Punk prosthetics: the mesmerising art of living sculpture Mari Katayama', *The Guardian*, 6 March 2017.
-

59 Correspondence with the artist, September 2024.
-

60 For more about the project see: Toyin Ojih Odutola, *The UmuEze Amara Clan and the House of Obafemi*, 2021.
-

61 Zanele Muholi, 'Faces and Phases', artist statement to accompany exhibition at Brodie/Stevenson, Johannesburg, South Africa, 9 July – 8 August 2009, later published in book form as (*Zanele Muholi, Faces and Phases*, Munich: Prestel, 2010). Full statement here: http://archive.stevenson.info/exhibitions/muholi/facesphases.htm
-

62 For more, see *Paradise Camp by Yuki Kihara*, edited by Natalie King, 2022.

63 Ziggurats are pyramidical stepped tower temples built in ancient Mesopotamia (present-day Iraq).

-

64 See Catherine McCormack, *Women in the Picture*, 2021, pp. 175–186 for more about the changing Medusa myth and the symbolism of snakes.

-

65 Quoted in Jonathan Jones, 'How Tracey Emin is giving Munch the mother he never had', *The Guardian*, 2 January 2020.

-

66 Quoted in Anna McNay, 'Peeled From a Private Life: Tracey Emin's New Bronzes', *Sculpture Magazine*, 2 September 2021.

-

67 'Apocalyptic theory is about survivalism and the intensity of trauma,' Simpson explains … 'We think we're stuck in some sort of story, but maybe we're not. That post-apocalyptic theory is so much like the victimhood of colonization … So how do I change that story to: "Actually, no, we are surviving, we are thriving, we are beautiful, we are powerful, we are stronger than ever because of the trauma we've been through." I'm going to focus on that instead.' Simpson in Amy Funderburk, 'Vessels, Interconnectedness, and the Beauty of Boundaries With Rose B. Simpson', *Art & Object*, 7 October, 2024 https://www.artandobject.com/news/vessels-interconnectedness-and-beauty-boundaries-rose-b-simpson

-

68 *Ebony* was founded in 1945 as a monthly news and lifestyle magazine geared to a middle-class Black American readership. *Jet* was founded in 1951 as a weekly lifestyle magazine featuring news and entertainment for young adult Black Americans.

-

69 Julie Rrap in conversation with Jennifer Higgie, 'Julie Rrap on Standing on Her Own Shoulders', *Ocula*, 12 February 2024. https://ocula.com/magazine/conversations/julie-rrap-standing-on-her-own-shoulders/

-

70 Julie Rrap in conversation with Jennifer Higgie, 'Julie Rrap on Standing on Her Own Shoulders', *Ocula*, 12 February 2024. https://ocula.com/magazine/conversations/julie-rrap-standing-on-her-own-shoulders/

-

71 Liv Clayworth, 'MCA art exhibition by Julie Rrap challenges perceptions of the female body', 21 August 2024. https://www.sydney.edu.au/news-opinion/news/2024/08/21/mca-art-exhibition-by-julie-rrap-challenges-perceptions-of-the-female-body.html

ARTISTS' BIOGRAPHIES

Marina Abramović (Serbian-American, b. 1946)
*Born Belgrade, Serbia; lives and works in New York,
New York, USA*

-

Sofonisba Anguissola (Italian, *c.* 1532-1625)
*Born Cremona, Italy; lived and worked in Madrid,
Spain and Genoa and Palermo, Italy*

-

Eve Arnold (American, 1912–2012)
*Born Philadelphia, Pennsylvania, USA; lived
and worked in New York, New York, USA and
London, UK*

-

Hans Baldung (German, 1484/85–1545)
*Born Schwäbisch Gmünd, Germany; lived
and worked in Strasbourg, Germany (now
France)*

-

Romare Bearden (American, 1911–1988)
*Born in Charlotte, North Carolina, USA; lived and
worked in New York, New York, USA*

-

John Bell (British, 1811–1895)
*Born Hopton Hall, Suffolk (now Norfolk), UK; lived and
worked in London, UK*

-

Marie-Guillemine Benoist (French, 1768–1826)
Born, lived and worked in Paris, France

-

Sandro Botticelli (Italian, *c.* 1445–1510)
*Born Florence, Italy; lived and worked in Florence
and Rome, Italy*

Louise Bourgeois (French-American, 1911–2010)
*Born Paris, France; lived and worked in New York, New
York, USA*

-

Alexandre Cabanel (French, 1823–1889)
*Born Montpellier, France; lived and worked in
Paris, France*

-

Annibale Carracci (Italian, 1560–1609)
*Born Bologna, Italy; lived and worked in Bologna
and Rome, Italy*

-

Mary Cassatt (American, 1844–1926)
*Born Allegheny City, Pennsylvania, USA; lived and worked in
Paris, France*

-

Walter Crane (British, 1845–1915)
Born Liverpool, UK; lived and worked in London, UK

-

Edgar Degas (French, 1834–1917)
Born, lived and worked in Paris, France

-

Tracey Emin (British, b. 1963)
*Born London, UK; lives and works in London and Margate,
UK and South of France*

-

Jeremiasz Falck (Polish, 1610/19–1677)
*Born Danzig (now Gdańsk, Poland); lived and worked in the
Polish–Lithuanian Commonwealth*

-

Leonor Fini (Argentinian-Italian, 1907–1996)
*Born Buenos Aires, Argentina; lived and worked in Paris,
France; Monte Carlo, Monaco and Rome, Italy*

-

Henry Fuseli (Swiss, 1741–1825)
Born Zurich, Switzerland; lived and worked in London, UK

Thomas Gainsborough (British, 1727–1788)
Born Sudbury, Suffolk, UK; lived and worked in Bath and London, UK

-

The Gansevoort Limner (unknown artist active in America 1730–1745)
Unidentified painter active in the USA 1730–1745. Possibly Pieter Vanderlyn, American painter born in Holland in 1687, who moved to New York around 1718 and died 1778

-

Paul Gauguin (French, 1848–1903)
Born Paris, France; lived and worked in France, Martinique, Tahiti and Marquesas Islands

-

Artemisia Gentileschi (Italian, 1593–c. 1654)
Born Rome, Italy; lived and worked in Florence, Rome, Venice, Naples, Italy and London, UK

-

Guerrilla Girls (American, formed 1985)
Based in New York, New York, USA

-

Frans Hals (Dutch, 1582/3–1666)
Born Antwerp, Spanish Netherlands (now Belgium); lived and worked in Haarlem, Netherlands

-

Barkley L. Hendricks (American, 1945–2017)
Born Philadelphia, Pennsylvania, USA; lived and worked in Hartford, Connecticut, USA

-

Nicholas Hilliard (British, c. 1547–1619)
Born Exeter, UK; lived and worked in London, UK

-

Hannah Höch (German, 1889–1978)
Born Gotha, Germany; lived and worked in Berlin, Germany

Jean-Auguste-Dominique Ingres (French, 1780–1867)
Born Montauban, France; lived and worked in Rome and Florence, Italy and Paris, France

-

Graciela Iturbide (Mexican, b. 1942)
Born, lives and works in Mexico City, Mexico

-

Frida Kahlo (Mexican, 1907–1954)
Born Coyoacán, Mexico City, Mexico; lived and worked in Cuernavaca and Mexico City, Mexico and San Francisco, California; Detroit, Michigan and New York, New York, USA

-

Hayv Kahraman (Iraqi-Swedish, b. 1981)
Born Baghdad, Iraq; lives and works in Los Angeles, California, USA

-

Mari Katayama (Japanese, b. 1987)
Born Saitama, Japan; lives and works in Gunma, Japan

-

Yuki Kihara (Sāmoan/Aotearoa New Zealand, b. 1975)
Born, lives and works in Sāmoa

-

Yves Klein (French, 1928–1962)
Born Nice, France; lived and worked in Nice and Paris, France

-

Gustav Klimt (Austrian, 1862–1918)
Born Baumgarten, Empire of Austria; lived and worked in Vienna, Austria-Hungary

-

Barbara Kruger (American, b. 1945)
Born Newark, New Jersey, USA; lives and works in New York and Los Angeles, California, USA

-

Dorothea Lange (American, 1895–1965)
Born Hoboken, New Jersey, USA; lived and worked in San Francisco, California, USA

Frederic, Lord Leighton (British, 1830–1896)
*Born Scarborough, Yorkshire, UK; lived and worked in
London, UK*

-

Tamara de Lempicka (Polish, 1898–1980)
*Born Warsaw, Poland; lived and worked in Paris, France;
Los Angeles, California and New York, New York, USA and
Cuernavaca, Mexico*

-

Leonardo da Vinci (Italian, 1452–1519)
*Born Anchiano, near Vinci, Italy; lived and worked in
Florence, Milan and Rome, Italy and Amboise, France*

-

Edmonia Lewis (American, 1844–1907)
*Born in Greenbush (now Rensselaer), New York, USA; lived
and worked in Boston, Massachusetts, USA; Rome, Italy and
London, UK*

-

Édouard Manet (French, 1832–1883)
Born, lived and worked in Paris, France

-

Ana Mendieta (Cuban-American, 1948–1985)
*Born Havana, Cuba; lived and worked in New York,
New York, USA*

-

Lee Miller (American, 1907–1977)
*Born Poughkeepsie, New York, USA; lived and worked in
Paris, France; New York, New York, USA and London, UK*

-

Amedeo Modigliani (Italian, 1884–1920)
Born Livorno, Italy; lived and worked in Paris, France

-

Zanele Muholi (South African, b. 1972)
*Born Umlazi, Durban, South Africa; lives and works in Cape
Town, South Africa*

Vera Mukhina (Russian, 1889–1953)
*Born Riga, Russian Empire (now Latvia); lived and worked
in Moscow, USSR*

-

Edvard Munch (Norwegian, 1863–1944)
*Born Ådalsbruk, Norway; lived and worked in Berlin,
Germany; Paris, France and Oslo, Norway*

-

Shirin Neshat (Iranian-American, b. 1957)
*Born Qazvin, Iran; lives and works in New York,
New York, USA*

-

Toyin Ojih Odutola (Nigerian-American, b. 1985)
*Born in Ife-Ife, Nigeria; lives and works in New York,
New York, USA*

-

Michelangelo Pistoletto (Italian, b. 1933)
Born, lives and works in Biella, Italy

-

Hiram Powers (American, 1805–1873)
*Born Woodstock, Vermont, USA; lived and worked in
Cincinnati, Ohio and Washington, D.C., USA and
Florence, Italy*

-

Raphael (Raffaello Sanzio, Italian, 1483–1520)
*Born Urbino, Italy; lived and worked in Florence and
Rome, Italy*

-

Man Ray (Emmanuel Radnitzky, American,
1890–1976)
*Born Philadelphia, Pennsylvania, USA; lived and
worked in New York, New York and Los Angeles,
California, USA and Paris, France*

-

Paula Rego (Portuguese-British, 1935–2022)
*Born Lisbon, Portugal; lived and worked in
London, UK*

Germaine Richier (French, 1902–1959)
Born Grans, France; lived and worked in Paris and Provence, France

-

Julie Rrap (Australian, b. 1950)
Born Lismore, Australia; lives and works in Sydney, Australia

-

Peter Paul Rubens (Flemish, 1577–1640)
Born Siegen, Holy Roman Empire (now Germany); lived and worked in Antwerp, Spanish Netherlands (now Belgium)

-

Niki de Saint Phalle (French-American, 1930–2002)
Born in Neuilly-sur-Seine, France; lived and worked in Paris and Soisy-sur-Ecole, France; Garavacchio, Italy and San Diego, California, USA

-

John Singer Sargent (American, 1856–1925)
Born in Florence, Italy; lived and worked in Paris, France and London, UK

-

Jenny Saville (British, b. 1970)
Born Cambridge, UK; lives and works in Oxford, UK

-

Egon Schiele (Austrian, 1890–1918)
Born Tulln, Austria; lived and worked in Neulengbach and Vienna, Austria

-

Carolee Schneemann (American, 1939–2019)
Born Philadelphia, Pennsylvania, USA; lived and worked in New York and New Paltz, New York, USA

-

Amrita Sher-Gil (Hungarian-Indian, 1913–1941)
Born Budapest, Hungary; lived and worked in Paris, France; Simla and Saraya, India

Cindy Sherman (American, b. 1954)
Born Glen Ridge, New Jersey, USA; lives and works in New York, USA

-

Lorna Simpson (American, b. 1960)
Born, lives and works in Brooklyn, New York, USA

-

Rose B. Simpson (American, enrolled member of the Santa Clara Pueblo (Kha'po Owingeh) b. 1983)
Born Santa Fe, New Mexico, USA; lives and works in Santa Clara Pueblo, New Mexico, USA

-

Dorothea Tanning (American, 1910–2012)
Born Galesburg, Illinois, USA; lived and worked in New York, New York and Sedona, Arizona, USA and Provence, France

-

Mickalene Thomas (American, b. 1971)
Born in Camden, New Jersey, USA; lives and works in Brooklyn, New York, USA

-

Titian (Tiziano Vecellio, Italian, *c.* 1488–1576)
Born Pieve di Cadore, Italy; lived and worked in Venice, Italy

-

Henri de Toulouse-Lautrec (French, 1864–1901)
Born Albi, France; lived and worked in Paris, France

-

Toyen (née Marie Čermínová, Czech, 1902–1980)
Born in Prague, Bohemia (now Czechia); lived and worked in Prague, Czechia and Paris, France

-

Kitagawa Utamaro (Japanese, 1753–1806)
Born, lived and worked in Edo (now Tokyo), Japan

-

Diego Velázquez (Spanish, 1599–1660)
Born Seville, Spain; lived and worked in Madrid, Spain

Johannes Vermeer (Dutch, 1632–1675)
Born, lived and worked in Delft, Netherlands

-

Élisabeth Vigée Le Brun (French, 1755–1842)
Born Paris, France; lived and worked in Paris, France; Italy, Austria, Russia and Germany

-

Andy Warhol (American, 1928–1987)
Born Pittsburgh, Pennsylvania, USA; lived and worked in New York, New York, USA

-

George Frederic Watts (British, 1817–1904)
Born London, UK; lived and worked in London and Compton, Surrey, UK

-

Gerda Wegener (Danish, 1886–1940)
Born Hammelev, Denmark; lived and worked in Copenhagen, Denmark and Paris, France

-

Kehinde Wiley (American, b. 1977)
Born in Los Angeles, California, USA; lives and works in New York, New York, USA

FURTHER READING

Art and Sexual Politics, edited by Thomas B. Hess and Elizabeth C. Baker, New York: MacMillan, 1971

-

Jill Burke, *How to be a Renaissance Woman: The Untold History of Beauty & Female Creativity*, London: Profile Books, 2023

-

Whitney Chadwick, *The Militant Muse: Love, War and the Women of Surrealism*, London: Thames & Hudson, 2017

-

Whitney Chadwick, *Women, Art and Society*, sixth edition, London: Thames & Hudson, 2020

-

Ann Coxon, *Motherhood*, London: Tate Publishing, 2023

-

Emma Dabiri, *Disobedient Bodies: Reclaim Your Unruly Beauty*, London: Profile Books, 2023

-

Amy Dempsey, *Surrealism*, London: Thames & Hudson, 2019

-

Doing Feminism – with Art!, booklet to accompany exhibition 'FEMME FATALE: Gaze – Power – Gender', Hamburger Kunsthalle, Hamburg, Germany, 9 December 2022–10 April 2023 https://www.hamburger-kunsthalle.de/sites/default/files/begleitheft_femme-fatale.pdf

-

Flavia Frigeri, *Women Artists*, London: Thames & Hudson, 2019

Guerrilla Girls, *Guerrilla Girls: The Art of Behaving Badly*, San Francisco, California: Chronicle Books, 2020

-

Karen Hearn, *Portraying Pregnancy: from Holbein to Social Media*, London: Paul Holberton Publishing, 2020

-

Katy Hessel, *The Story of Art Without Men*, Hutchinson Heinemann, 2022

-

Hettie Judah, *Acts of Creation: On Art & Motherhood*, London: Thames & Hudson, 2024

-

Catherine McCormack, *Women in the Picture: Women, Art and the Power of Looking*, London: Icon Books, 2021

-

Modern Couples: Art, Intimacy and the Avant-Garde, edited by Jane Alison and Coralie Malissard, London: Prestel, 2018

-

Linda Nochlin, *Representing Women*, London: Thames & Hudson, 2019

-

Griselda Pollock, *Woman in Art: Helen Rosenau's 'Little Book' of 1944*, London: Paul Mellon Centre for Studies in British Art, 2023

-

Re/Sisters: A Lens on Gender and Ecology, edited by Alona Pardo, London: Prestel, 2023

-

Liz Rideal and Kathleen Soriano, *Madam & Eve: Women Portraying Women*, London: Laurence King Publishing, 2022

-

Natalie Rudd, *The Self-Portrait*, London: Thames & Hudson, 2021

H. Diane Russell, *Eva/Ave: Woman in Renaissance and Baroque Prints*, New York: The Feminist Press at The City University of New York, 1990

-

Soul of a Nation: Art in the Age of Black Power, edited by Mark Godfrey and Zoé Whitley, Tate Publishing, 2017

PICTURE CREDITS

pp. 16–17   Photo: IanDagnall Computing/Alamy Stock Photo

p. 19   Photo: Peter Horree/Alamy Stock Photo

p. 21   Gift of Felix M. Warburg and his family, 1941/The Metropolitan Museum of Art

p. 23   Photo: incamerastock/Alamy Stock Photo

pp. 26–27   Photo: World History Archive/Alamy Stock Photo

pp. 30–31   Photo: Artefact/Alamy Stock Photo

p. 33   Photo: IanDagnall Computing/Alamy Stock Photo

p. 35   ART Collection/Alamy Stock Photo

p. 37   Photo: IanDagnall Computing/Alamy Stock Photo

p. 39   Peter Paul Rubens (German, 1577–1640), The Three Graces, 1630-35, Public Domain: https://artvee.com/dl the-three-graces-6/#00

p. 42–43   Photo: IanDagnall Computing/Alamy Stock Photo

p. 45   Etching attributed to J. Falck after B. Strozzi. Wellcome Collection. Public Domain Mark. Source: Wellcome Collection. https://wellcomecollection.org/works/ m477skh5

pp. 48–49   Photo: The Picture Art Collection/Alamy Stock Photo

p. 51   Photo: Giorgio Morara/Alamy Stock Photo

p. 53   Gift of Edgar William and Bernice Chrysler Garbisch, The National Gallery of Art

p. 55   Henry Fuseli, The Nightmare, 1781, oil on canvas. Detroit Institute of Arts, Founders Society Purchase with funds from Mr. and Mrs. Bert L. Smokler and Mr. and Mrs. Lawrence A. Fleischman, 55.5.A

p. 57   Reproduced by permission of Chatsworth Settlement Trustees Bridgeman Images

p. 59   Photo: Historic Images/Alamy Stock Photo

p. 61   Photo: PAINTING/Alamy Stock Photo

p. 65   Photo: ACTIVE MUSEUM/ACTIVE ART/Alamy Stock Photo

pp. 68–69   Photo: incamerastock/Alamy Stock Photo

p. 71   Corcoran Collection (Gift of William Wilson Corcoran), The National Gallery of Art

pp. 74–75   © Watts Gallery/© Trustees of Watts Gallery/ Bridgeman Images

p. 77   Photo: The National Trust Photolibrary/James Dobson Alamy Stock Photo

pp. 80–81   Gift of John Wolfe, 1893/The Metropolitan Museum of Art

pp. 84–85   Photo: incamerastock/Alamy Stock Photo

p. 87   Smithsonian American Art Museum, Gift of the Historical Society of Forest Park, Illinois, 1994.17

p. 89   Photo: Steeve-x-art/Alamy Stock Photo

p. 91   Gift of Mr. and Mrs. Nate B. Spingold, 1956/The Metropolitan Museum of Art

p. 93   Photo: Universal History Archive/UIG/Bridgeman Images

p. 95   Photo: Art Library/Alamy Stock Photo

pp. 98–99   Photo: The Picture Art Collection/Alamy Stock Photo

p. 101   Edvard Munch "Madonna", 1894. Foto: Munchmuseet/ Rena Li

p. 103   The Luis A. Ferre Foundation Inc., Ponce, Puerto Rico/ Christie's Images/Scala, Florence

p. 105   "A Garland for May Day 1895, original relief print." In the digital collection Political Posters, Labadie Collection, University of Michigan

p. 109   Photo: Heritage Image Partnership Ltd/Alamy Stock Photo

p. 111   Bequest of Scofield Thayer, 1982, The Metropolitan Museum of Art, Accession Number: 1984.433.316

p. 113   Photo © Barnes Foundation/Bridgeman Images

p. 115   ART: © DACS 2024 PHOTO: © Israel Museum, Jerusalem Vera & Arturo Schwarz Collection of Dada and Surrealist Art Bridgeman Images

p. 118   Art: © Man Ray 2015 Trust/DACS, London. Photo: Digital image, The Museum of Modern Art, New York/ Scala, Florence

p. 119   Art: © Man Ray 2015 Trust/DACS, London. Photo: © MAN RAY 2015 TRUST

p. 121   Photo: steeve-x-art/Alamy Stock Photo

p. 123   Art: © Tamara de Lempicka Estate, LCC/DACS 2024. Photo: Artepics/Alamy Stock Photo

p. 125   Photo: ARTGEN/Alamy Stock Photo

p. 127   Library of Congress, Prints & Photographs Division, Farm Security Administration/Office of War Information Black-and-White Negatives. Photograph: https://www.loc.gov/ item/2017762891/

p. 129   Photo: Peter Phipp/Travelshots/Bridgeman Images

p. 131   Art: © ADAGP, Paris and DACS, London 2024. Photo: GAVU Cheb

p. 133   Digital image, The Museum of Modern Art, New York/ Scala, Florence

p. 135   Art: © ADAGP, Paris and DACS, London 2024. Photo: Peggy Guggenheim Collection, Venice (Solomon R. Guggenheim Foundation, New York)

p. 138   © Lee Miller Archives, England 2024. All rights reserved. leemiller.co.uk

p. 139   © Lee Miller Archives, England 2024. All rights reserved. leemiller.co.uk

p. 141   Art: © ADAGP, Paris and DACS, London 2024. Photo: Purchased with assistance from the Art Fund and the Friends of the Tate Gallery 1995

pp. 144, 145   © Eve Arnold/Magnum Photos

p. 149   Art: © Succession Yves Klein c/o ADAGP, Paris and DACS, London 2024. Photo: ROBERT/Alamy Stock Vector

p. 152   Art: © Niki de Saint Phalle Charitable Art Foundation/ADAGP, Paris and DACS, London 2024. Photo: © 2024 NIKI CHARITABLE ART FOUNDATION

p. 153   Art: © Niki de Saint Phalle Charitable Art Foundation/ADAGP, Paris and DACS, London 2024. Photo: © 2024 NIKI CHARITABLE ART FOUNDATION

p. 155   Art: © 2024 The Andy Warhol Foundation for the Visual Arts, Inc./Licensed by DACS, London. Photo: Christie's Images/© 2024 The Andy Warhol Foundation for the Visual Arts, Inc./Licensed by DACS, London/Bridgeman Images

p. 157   Art: © Carolee Schneemann Foundation; ARS, NY; and DACS, London 2025. Photo: Al Giese. Courtesy of the Carolee Schneemann Foundation; Lisson Gallery; and P·P·O·W, New York

p. 160   Art: Courtesy Archivio Cittadellarte – Fondazione Pistoletto. Photo: Purchased with assistance from Tate International Council 2006

p. 161   Art: Courtesy Archivio Cittadellarte – Fondazione Pistoletto. Photo: Mike Greenslade/Alamy Stock Photo

p. 163   © Barkley L. Hendricks. Courtesy of the Estate of Barkley L. Hendricks and Jack Shainman Gallery, New York

p. 165   Art: © ADAGP, Paris and DACS, London 2024. Photo courtesy The Dorothea Tanning Foundation

pp. 168, 169   © Marina Abramovic. Courtesy of the Marina Abramovic Archives/DACS 2024

p. 171   Ana Mendieta, Tree of Life, 1976 © The Estate of Ana Mendieta Collection, LLC. Licensed by DACS, London. Courtesy Alison Jacques, London

p. 173   Art: © Romare Bearden Foundation/VAGA at ARS, NY and DACS, London 2024 / Colonel Rex W. and Maxine Schuster Radsch Endowment fund purchase. Photo: Chazen Museum of Art, University of Wisconsin

pp. 176, 177   © Cindy Sherman. Courtesy the artist and Hauser & Wirth

p. 179   Art: © Graciela Iturbide. Photo: San Francisco Museum of Modern Art/Bridgeman Images

p. 181   Copyright © Guerrilla Girls, courtesy guerrillagirls.com

pp. 184, 185   Courtesy the artist, The Broad Art Foundation and Sprüth Magers

p. 187   Art: © Jenny Saville. All rights reserved, DACS 2024. Photo: © Courtesy Gagosian

p. 189   © Shirin Neshat. Courtesy of the artist and Gladstone Gallery

pp. 192–193   Paula Rego. All rights reserved 2024/Bridgeman Images

p. 195   Louise Bourgeois, Do Not Abandon Me, 1999. Pink fabric and thread, 12 x 52 x 21.5 cm. Ursula Hauser Collection, Switzerland. Photo: Christopher Burke, © The Easton Foundation/Licensed by DACS, UK and VAGA at Artists Rights Society (ARS), NY

p. 199   Art: © ARS, NY and DACS, London 2024. Photo: © Mickalene Thomas (the "Artist")

p. 201   © Mari Katayama, courtesy of Mari Katayama Studio and Galerie Suzanne Tarasieve, Paris

p. 203   © Zanele Muholi. Courtesy of the artist and Yancey Richardson, New York

p. 205   © Toyin Ojih Odutola. Courtesy of the artist and Jack Shainman Gallery, New York

p. 207   © Yuki Kihara. Nafea e te Fa'aipoipo? When Will You Marry? (after Gauguin), from the series Paradise Camp, 2020, c-print, 1010 x 770 mm. Courtesy of Yuki Kihara and Milford Galleries Aotearoa New Zealand

p. 209   © Hayv Kahraman. Courtesy of the Artist, Pilar Corrias, London, Jack Shainman Gallery, New York, and Vielmetter Los Angeles

p. 211   Art: © Tracey Emin. All rights reserved, DACS 2024. Photo: Shoults/Alamy Stock Photo

pp. 214, 215   © Rose B. Simpson. Courtesy the artist, Jessica Silverman, San Francisco, and Jack Shainman Gallery, New York. Photo: Stephanie Zollshan

p. 217   Kehinde Wiley, The Three Graces (Coumba, Mariama, Rokhaya), 2023. © Kehinde Wiley. Courtesy of Stephen Friedman Gallery, London

p. 219   © Lorna Simpson. Courtesy the artist and Hauser & Wirth. Photo: James Wang

p. 221   Art: © Julie Rrap/DACS 2024. Photo: Zan Wimberley for Roslyn Oxley9 Gallery, Sydney

INDEX

ACKNOWLEDGEMENTS & BIOGRAPHIES

Many thanks to Laura Paton at Laurence King for coming to me with the idea and letting me run with it, and to those who helped along the way: Aliki Braine, Cathy Haruf, Ethan Hedayat, Jessica Hedayat, Stephanie Lundy, Sophie Perkins, Pippa Roberts, Charlie Saunders and Justin Saunders.

Amy Dempsey is an art historian who studied at Hunter College in New York and received her doctorate from the Courtauld Institute of Art in London. A Fellow of the Royal Society of Arts, Dempsey is the author of the international bestseller *Styles, Schools & Movements: The Essential Encyclopaedic Guide to Modern Art* (2002, 2010, updated and revised edition 2026), the groundbreaking *Destination Art* (2006, 2011), the first monographs on *Almuth Tebbenhoff* (2025) and *Alfio Bonanno* (2020), and three titles in Thames & Hudson's Art Essentials series: *Modern Art* (2018), *Surrealism* (2019) and *Destination Art* (2021).

www.destination-art.org

Hettie Judah is a writer and curator. She is a regular contributor to *The Guardian, Frieze, The Times Literary Supplement*, and *Apollo* magazine. Her recent shows include the Hayward Gallery Touring exhibition 'Acts of Creation: On Art and Motherhood,' which opened at the Arnolfini in Bristol in March 2024. As a public speaker and broadcaster, she can be heard on programmes such as BBC Radio 4's *Front Row*. Her recent books include *How Not To Exclude Artist Mothers (and other parents)* (Lund Humphries, 2022), *Lapidarium: The Secret Lives of Stones* (John Murray, London, 2022) and *Acts of Creation: On Art and Motherhood* (Thames & Hudson, 2024).